Mother/Nature

Catherine M. Roach

Mother/Nature

Popular Culture and
Environmental Ethics

INDIANA
University Press
Bloomington & Indianapolis

Excerpt from *Chapter 10* from HOUSEKEEPING by Marilynne Robinson. Copyright © 1981 by Marilynne Robinson. Reprinted by permission of Farrar, Straus and Giroux, LLC.

Excerpt from "The Hollow Men" from COLLECTED POEMS 1909–1962 by T. S. Eliot, copyright 1936 by Harcourt, Inc., copyright © 1964, 1963, by T. S. Eliot, reprinted by permission of the publisher.

This book is a publication of

Indiana University Press
601 North Morton Street
Bloomington, IN 47404-3797 USA

http://iupress.indiana.edu

Telephone orders   800-842-6796
Fax orders   812-855-7931
Orders by e-mail   iuporder@indiana.edu

© 2003 by Catherine M. Roach

The paper used in this publication meets the minimum requirements of American National Standard for Information Sciences—Permanence of Paper for Printed Library Materials, ANSI Z39.48-1984.

Manufactured in the United States of America

Library of Congress Cataloging-in-Publication Data

Roach, Catherine M., date
   Mother/nature : popular culture and environmental ethics / Catherine M. Roach.
      p.   cm.
   Includes bibliographical references and index.
      ISBN 0-253-34178-7 (alk. paper) — ISBN 0-253-21562-5 (pbk. : alk. paper)
   1. Philosophy of nature. 2. Ecology—Philosophy. 3. Popular culture.
4. Environmental ethics. I. Title.
   BD581 .R59 2003
   304.2—dc21

                                                          2002007644

1 2 3 4 5   08 07 06 05 04 03

With love, respect, and gratitude

to my parents

Diane Roach and Joseph E. Roach

and to my mother in academia

Naomi R. Goldenberg

Cain murdered Abel, and blood cried out from the earth; the house fell on Job's children, and a voice was induced or provoked into speaking from a whirlwind; and Rachel mourned for her children; and King David for Absalom. The force behind the movement of time is a mourning that will not be comforted. That is why the first event is known to have been an expulsion, and the last is hoped to be a reconciliation and return. So memory pulls us forward, so prophecy is only brilliant memory—there will be a garden where all of us as one child will sleep in our mother Eve, hooped in her ribs and staved by her spine.

—Marilynne Robinson, *Housekeeping*

Contents

Illustrations

Preface

This book began as a bad poem. It has its deepest roots, that is, in the poetry and prose fragments I wrote while working one summer as a Junior Ranger for the Ministry of Natural Resources in Northern Ontario. My band of fellow rangers and I were based in Esker Lakes Provincial Park, near the town of Swastika. I was seventeen.

While I had always enjoyed summer cottages, canoeing, and nature walks, I think it was during that summer in the forests and by the lakes of the Canadian Shield that I developed a keener awareness of nature and a concern for environmental degradation. The beauty and force of nature deeply impressed me. I got up at dawn to go canoeing on mist-covered lakes, seized with adolescent fervor to write *something* to convey what I saw and felt—hence the bad poetry. I also developed—from solitary walks out on the hiking trails—a fear of bears that endures today. And from Northern Ontario, where towns are small and widely scattered, came a sense of the smallness of humans and of nature's power and vastness, enduring despite our encroachments.

The September after that summer at Esker Lakes I entered university, first at the University of Ottawa in Canada and then, six years later, at Harvard. My studies soon fell in line with my Northern-born interests and came to revolve largely around themes of human perceptions of nature and the expression of these perceptions in religion and culture. A long-standing feminist concern (evident in the youthful dramatics of that same summer when I defiantly tossed a brassiere into the bonfire of a cool Northern evening) led me to ask why nature is so often seen as female. And why, I asked, in our Western religious and philosophical traditions, are women so often seen as closer to nature than men? What do these associations mean for the treatment of both women and nature? These questions eventually bore fruit in a masters degree and then in a doctoral dissertation. My explorations continue now at the University of Alabama, where I have pursued this research into its present form in this book. Here, I teach interdisciplinary humanities courses as Assistant Professor in New College (a program where undergraduates design their own majors) and religion and culture courses in the Department of Religious Studies. I also set up and now direct the university's minor in Interdisciplinary Environmental Studies.

Most broadly expressed, my experiences and concerns have led me into and keep me inside this large question:

How can we think about and live the differences and commonalities of being female and male and the complexities of being human-in-nature so as, on the one hand, to be more just and supportive within the human community and, on the other (connected) hand, to be more environmentally sound?

The methods I use to explore this question have evolved over time. All of my work has occurred within the context of religious studies, but encounters with influential teachers and the interpretive power of psychoanalytic theory encouraged me to engage in interdisciplinary research in that field as well. All along, I have drawn on feminist theory and addressed myself to environmental thought.

This work, then, is the fruit of a long journey—indeed, an unexpectedly southward migration—from Northern Ontario; to Ottawa; to Cambridge, Massachusetts; to Tuscaloosa, Alabama. Its roots stretch back over more years than I now care to count. Both Canadian and American soils have nourished the book, as have friends and teachers in both places. It is nourished above all by the sensual and spiritual pleasures of nature and by the intellectual pleasures of working out the ideas presented herein. It is fed, ultimately, by my hope of playing a small part in the crucial task of protecting the environment, a task that may well become the most pressing of the twenty-first century.

I invite readers to share these pleasures and this task with me.

Acknowledgments

One of the things about this book that I know most deeply to be true is that I could not have written it alone. I am grateful to many who have helped me think through its ideas and live through its writing.

I offer particular thanks to Naomi R. Goldenberg, an inspirational mentor and goddess *extraordinaire*, who has been teacher, role model, friend, and partner in enjoying the Canadian outdoors. Other teachers and advisors to whom I am very grateful include Richard R. Niebuhr, John McDargh, Everett Mendelsohn (whose sage advice, "be expansive," has proven useful in any number of contexts), Mark U. Edwards, Judith Van Herik, Harriet Lutzky, and George Goethals. My peer colleagues have provided me with the best of friendship, conversation filled with intelligence and humor, and the all-important lesson that life is much bigger than academia. In particular, I mention Courtney Bickel, Marie Griffith, and Ted Trost. I offer special thanks to Ted—my husband now after love bloomed wild in the angst-ridden corridors of academia—for his constant support and sound critical feedback. Kelley Raab was insightful in our discussions of the material and is a wonderful friend. My junior faculty colleagues in the Interdisciplinary Writing Group at the University of Alabama have proven invaluable both for their critiques of drafts of this manuscript and for their delightfully quirky selves. Editors (Bob Sloan and Nick Street, in particular) and several anonymous reviewers provided detailed and thoughtful criticism in the revision process that helped me to see my text more clearly. Other colleagues, professors, and friends have helped and taught me along the way: Carole Bundy, Adam Chippindale, Nalini Devdas, David Gewanter, Elizabeth Dodson Gray, Philip Holzman, Diane Jonte-Pace, Dave Klemmack, Elisabeth Lacelle, Margaret Miles, Ed Passerini, Carol Pierman, Bennett Simon, Georges Tissot, Karen Warren, Joy Young, and the Women's Caucus of Harvard Divinity School. I owe them all my thanks. I extend gratitude as well to the staff in imaging and video services at the campus Faculty Resource Center who graciously helped with the book's illustrations on a very tight schedule and to my student Amanda Houser, who took my photograph for the book. Finally, I thank my family in Ottawa, Michigan, and Tuscaloosa: what fun we have together!

I tested out sections of the book's argument in presentations at national meetings of the American Academy of Religion (AAR) in 1989, 1993, 1998, and 2000; at a regional AAR meeting in Boston in 1998; as a member of a panel on ecopsychology at the Center for Psychology and Social Change at the Cambridge Hospital in 1994; at a conference on Environmental Worldviews and the Academy at Harvard Divinity School in 1997; at a Women's Studies Research Colloquium of the University of Alabama in 1999; and at the Third International Conference on Media, Religion, and Culture at the University of Edinburgh, Scotland in 1999. In all cases, I thank audience members for comments and questions that spurred me in my thinking and encouraged me in my work. Parts of the book's argument appeared previously in different forms in *Journal of Feminist Studies in Religion* (Spring 1997) and in *Hypatia: A Journal of Feminist Philosophy* (Spring 1991).

I gratefully acknowledge the financial support that made this work possible. Funding came from the Social Sciences and Humanities Research Council of Canada (I applaud their commitment to the graduate education of Canadians), the Frank Knox Memorial Fellowship, the Harvard Mellon Fellowship, the Research Advisory Council of the University of Alabama, and the Dean's Office of the College of Arts and Science at the University of Alabama.

Mother/Nature

ONE

Wilderness— Within and Without

I wish to explore what remains for most—and has been for me—a terra incognita, a forbidden place, a heart of darkness that civilized people have long attempted to repress—that is, the wilderness within the human soul and without, in that living profusion that envelops all creation.

—Max Oelschlaeger, The Idea of Wilderness

From our perch on the edge of the new millennium, we hear the daily litanies of environmental destruction. The damage includes extinction or near-extinction of species; depletion of what we like to call "our natural resources"; major worldwide disruptions such as ozone thinning and climate change; pollution of air, water, soil, and living creatures. To cite just one disquieting example, the internationally renowned annual report on the planet's health called *State of the World* announced in its 2000 edition that five hundred synthetic chemicals are presently found in the human body, chemicals that did not even exist before 1920.[1] As a new mother, I was particularly disturbed to learn that I was passing some of these chemicals on to my baby through my breast milk. In one sense, the twentieth century had turned my very body into a source of pollution to my newborn son. As I rocked my suckling child, had I become a living metaphor or avatar of besmirched Mother Nature? A bizarre image, but reflecting on it nonetheless during those endless 3 A.M. feedings, I could feel my anger and fear simmering (along with, of course, my exhaustion and amazement at my expanded bustline—Mother Nature indeed).

A HEART-OF-DARKNESS ENVIRONMENTALISM
This book is about nature imagery and environmental ethics. I wrote it to try to understand how we got ourselves into such a mess and what we might do to get ourselves out of it. By "we" I mean the people of the modern industrialized West, and more particularly the

1

people of contemporary America, who as a whole are the world's hyper-consumers. I write out of specific ethical concerns: I am a feminist concerned about sexism and an environmentalist concerned about ecological degradation. I find both sets of problems to be of grave ethical concern—and also related; thus, I am an ecofeminist too. I write as a university professor trained in the academic study of religion (mainly Christianity), who sees religion as implicated in both of these sets of problems as well as in their solutions. Furthermore, I write as an academic trained in the interplay of religion and psychology who finds Christian theology (regardless of what it has to say about God's existence) and psychoanalysis (regardless of what it has to say about God's nonexistence or irrelevance) to offer two complementary and penetrating insights into what it means to be human. Together, these insights strike me as being helpful in tackling the ethical concerns of my book. Finally, I write as someone who, like pretty much everyone else in America today, lives her life saturated in popular and consumer culture: surrounded by advertising, media campaigns, popular music, Hollywood films, bumper stickers, and billboards. (Studies show that Americans are now subjected to 3,600 "commercial impressions" every day.)[2] This cultural surround tells us something significant about who we are, about our deepest anxieties and fantasies, and also about what we must resist becoming. More specifically, since pop culture is filled with nature imagery—including powerful images of Mother Nature—it tells us something about common ways of conceptualizing nature. Thus, this book is partly a critique of pop culture as well as a celebration of its creativity, from the point of view of environmental ethics.

The intended audience of this book emerges from these aspects of my professional identity and concerns. I write primarily from a base in religious studies—the area in which I am trained—for a dual audience. Within religious studies, the book is aimed at people interested in the area of religion and ecology, whether they are ecotheologians from a particular faith tradition or those engaged by critical and comparative studies of the interplay of environmental issues with any of the world's religions. Outside the field of religion, I write primarily for ecofeminists and others interested in gender analyses of culture and society. For the informed general reader with interest in environmental issues, I have tried to make the book as accessible as possible.

Because I draw on pop culture and media imagery for my primary case study material, the book also has intersections with popular culture studies and with communication and media studies. (One way to describe this book is, indeed, as a type of green cultural studies.) But to scholars who specialize in these fields, I confess I am a novice. I have relied here for a model on the leading-edge work of communications scholar Sut Jhally, whose research on the social role of advertising in the consumer culture has served as an inspiration to me.[3]

This book is an effort to bring closer together my two central audiences—those people in religion and ecology, and those in ecofeminism—and have them turn their attention to a common problem. As the project developed, I came to call this, at first somewhat facetiously, the problem of "a heart-of-darkness environmentalism." This book is an attempt to develop such an environmentalism and to use contemporary Mother Nature imagery to illustrate the value of this perspective. My vision here grew from the quote by ecophilosopher Max Oelschlaeger that serves as epigraph to this chapter, as well as from Joseph Conrad's novel, *Heart of Darkness*. Oelschlaeger expresses the desire, which I share, to explore "the heart of darkness . . . that is the wilderness within the human soul and without."[4] In Conrad's story, there is a darkness to the wilderness and a darkness to humans. For the wilderness, the heart of darkness is the Upper Congo; for humans, it is the heart and soul. Conrad suggests that the two are related in that wilderness can make the human heart dark. It can corrupt us, or more accurately, can bring out corruption that is already there. I am also aware that some people see metaphorical equations of darkness with the unconscious and especially with destructiveness or evil as racist and as part of the oppressive colonial backdrop of Conrad's novel. Although I intend no racist implications, I may nevertheless perpetuate them. However, for me the metaphor draws on the darkness of night when it is cold and hard to see, when danger lurks and nocturnal beasts hunt, when the ghosts come out to haunt us.[5]

I find this talk of nature and the heart of darkness suggestive. There is certainly something very powerful about wilderness: it evokes strong emotions, responses, and fantasies. In human experiences with nature, we see both our best and our worst capabilities. The best includes such varied works of beauty as the poetry of Wordsworth;

the prose of Annie Dillard; the life work of environmentalists like Rachel Carson and John Muir; and vineyards, gardens, and olive groves tended carefully for hundreds of years. But the history of attitudes and behaviors in nature has also too often been a history of rapacious abuse, and imagery of conquered or wounded Mother Nature reflects this rapacity. As I will explain in this book, I believe that part of the reason for environmental destruction and for the negativity in much nature imagery is the influence of this "heart of darkness." This claim is not intended to imply that humans are all or only evil. It does, however, attempt to do justice to the bloody facts of history and of the history of environmental abuse, as well as to the general human difficulty in determining and keeping to the moral path. It is to acknowledge a tendency, to face a deep truth. It is to explore what Oelschlaeger calls "the wilderness within the human soul," so as to better understand our relations to the wilderness without. This exploration is important because of my further conviction that the effects of the darkness are best countered through encounter with it, by shedding light on it, by heading up the Congo.

I came to these convictions from an initial question that seems in some ways simple or even naïve. It is fairly widely accepted today that environmental destruction ultimately becomes self-destruction as a sick and impoverished global environment in turn sickens and impoverishes the human members of that ecosystem. My question, then, was the following: *Why, despite warning signs from a stressed global ecosystem, mounting scientific evidence, and public education campaigns, does degradation of the environment continue to persist and mount?* On the political, industrial, and individual levels, the will to make major systemic changes often seems weak (and despite my efforts, I should probably include myself here as well). Americans in particular seem reluctant to commit themselves fully to the search for solutions (witness President Bush's recent refusal to ratify the 1997 Kyoto Protocol's targets for reducing emission of greenhouse gases in the United States). For example, *State of the World 1996* notes this dangerous contradiction: "Securing food supplies for the next generation depends on an all-out effort to stabilize population and climate, but we resist changing our reproductive behavior, and we refrain from converting our climate-destabilizing, fossil-fuel-based economy to a solar/hydrogen-based one."[6]

Again, my question was: *Why do we resist and refrain in this way? Why continue to engage in environmental destruction, when such destruction seems clearly not in our own long-term best interests?* At first glance, this question might seem rather obvious and naïve. First of all, there is no monolithic "we." While environmental protection is a wasteful false alarm for some, for others it is an urgent priority to which they have committed themselves wholeheartedly. Relations to the environment and consumption of resources differ significantly among the developed and developing countries and between rich and poor in all countries. People do not all bear equal responsibility for ecological abuse, nor do all relate to nature in the same way. There are important differences among CEOs of multinational corporations, environmental activists, Third World slum dwellers, and First World suburbanites; gender, race, class, and a host of differences in personal sensibility all matter enormously. Furthermore, one might protest, surely no one sets out to actively destroy the environment. Societies instead suffer such destruction as the unintended side effect of lack of ecological knowledge, an intransigent industrial complex, badly applied or insufficient technology, and the huge population explosion of the twentieth century. Or ecological degradation may seem the tragic but necessary trade-off for short-term economic gains and immediate survival needs.

While all of this may be true, the question stayed with me as one not so easily dismissed. It seems, in fact, quite a complicated question that invites closer analysis of the "we" and of the varieties of relationships—loving, hateful, envious, fearful, remorseful—that human beings have with what we call "nature." The question requires exploration of the complex factors shaping how people represent, value, and interact with their environments. It is a question that reveals the "clearly" to be in fact quite murky and dark. And this question has a crucial corollary concerning what then to do in order to prevent and heal environmental destruction. How are we to understand complexities of human response to nature, and how are we to work toward environmental healing? Together, these tasks define the problem of this book.

The book investigates this problem within the cultural complex of contemporary America. It does so through a close examination of nature imagery, and especially images of Mother Nature, in American popular culture. I refer here to pictorial representations of nature and also to imagistic or metaphoric language about nature as such imagery is found in the popular culture forums of print and television advertising, the media campaigns of environmental groups, and cartoons or comic strips. Such imagery provides primary data on widely shared and deeply held attitudes about the value of nature and about the human relation to it. (I will say more in the next section about this choice of Mother Nature imagery and pop culture as my study ground). From the evidence of the imagery, this relation seems to be one of intense ambivalence in American society. The ambivalence encompasses fearful desires for control over an environment cast as a threatening—and often female—other as well as reparative impulses toward a life-giving, beloved surround imbued with the nurturance of mother. The book's central argument is that the intransigence of environmental degradation—people's reluctance to fully face the problem and to make changes—results partly from the deadlock of this ambivalence. The problem seems further exacerbated by the largely unconscious function of the ambivalence in contemporary culture. My hope is to ease the intransigence by shedding some light on this ambivalence as it is portrayed in and uncovered by the nature imagery examined in the book.

I work, then, within the highly interdisciplinary field of environmental studies, as a humanist investigating how semiconscious and ambivalent attitudes toward nature act as one deep root of ecological degradation.[7] Digging after this root entails both a sympathetic critique of where I think more can be done in environmental studies and a contribution toward these new directions. More specifically, as I read the literature of the field, I wondered if environmental studies could grapple more deeply with the question of *why*. I saw evidence of so much ambivalence in popular nature imagery and in continuing realities of environmental degradation. Could not environmental studies do more to probe the meaning of this ambivalence, to explain the reason for its depth? Perhaps by focusing on the wilderness around us, environmental studies was slighting the wilderness within. Yet as Oelschlaeger points out in the epigraph, the wilderness within and without are deeply connected. This connection means that response to nature is necessarily shaped by the varieties of human identity and experience, by what it means to be human. A fundamental starting point for this book, then, is the conviction that environmental thought requires deeply insightful notions of personhood and sustained critical attention to "human nature," to questions of how and why people respond as they do in the patterns of environmental behavior and imagery that they create and use.

Environmentalists do often argue that people engage in ecological destruction partly because they operate out of false self-understandings that claim humans to be separate from and superior to nature. These environmentalists instead present visions of humans as inextricably connected to a web of life in order to motivate our loving, reparative participation in this web. They may, however, move too quickly to encourage better harmony with nature and pass too quickly over the questions of why there is such *dis*harmony and why it seems so hard and perhaps in some ways so undesirable to live in the suggested harmony. Their notions of the self, in other words, can seem too simple and rosy. Environmental thought may suffer from too easy an optimism that elides the deeper challenges posed to the environmentalist project by intractable aspects of human destructiveness and dividedness, attested to by the nature imagery I examine in this book. As Frederic Bender says in a review of ecophilosopher J. Baird Callicott's *Earth's Insights,* "Its chief shortcoming, in this reviewer's opinion, is one that is endemic to environmental ethics per se, a discipline that seems to wish only that everyone would stop harming the Earth in order that all our ecological problems might be solved."[8] Clearly, the encouragement of loving impulses does not go far enough. This "good news" message is incomplete and weakened unless placed in the context of dynamics of love *and* hate and unless it recognizes the extent to which behavior is shaped by factors of which we are not always aware and that can be painfully elusive to conscious control.

The project of this book is to pay attention to these angry and obscure desires to control and conquer nature. I take such desires seriously—not as a false impulse that must be denied in favor of the interconnected self, but as an impulse, whether personal or collective, conscious or unconscious, that may be to some degree inevitable and that must be faced and integrated. My perspective here leans toward the tragic, although it is by no means without hope. Humans are not solely loving, but neither are we inevitably brutish. We are not solely rational beings whose good intentions determine our actions, but neither are we blindly controlled by hidden and selfish agendas that we can never hope to access or change. Probing the deep roots of our ambivalent and aggressive response to nature can help mitigate feelings of hate toward it. I thus want to build on or stretch my two central audiences of ecofeminism and of religion and ecology by adding a depth perspective, by proposing an environmental ethic that peers into the heart of darkness. Such a heart-of-darkness environmentalism balances the quest to love and heal nature with attention to the dark or destructive side of human relations, to angry passions of rage and violence.

MOTHER NATURE IN POPULAR CULTURE

All these passions—the desire to love, to hurt, and to heal nature—are found in Mother Nature imagery. In fact, this imagery exposes more clearly than anything else in the culture, I became convinced, the turbulence and conflict in popular sensibilities toward the environment. Nowhere else is there found such a passionate confluence of contradictory attitudes. "Mother Nature" thus functions as a particularly telling form of nature representation. Although it might seem paradoxical to develop a book on environmental ethics out of consumerist advertising that commodifies nature, such imagery reveals much about the ways that human relations shape relations to nature. Precisely for this reason the imagery provides fertile material for a heart-of-darkness environmental ethic. If a key to motivating environmental action lies in revealing and resolving ambivalence toward nature, then a prime site for the work is exactly this Mother Nature imagery.

Nature is our sweet mother; she loves us, and we her.
Nature is our treacherous enemy; she needs taming, now.
Nature is our wounded victim; we must heal her who has given us life.

These three motifs emerge as recurring patterns in popular American imagery. I refer to them as the *Good Mother, Bad Mother,* and *Hurt Mother* and capitalize these motifs throughout the book in order to indicate their mythic stature.

Several questions fascinate me: Why is nature so often and easily portrayed as a maternal figure? Nature seems "naturally" cast as mother, for example, whereas "Father Nature" has no cultural meaning or resonance at all. Why does the imagery take the form of these intense and contradictory motifs that reveal so much ambiguity, so much passionate concern as well as thinly veiled aggression? What, overall, is the meaning of Mother Nature imagery? In purely practical terms, does it support an environmental and feminist agenda or not?

That these passions are found most intensely in Mother Nature imagery is no mere coincidence. In this book I develop an argument that the imagery works like a lens to focus patterns of response to the environment that are (1) ambivalent, (2) gendered, and (3) semiconscious. The imagery reflects these patterns so well because of the way "mother" functions as a prime symbol of nature and, at the same time, as a prime locus of ambivalence in patriarchal culture. "Mother Nature" comes to function, then, as a screen *par excellence* for the projection of this ambivalence. The argument, as noted, is threefold: first, that the images reveal not simply connection but complex, ambivalent tendencies toward both violent control and loving repair. The imagery expresses these conflicts in human response to nature and reveals them within human relations themselves. Second, the imagery shows that gendered family relations inflect this response in significant ways. By condensing mother-child dynamics together with relations to nature, "Mother Nature" produces particularly evocative and powerful images of what it means to live in a natural environment. The imagery also evokes a whole range of both patriarchal and feminist notions of what "mother" means and then projects these meanings onto the environment. Third, Mother Nature imagery seems to have unconscious or semiconscious roots, by which I mean that unconscious or semiconscious projections shape the content and emotional tone of the imagery. The imagery is thus multivalent, overdetermined, and often works on more than one level. We are not always aware of all these levels and of how they can work against each other. Nor, often, are we fully aware of the emotions and associations the imagery evokes and of the sources and influence of these evocations. Overall, then, images of Mother Nature—even when putatively environmentalist—can portray a response toward nature that is ambiguous and uneasy. Such imagery can undermine its own activism and support a non-environmentalist stance. Given the ubiquity of the imagery and the ecofeminist argument that it not

only expresses but can reinforce negative attitudes toward both nature and women, in-depth analysis of it seems timely.[9]

But if it is true that Mother Nature imagery acts like a lens that
allows one to peer closely at the ambivalent, gendered, and semiconscious patterns of response toward nature that brew "in the wilderness within," why focus in particular on imagery from contemporary popular culture? My choice of pop culture, and especially
of consumer culture, was quite deliberate, although as I have con-
fessed, I made this initial choice as a non-specialist in communications and media studies. My interest in media images began inno-
cently enough. When this project was first taking shape, I saw a
poster that said, "Love Your Mother." (The poster becomes my central
case study in chapter 2.) Soon I noticed the ecological slogan showing up on T-shirts, bumper-stickers, and backpack buttons. My consciousness raised, as it were, I began to notice how often nature
imagery, and particularly Mother Nature imagery, appeared in the
public realm. I suddenly saw it everywhere! I experienced in the form
of an epiphany, so to speak, what is widely known among pop culture, media, and communications scholars: artifacts of popular and
consumer culture can be read as a text of the social construction of
reality. From this angle, something as common as a television commercial becomes a cultural representation and a way of interrogating
the human psyche. Advertising, in the words of Jhally, both reflects
and creates our collective dream life. It is a "fantasy factory" and can
be dissected as a way of studying popular cultural fantasies. Little of
this pop culture approach is practiced in environmental studies, although it strikes me as a very fruitful avenue of work.[10] My interest
focused on how I could use popular nature imagery to access how
American society constructs concepts of nature and to study widespread or influential fantasies and attitudes toward the environment
in this society.

Accordingly, the main images examined in this book are contemporary instances of the Mother Nature motif that have received major
public exposure—and in some cases even critical acclaim. They come
from popular culture and from sources such as television commercials, print advertising, public service announcements, and slogans
created by both business and environmental groups. The authors of
the nature imagery considered here are obviously diverse and often

share no common agenda. However, they all address the public, the constituency of American consumers and popular culture. By referring to this public, I do not mean to efface differences among people or groups within American society or to claim any cultural homogeneity. I merely point out that this society as a whole shares a common status as the intended audience of the messages and imagery examined in this book.

I count myself as part of this constituency of American popular culture and assume that most of my readers do as well, even if they, like I, watch little television and try self-consciously to resist the lures of consumer culture. (I often feel, however, that it makes little difference: billboards, storefront signs, and the corporate logos emblazoned on everything are so omnipresent as to form the subtext of our culture; with those 3,600 commercial impressions a day, one does not have to watch TV to "get the message.") I also identify myself with this constituency even though I am not an American but a Canadian living in the United States. Indeed, many Canadians feel both pleasure and despair that our pop culture is largely American in content. It is, in fact, notoriously difficult to escape the influence of American popular culture: in a world where America is the last superpower and where globalization seems to mean the spread of American-style capitalism, democracy, and free markets, *Bay Watch* and *Dallas* are in reruns all over the planet, spreading the gospel—or the fantasy—of the good life to be had here.

Contemporary Americans are not merely the audience or receivers of this media imagery but also its authors and users. References to "Mother Nature" are ubiquitous and are found in casual conversations about the weather, gardening, or, more ominously, about disasters such as floods and earthquakes. We all use this imagery or know what it means when we hear it. Were this not so, companies such as Nissan ("She will try to drown you . . . ") and the manufacturers of Chiffon margarine ("It's not nice to fool Mother Nature") would not invest heavily in advertising campaigns designed to sell their products by evoking everyday people's emotional responses about nature— often the pleasures of human victory over threatening nature. Corporate marketing departments, advertising agencies, and environmental organizations conduct careful research to ensure that their ad campaigns will have the broadest public appeal, the most "bang for their buck." Their images are designed both to reflect and to evoke widely held responses toward nature. My method is to read these advertisements as a valuable text of feelings about nature that are common but are often unarticulated or even only semiconscious at the level of the individual. The ad campaigns tap into these feelings and give them voice. I use the creators of the advertising, in other words, as social scientists felicitously doing research for me to identify the public's most evocative notions of human-nature relations.

It may be that this method works particularly well in America. This is a country that continues to live and breathe its founding myth that it is the land of freedom and opportunity. I came to the United States from Canada to do my Ph.D. partly because of the power—and to some degree the reality—of that myth. But from an environmental standpoint, the land of opportunity has become today the superpower of capitalism, consumerism, and commodification. These value systems operate at a fever pitch, and advertising is a $175 *billion* dollar a year industry focused assiduously on the support and exploitation of those values. We may well wonder about the status of freedom in a land where Jhally describes advertising as "the most powerful and sustained system of propaganda in human history." Shopping in the United States is therapy, recreation, socializing—it is practically a sport. Everything and anything is for sale, either in the mall or online. Friends recently showed off a wall-mounted plastic trout that wiggled, sang, and even burped, all rather charmingly. They had bought it for other friends in England, as a memento of a recent trip to America. I can really think of no better reminder.[11]

As should be clear by now, my focus on Mother Nature imagery does not serve to claim that nature *is* our mother, but instead to analyze and make problematic such claims. "Mother Nature" in the book's title refers to the environment, but it is also intended to evoke "mother-nature," or the nature of the mothering experience—both of being a mother and of being mothered. The book explores the ambivalence felt toward these double senses of mother-nature and the links between them in contemporary environmental imagery.

But what, then, is meant by "nature," a dense word loaded with layers of history and meaning?[12] The term is a problematic one if it automatically implies female as exploitable or conquered, as I will show that nature imagery not infrequently suggests. Traditional Western definitions of nature as "that which is not human nor produced by humans" and of culture as "that which is human or produced by humans" are also problematic if they maintain a separation that violates ecological lessons of interdependence. Indeed, a significant trend in environmental thought seeks to break down rigid distinctions between the two categories.[13] An irony here, however, is the difficulty of finding a term for nature that does not imply our separation from that to which it refers. We are bound by, even trapped within, the language and history of the Western modernism that has set up this separation.[14]

The resolution, I suggest, is not to seek "environmentally correct" terms from a list of alternatives such as "wilderness," "the earth," "the land," "the planet," "the biosphere," or "the nonhuman world" but instead to become more conscious of the images, actions, emotions, and desires that are ascribed to nature. We can then be more deliberate in our use of symbolic language and imagery, more aware of what these ascriptions say about ourselves and our response to that which we name. In the absence of any agreed-upon right name, then, I use "nature" and other similar vocabulary interchangeably, both to reflect the varied usage within environmental thought and to point out this problem of naming. After all, as cultural historian Clarence Glacken fondly notes about "nature": "With all of its failings, it is a grand old word."[15]

"Nature," of course, can refer also to "human nature." References to "Mother Nature" and "human nature" highlight this amphibolous potential of the word to carry meanings of both "it" and "us." This amphiboly is a bridge of the separation just noted, in that a focus on human relations and experience—as my central argument maintains —can help to decode popular nature imagery. In this sense, I agree with Andy Fisher, an environmental engineer turned ecopsychologist, when, in his discussion of ecopsychology, he clarifies that "'nature' is meant here in two senses: the human nature studied by psychologists (among others) and the more-than-human nature that concerns ecological scientists, thinkers, and activists. Ecopsychology brings these two natures together to study how they are interrelated: how the 'inner' or psychological dimensions of the ecological crisis are linked to the more visible 'outer' manifestations."[16] My project is ecopsychological in this sense, although I do not intend to reify "human nature" as a universal constant, or to make any cross-cultural claims about the human relationship to the natural environment.

Issues of universalism do arise, however, and they are at the heart of two of the tensions in this book. First, I have talked about "the human relationship to nature." The tension here is whether the analysis applies only to America today, or to all of the modern West, or even to global human history. The question is raised: Can one say anything about the "nature of being human in nature" as a cross-cultural, pan-historic phenomenon? Or can one only ever speak about culturally specific and historically located aspects of such a relation? I certainly do not posit that human-nature relations are always and everywhere the same, or that "Mother Nature" functions similarly in all cultural contexts. At the same time, however, I am convinced that the Mother Nature imagery I examine speaks to something more than merely the cultural imagination of America at the turn of the millennium. Current imagery is consistent with images that are older and that come from different cultural contexts (as I will discuss in chapter 2). To be completely honest, I am not sure how widely my argument applies. I do think that analysis of this imagery yields insight into ambivalent attitudes toward nature that, while intensified by the present hyperconsumerism of American culture, are generally characteristic of Western modernity as a whole. However, I am content to limit my conclusions to the context of the material upon which I draw, namely contemporary America. I resolve this tension, then, between a culturally specific analysis and one with wider applications by holding the door open for further research and cross-cultural media studies about Mother Nature.

A second tension arises because some of the theory I use makes universal claims about human identity and experience. For example, psychoanalysis refers to the Oedipus complex or attachment needs as potentially true of all humans; feminism talks about the cross-cultural subordination of women by men; Christian theology describes the human soul and the creation of all humanity. These claims are to varying degrees controversial, and to the extent that they impose as universal what may be only one society's limited view, they are problematic. While my argument does not depend on accepting the claims, I do make certain assertions in the book about what it means to be human. The way I try to resolve this tension between universalist tendencies or essentialism, on the one hand, and complete cultural relativism, on the other hand, is by eschewing notions of "human nature" and instead asking about "human riddles." As generally used, "human nature" tends to be an ahistorical concept that fails to recognize the influence of cultural embeddedness.[17] I do, however, think one can say something about human identity and experience, or as anthropologist Sherry Ortner puts it, one can ask about the "existential questions, even riddles, which humanity everywhere must face."[18]

One of the most central of these riddles, Ortner explains, is "the confrontation between humanity and nature" or "the problem of the relationship between what humanity can do, and that which sets limits upon those possibilities."[19] I agree that part of what it means to be human is to confront the meaning of our "creatureliness," of our existence as human beings within the context and constraints of a natural environment. From the first riddle of this confrontation, there arise at least four other riddles—the further assertions that I develop in this book about what it means to be human. The second riddle is that of relationship itself. Humans are relational beings. Our identity is shaped in and through experience with others. What does it mean to have identity as an individual, yet always to exist in a network of relations? Third, what does it mean that there are things about ourselves that we do not or cannot easily know, or that we find painful to face? My claim here is that there is an element of depth to the human psyche. This is part of what I mean by "the heart of darkness" and what I take Oelschlaeger and Conrad to mean as well. The fourth riddle asks, What is the meaning of gender difference? In all societies, although in different ways, gender acts as a significant lens for structuring social relations. Why is this the case, and why do patterns of subordination result? The fifth riddle is the problem of evil. Tendencies toward what is variously construed as destructiveness or violence or selfishness or sinfulness seem woven into the fabric of being human. This is not to say that we are all or only wicked, but that all societies have regulative moral principles and that people nevertheless hurt one another. This is the other and most painful part of the heart of darkness.

Together, these five riddles or universal problems constitute my claim about what it means to be human. Mother Nature imagery is so rich, so provocative, and so imagistically intense precisely because it embodies all five riddles.

TOOLS OF ANALYSIS:
RELIGION, PSYCHOLOGY, AND GENDER

How, then, can one proceed to decode this imagery? As I attempted to untangle the meaning and function, the roots and fruit, of the pervasive but under-examined Mother Nature imagery, the three theoretical tools of analysis that proved most helpful to me in the task were (1) religious studies, (2) psychology, and (3) gender studies or feminism, all combined together in an interdisciplinary confluence. From religious studies, I draw on Christian thought (mainly Augustinian and neo-orthodox theology and contemporary ecotheology), as well as on critiques of the role of religion in shaping Western cultural concepts of nature and the female. From psychology, I use psychoanalysis (Freud); object relations theory, which is a form of psychoanalytic thought (mainly the important theorist Melanie Klein and some of her present-day interpreters); as well as the work of current ecopsychologists. From feminism, I draw on feminist Christian theology, feminist ethics, psychoanalytic feminism, and ecofeminism.

These three bodies of theory may seem at first to form a rather strange ménage à trois, yet in much of the analysis they get along surprisingly well. All stem from the perennial riddles—posed also by philosophy and literature—about what it means to be human. All ask, What are the tasks and challenges of being human? How can we heal the fractures and failings of being human? All engage profoundly with issues of human destructiveness or evil. A common perspective emerges from the Christian thought and psychoanalysis in particular. Both see humans as divided against ourselves, explore possibilities for healing, and ask whether life can triumph over death. Both focus on ambivalence, on the depths or wilderness of the human heart, on central passions of love and hate, on impulses to connect and repair as well as to destroy. I make this comparison, not to deny the very real differences between Christian theology and psychoanalysis (e.g., a theist vs. an atheist or agnostic stance) or to use either as proof for the other, but simply to argue that they both address key riddles or universal problems about human life. Psychologist of religion James Forsyth, for example, concurs that the "common ground" of theology and psychology "consists not so much in what each discipline has to say about God and religion but in what each says about human existence."[20] Where their considerations are gender-blind or sexist, I use feminist theory as an important corrective.

My approach is thus purposely interdisciplinary because of my conviction that ecological problems and response to nature are so complex that work on these issues needs to draw on more than one field. The resulting cross-pollination of fields yields a harvest of richer fruit.[21] The new and specific contributions I see arising here are: the use of Christian thought for insight into the riddles of evil and the hard-to-know depths of the human heart, insight that helps analyze why patterns of environmental abuse—or other forms of abuse—are so hard to shift; the new use of psychoanalysis as a tool that allows greater explanatory rigor in figuring out the psychosocial roots of the Mother Nature imagery and the resultant development in this text of a psychoanalytic ecopsychology; the application of gender and (eco)feminist analysis of Mother Nature to the under-examined area of pop culture; and, finally, an overall focus from all three theoretical perspectives on the critical but neglected issue of dark or negative passions of anger, resentment, and violence toward nature. By drawing on these three paddles of religious critique, psychoanalytic thought, and feminist theory, I work my way up the Congo to a heart-of-darkness environmentalism.

To say a bit more about each paddle: in general, I draw on religious critique because an important part of many people's relationship to nature is some sense of religion or spirituality. People often report wilderness experience—even a stroll in a city park—to be transformative, uplifting, and inspiring. For example, a poster available online pictures a gorgeous forest scene and carries the caption "Cathedral of Life," reflecting (and seeking to cash in on) this popular sense of nature as spiritually fulfilling and even as itself hallowed or sacred.[22] The transcendent quality of such wilderness experience can be an important motivation to environmentalism, and religious organizations can provide environmental leadership. I suspect that religion or spirituality—very widely defined and variously practiced—is a significant part of the picture for a sound environmental future.

More specifically, in this book I draw on *Christian* thought. My use of it implies no claim here about this tradition's exclusive ability to address issues of ambivalence and human-nature relations. Other religious traditions obviously address these points as well; however, comparative work is not my task here, and there are other texts in environmental studies that already do that task well.[23] Neither is it my point that Christianity offers a particularly reparative vision of the relationship between humans and nature. From an environmental perspective, the tradition is actually burdened by a deep ambivalence toward nature. According to Lynn White's famous thesis, Christianity is even at the root of the present ecological crisis.[24] Genesis 1:28 may legitimate a dominion model in which humans are only following God's divine will by "subduing" the earth and carrying out a program of environmental exploitation.

Instead, I focus on Christianity among the richness of the world's religions because it has been the most influential tradition—for better or worse—in shaping understandings of nature in the modern West. The "for better" is lauded in current Christian ecotheology as the great potential of Christianity's "ecological promise," as in, for example, some form of a stewardship model based instead on the paradigmatic verse of Genesis 2:15 ("The Lord God then took the man and settled him in the garden of Eden, to cultivate and care for it"). At the same time, these ecotheologians often agree with much of the "for worse" in White's critique, and with the historic and contemporary predominance of the dominion model.[25] I am interested in Christianity, in other words, not because I think it provides the answers to life's ultimate questions, but because so many other people have found its answers compelling. Christianity has shaped much of Western culture, including its environmental practices, and is one of the keys to understanding the workings of our culture and to achieving better practices within it. (While I am an occasional churchgoer—raised Catholic and presently becoming involved with a liberal Protestant neighborhood church—I am more of a pantheist than a theist, with a nonpersonal concept of God as the sustaining and transformative "resurrection" power of life, justice, and love in this world.)

I also draw on Christian thought because it is, in my judgment, a particularly powerful tool in Western analytic discourse for addressing the riddles of evil and the hidden depths of the human heart, as well as the hope for healing and for loving relation. Accordingly, I see theology as a perceptive means of analyzing the central problematic of this text: Why does popular environmental imagery evince such ambivalence, anger, and violence toward nature? Almost all eco-theology has relation as its moral aim, whether stated or implied, and demonstrates the need for reparative relations toward the earth. But it much less often draws on its own theological traditions about sin to explain the depth and persistence of ecological sin, to ask questions about why relation seems so problematic for us humans. While Christian thought is not unique in its insight into these dynamics, its discourse on sin and evil as central aspects of human identity is profound. In particular, I find the classical Augustinian and the twentieth-century Protestant neo-orthodox traditions to be helpful (although not entirely unproblematic) on these points. As I will explain, they grant insight—compatible in many ways with psychoanalytic insight—into the fantasy of humans-as-god that animates some of the imagery and the fantasy's attendant themes of sin and dividedness, of reconnection and repair.

There is, however, a tension in my use of Christian thought that needs acknowledging. I am comfortable calling myself an ecofeminist and working within the fold of ecopsychology, but I do not consider myself to be a Christian theologian or an ecotheologian, nor do I intend this book as a work of constructive ecotheology. I draw on Christian theology and ecotheology, not as a theologian, but as a cultural critic working on the boundaries of theology.[26] I do not *do* theology, but instead I engage in theological criticism. I am not primarily interested in what theological discourse has to say about God, but instead in what it has to say about conflicts in human identity and society. I focus on the human side of theology's interest in the God-human relation (in technical terms, I am interested in what is called "theological anthropology," or theological notions of personhood). In other words, whether or not Christian theology is right about the existence of God, I think it gets much right about the riddles of human nature. Theology thus functions for me as one critical discourse among others in this text and as an astute form of cultural criticism and psychosocial theory. It is no new observation to say that Christian theology engages in much "psychology," in that it is study of the *psyche,* or soul, as much as it is study of God and God's revelation. William James wrote that the "common nucleus" of all religions is a two-part feeling of something being *"wrong about us* as we naturally stand" and of salvation coming through "proper connection with the higher powers."[27] To the extent that Christian theology focuses on this first part of the uneasiness of the human condition, it shares common ground with psychology. I thus draw equally on Christian theology and psychoanalysis in a psychosocial method that neither subsumes theology under the rubric of psychology nor privileges theology.[28]

My second paddle in this psychosocial method is psychoanalysis. As I have said, I believe that key human riddles are as relevant as notions about nature in any analysis of human relations to the environment. Theorists gain a more complex understanding of representations of nature and motives for environmental abuse by exploring the psychological—and theological—territory of the "wilderness within the human soul." But this individual territory is always also the social. I am interested in both the psychological and the social dimensions of environmental issues and in the interplay between these dimensions. Individuals always participate—sometimes unwittingly or unwillingly—in groups, institutions, and larger social structures and processes. As such, much environmental imagery and damage operates at a level higher than that of the individual. From this perspective, environmental abuse is a form of what feminist theorist Nel Noddings calls "cultural evil."[29] It is often neither committed by the individual nor resolvable by the individual. Dorothy Dinnerstein—whose brilliant work encompasses psychoanalytic, feminist, and environmental concerns—is particularly helpful on this point. Speaking about our "murder of nature," she writes: "Our predicament clearly also has to do with societal factors of the blind kind that Tolstoy described in *War and Peace*—historical and sociological processes whose overall shape does not at all coincide with any participant's motives, and only fragments of which are represented in any participant's awareness. But psychological processes of the kind referred to here—processes rooted deep in 'normal' personality, and mutable only if confronted—must be an important part of the explanation."[30]

In line with Dinnerstein, my use of psychoanalysis is not intended as an argument that either environmental damage or nature imagery should be understood in purely individual, psychological terms. My point is that collective, societal factors (economic, technological, demographic, etc.) do not tell the whole story. I am less interested in the responsibility of government or multinational corporations for environmental abuse and more interested in a wide-shared individual responsibility deducible from the patterns of response toward nature portrayed and elicited by the imagery of popular culture. Social ecology locates problems of environmental destruction in society, in social domination and capitalist exploitation.[31] But psychoanalytic theory argues that internal processes help underpin such hierarchy and exploitation. This theory shows how the psychological and the social are intimately related, as the internal world creates meaning in the external world, as intrapsychic or unconscious processes interplay with external relations. Accordingly, the method I pursue with the help of psychoanalytic object relations theory is psychosocial. Our understanding of environmental problems deepens when we pay attention to intrapsychic and interpersonal dynamics, to unconscious motivation, to fantasy and emotion—for such factors help shape responses to nature.

The final paddle powering my journey up the Congo to the heart of darkness is feminist theory, used in this text in a variety of forms. As one of my colleagues remarked, there is a warmth and reassurance to the image of "good ol' Mom." Mother Nature imagery speaks directly to the experience many of us have of nature providing both physical and spiritual refueling—there is nothing quite so rejuvenating as a walk in the woods—two things that the real "good ol' Mom" often provided as well.[32] But a feminist perspective asks about the negative effects on mom and on women in general of using her as a "fuel source." Ecofeminists add the argument that casting nature as mother can easily compound environmental problems if all of nature is then viewed as a never-ending source of energy and resources. No reading of Mother Nature is complete without careful attention to these gender dynamics.

As I trace expressions of nature in popular culture, I focus in particular on how human gender relations and gendered childcare arrangements (where men "father" children but women still overwhelmingly do the "mothering") matter for the environment. I draw on feminist psychoanalytic theory to probe why Mother Nature imagery holds such power and to uncover some of the dangers of its operation in the cultural imagination. Object relations theorists like

Klein are particularly relevant here since so much of their analysis focuses on mother-child dynamics. Feminist theologians and eco-theologians critique patriarchal religion that links woman and nature and that too often finds both to be morally suspect. Such feminist theology, with its deep commitment to relationality and its critique of oppression, also aids in the construction of an alternate and more healing vision of human-nature relations.

Overall, then, my method in this book is to engage in a close reading of nature imagery in popular American culture as a way to build a vision of earth healing, a heart-of-darkness environmental ethic that incorporates insights of ecotheology, ecopsychology, and ecofeminism. The book is divided into three parts of two chapters each. Each part focuses on a major motif of Mother Nature imagery and is structured around a case study of that motif. Part I, "Nature as Good Mother," examines the notion that nature is, or is like, a beneficent and nurturing mother who provides and maintains all life. Chapter 2 starts with a case study of the green slogan "Love Your Mother." Here I draw on feminist and ecofeminist theory to ask about the effects, for women and for the environment, of imputing female gender to nature. Chapter 3 then adopts a psychological and feminist framework to dig deeper into some of the unconscious content of this imagery. What associations with motherhood and mothering does this imagery carry from a culture still shaped by patriarchy? I argue here that "Love Your Mother" backfires if "mother" evokes traditional meanings of a bountiful, self-sacrificing provider who herself requires no care.

Part II explores the flip side of this motif in "Nature as Bad Mother." Nature here becomes the violent, threatening, wrathful mother, as exemplified in the case study in chapter 4 of commercials for the Nissan Pathfinder and Chiffon margarine, where humans and their technology master unruly versions of Mother Nature. The chapter draws on theological reflection to analyze this ambivalence in terms of a fantasy that casts humans as gods and explores the contributions of (eco)theology and (eco)psychology to a heart-of-darkness environmentalism. Chapter 5 borrows from a psychoanalytic perspective to put forward a theory about why nature becomes mother in the cultural imagination and why this mother is then split into "good" and "bad."

Part III, "Nature as Hurt Mother," looks at possibilities and pitfalls of environmental healing in the image of nature as the mother we have wounded and now seek to heal. The environmental group Earth Communications Office produced an award-winning public service announcement called "Mother" that portrays this image well. Chapter 6 examines this case study and develops from it criteria for judging the effectiveness of healing imagery. Finally, Chapter 7 synthesizes the book's analysis in a feminist/theological/psychological environmental ethic that shows how, within limits, a relational model of self can help us work through ambivalence toward healing.

A final point about the book is that its ultimate purpose is pragmatic, in the tradition of the pragmatic philosophy of William James, which proves itself useful as an ethical basis for environmentalism. James advocates a deeply moral vision of commitment to the future based on his meliorist belief that our acts create meaning in the world and hold the possibility of creating the world's salvation. He judges the truth and value of ideas by their consequences, or the "fruits of their action." We should try out different ideas, he counsels, and, as the criterion of their usefulness, "listen to the cries of the wounded" that result from their implementation. The wounded determine which are "best," in the sense of which cause the least suffering. In an environmental context, such an ethic translates into attending carefully to signs of disruption or damage to ecosystems and their populations. It addresses the question of how humans can make decisions about what is best for the rest of nature—the test is one of time and the welfare of all the community's individuals.[33]

James's criterion of "listening to the cries of the wounded" also helps us judge the difficult question of what counts as environmentally sound, since problems of ecological degradation present enormous complexities we often seem ill-equipped to resolve. Our knowledge of ecology is often too limited to judge what is best for ecosystems where flux and complexity are the rule, where natural degradation occurs alongside human-caused damage, and where it is not always obvious how to judge what constitutes degradation. Should we allow wildfires to burn or battle to put them out? Should we reintroduce wolves and grizzly bears to Western states? Many such questions of ecological change are difficult to judge. Environmental scientists do, however, know something about what constitutes "sustainability." It is characterized above all by balance, such as between human population and the planet's carrying capacity; soil erosion and new soil formation; tree cutting and tree planting; the number of fish caught and fisheries' sustainable yield; the cattle on a range and the range's carrying capacity; water pumping and aquifer recharge; carbon emissions and carbon fixation; plant and animal species lost and those newly evolved. In a sustainable global system, all these factors are in balance, and neither side exceeds the other.[34] Anything that seems to support such balance—and this too is certainly a difficult judgment —is environmentally healthy or sound. Anything that does not raises instead "cries of the wounded" to which it behooves us to attend.

This book, then, is concerned with ideas' fruits and with earth healing. If representations of nature contain multiple, ambiguous, and sometimes domineering messages about human-nature relations, which images best support or inspire environmentally sound action? Which raise the fewest cries of the wounded? And how can we hope to halt destructive behaviors and motivate sound ones? On this, the ultimate pragmatic question for environmentalism, I am guided by Dinnerstein's earlier comment that the roots of "our murder of nature" are "mutable only if confronted." Accordingly, this book confronts in order to change.

In this book I trace deep roots of patterns of response to nature, roots that stretch down into the grounds of human identity and early family relations. Because these roots are largely unconscious, their influence is powerful and not always recognized. I try to bring them to light, out of a pragmatic conviction that awareness of unconscious influences and tendencies provides protection against these forces. Knowledge of the depths is transformative in a way that knowledge of conscious processes alone is not. As *State of the World* warns, "The roots of environmental damage run deep. Unless they are unearthed soon, we risk exceeding the planet's carrying capacity to such a degree that a future of economic and social decline will be impossible to avoid."[35] This project sheds light on one set of these roots by looking at what feeds popular imagery of nature produced and consumed in America.

Part One:
Nature as Good Mother

TWO

"Love Your Mother"

I will sing of well-founded Gaia, Mother of All, eldest of all beings, she feeds
all creatures that are in the world, all that go upon the goodly land and all
that are in the paths of the sea, and all that fly: all these are fed of her store.
                                    —*Homeric hymn to Earth, 7th century* B.C.

Throughout Western history, the answer to the question What is nature? has been, not infrequently, some version of "like a female." This
answer draws on cultural meanings of "nurturing" and "life-giving"
(the Good Mother), but also "quixotic" and "dangerous" (the Bad
Mother), as well as "frail" and "in need of male protection" (the Hurt
Mother). Gendered images and metaphors of nature are common,
both historically and presently. Furthermore, this gendering of nature
is not merely accidental or metaphorical, but it is central to how Western culture tends to understand both nature and women.[1]

A fundamental claim I make in this book is the ecofeminist one
that more attention needs to be paid to the complex ways that these
categories of "nature" and "female/mother" overlap. I begin the task
here by introducing the category of Mother Nature imagery through
its most familiar form: that of nature as a loving and kindly mother
whom we, as her human children, are called on to love in return.
What is the meaning of this link between nature and the female, especially in this form of the idealized Good Mother? To what degree
is the association real, beneficial, and something that both feminism
and the environmental movement should embrace? If the imagery
is problematic, how should we respond to it? Should we reclaim, rehabilitate, and embrace it as embodying a powerful feminine truth;
or should we instead reject it outright as irremediably sexist? I consider these first two options in this chapter in order to argue for a
third: that what we really need is to break down or "biodegrade" the
hierarchical dualisms implied in this Mother Nature imagery. By doing so, we start to get closer to what the imagery is all about.

Figure 1. *"Love Your Mother."* Environmental button.
Collection of author.

LOVING MOTHER EARTH:
CASE STUDY OF A BUMPER STICKER

The environmental movement has gathered such momentum that wherever one looks one can find posters, billboards, advertisements, and other eco-paraphernalia urging protection of the environment. Many people will be familiar, then, with a particular sign that also appears frequently on T-shirts, buttons, or bumper stickers (see Figure 1). It consists of a picture and a short phrase. The picture is the whole-earth image of the planet as seen from outer space. The phrase, printed on, underneath, or beside it reads, "Love Your Mother." This poster has become a leading American example of Mother Nature imagery.

The mother referred to in the poster is clearly "Mother Nature" or "Mother Earth." The slogan metaphorically equates the environment with childbearing women. In thus directing us to love our mother, environmentalists communicate three messages. The first, conveyed through use of the imperative "love," is the exhortation to care for and maintain the health of the earth. The question immediately arises, however: Why pass through the metaphor of loving one's mother in order to express a message of ecological soundness? The text is deceptive to the extent that although it makes no mention of real-life mothers, it does seek to take advantage of certain generally assumed ideas about motherhood and its connection to nature. These ideas lend the slogan its aura of aptness. Two such assumptions are that we all should love our real-life mothers, and that we all can intuitively grasp how the planet is, in a sense, our mother. This is indeed the second message of the slogan, carried by the phrase "your mother." It is the central environmentalist message that we are all closely tied to nature, that our very existence derives from and depends on a healthy environment, as life once derived from a mother. By imaging the earth this way, the poster seeks to play on our love for our mothers.

But how well does the metaphor of mother apply to the earth? How appropriate is it? On first consideration, nature does seem to fit reasonably enough into the metaphor. After all, it is from the environment that we draw our oxygen, food, water, and all of the raw materials from which we fashion the endless items making up the materiality of our culture. As a fetus in the womb or a nursling at the breast forms its body by drawing from the body of the mother, so too does material culture take shape through human transformation of the physical environment. This environment is certainly life-giving and life-sustaining, as were and are most mothers. Nature as mother seems, at least in these ways, an apt and felicitous metaphor.

These reflections uncover the third message of "Love Your Mother" and the real heart of its imagery: nature, the slogan tells us, is the *Good Mother.* American literary historian Annette Kolodny calls this "America's oldest and most cherished fantasy: . . . the land as woman, the total female principle of gratification—enclosing the individual in an environment of receptivity, repose, and painless and integral satisfaction."[2] The phrase "Love Your Mother" conveys a sense of nature as a bountiful, beneficent, and nurturing mother, whom we are directed to cherish in return, precisely because of the loving care she bestows upon us, her children. We frequently find "Mother Earth" or "Mother Nature" used as metaphor for this sense that nature attends to our needs and shares with us her riches. The allusion appears in the title of such diverse twentieth-century publications as a book on natural resources called *Enough and to Spare: Mother Earth Can Nourish Every Man in Freedom;* a Pennsylvania state map detailing "sources of primary wealth" subtitled *Plants, Animals, Minerals, Fundamental Products of Mother Earth;* a text on steam power plants titled *The Geothermal Steam Story: Or a Hot Tip from Mother Earth;* and a natural diet cookbook with the subtitle *Cookin' with Mother Nature!*[3]

Even such common phrases as "rape of the earth" and "virgin forest" or "virgin land" convey a message that nature has something valuable that humans want, whether or not she is willing to bestow it. Here violence enters into the narrative, and the Good Mother becomes the Hurt Mother. The ecofeminist book *Rape of the Wild* evokes this latter motif of the fertile but wounded earth by linking the violent treatment of women with violence against animals and the ecosphere. Or note the imagery in an essay about the shutdown of a formerly booming West Virginia coal town: Bimbo, an ex-miner, says "Yeah, this was it. This was the titty, where they sucked the black gold out the earth."[4] (Part III will examine the motif of the Hurt Mother in detail.)

This sense of the environment as bountiful female participates in an ancient tradition of association. The Mother Nature image, or nature as the Great Mother, appears to be almost timeless. It is found in figurines, cave paintings, and burial practices that date back to early human prehistory. Based on this evidence, nature as the Great Mother may, indeed, be the oldest human idea and the first religious practice. Although my focus in this book is on contemporary imagery, a few older examples reveal this rich historical context. These examples also raise a question about what, exactly, is the connection that links images of Mother Nature today with those from thousands of years ago. On the one hand, it is more than obvious that dramatically different social matrices are at play in the examples below drawn from Paleolithic times, classical Greece and Rome, seventeenth-century England, and contemporary America. These differences matter for cultural readings of nature imagery such as I am attempting here, and I want to avoid the anachronism or ahistoricity of pretending that the cultural differences do not matter. Mother Nature, or nature as Great Mother, does not carry the same meaning in these different cultural contexts. On the other hand, given these differences, what accounts for the transmission of "Mother Nature" as a cultural trope across cultures and centuries? Why does it endure, and in forms similar enough to be recognizable from the Paleolithic, or at least the classical period, to today? Is the apparent "naturalness" of the metaphor itself a sufficient explanation? Are the fertility of the earth, woman's biological role as child-bearer, and her social role as child-rearer together sufficient to account for the commonness of this imagery? My preliminary answer is a heavily qualified "yes," with much of this book about explaining the "yes." In this connection I will explore the implications of women's child-rearing role as a social role that only appears to be natural within patriarchal societies.[5]

Here, then, is a brief collage, somewhat randomly chosen from Western art, poetry, and prose to convey how powerful, long-standing, and widespread is the sense of the environment as bountiful female. Paleolithic peoples regarded nature as the Great Mother who nurtured them "much as a mother nourishes her baby at her breast."[6] The Goddess of Laussel, one of the earliest such images we have, was sculpted from a rock face at the entrance to the cave of Cap Blanc, near Les Eyzies in the valley of the Dordogne, France (see Figure 2). It has been dated 20,000–18,000 B.C.E. This Paleolithic figure holds up a notched bison horn, believed to represent the crescent moon and the thirteen-month lunar calendar. Her rounded, fleshy buttocks and belly are common for the goddess figurines of the time. The rock relief is painted with red ochre, "the magic color of menstruation and birth."[7] The Classical Greeks revered the Earth Goddess Gaia—as quoted in the chapter epigraph and in a usage currently resurrected by some scientists, environmentalists, and neo-pagans—as "Mother of All." The Romans sang a hymn to the holy goddess Tellus Mater (Mother Earth), Mother of Living Nature. This second-century Roman hymn reads in part:

> The food of life
> Thou metest out in eternal loyalty
> And, when life has left us,
> We take our refuge in Thee.
> Thus everything Thou dolest out
> Returns into Thy womb.[8]

Note that in all these uses, nature is not just the Good Mother but is actually a divine goddess, source of all food and indeed of all life.

Figure 2. *Goddess of
Laussel.* Paleolithic stone
carving. Les Eyzies,
Dordogne, France, ca.
20,000–18,000 B.C.E.
Photograph used
with permission
of Courtney Milne
www.CourtneyMilne.com.

It/she could hardly be more respected. Described as eternally loyal to
her creation, she seems loving and beneficent, although there is the
reminder that she is also the site of death when all return to her
womb. The first-century Alexandrian Jewish scholar Philo continues
the theme of nature as life-source. He identified nature with mother
as food-provider and focused on the breast as the font of "abundance":

> Nature has bestowed on every mother as a most essential
> endowment teeming breasts, thus preparing in advance food
> for the child that is to be born. The earth also, as we all know,
> is a mother, for which reason the earliest men thought fit to call
> her "Demeter," combining the name of "mother" with that of
> "earth"; for as Plato says, earth does not imitate women, but
> woman earth. . . . Fitly therefore on earth also, most ancient

and most fertile of mothers, did Nature bestow, by way of breasts, streams of rivers and springs, to the end that both the plants might be watered and all animals might have abundance to drink.[9]

Here the earth is a mother whom human women imitate. Earth and women alike share a "teeming" fertility and bountifulness that they offer freely to all offspring.

While in the previous examples, Mother Earth willingly "metest out the food of life" as the Good Mother, in another version of the theme, humans take that sustenance from her, sometimes violently. She then becomes the Bad Mother (since deliberately withholding) or the Hurt Mother (since wounded by man's taking). A famous chorus from Sophocles' play *Antigone* (c. 441 B.C.) celebrates man's conquest of nature:

> And she, the greatest of gods, the Earth—
> ageless she is, and unwearied—he wears her away
> as the ploughs go up and down from year to year
> and his mules turn up the soil.

This example highlights the ancient identification of the female and the plowed earth. The identification reoccurs later in the play when Antigone's uncle Creon—a character seemingly obsessed with the need for men to be in control over women—defends his decision to kill his rebellious niece, who is betrothed to his son, with the contemptuous line, "Oh, there are other furrows for his plough."[10] Nature is still a fertile mother who provides for humanity, but here that bounty is taken by force. Neither nature nor woman is in control of the giving but instead depicted as tamed and mastered by man/humans.

Another more benign take on this theme is found in a poem by the seventeenth-century English poet John Donne. He playfully compares his mistress to the rich mines and "new-found-land" of America:

> O my America! my new-found-land,
> My kingdom, safliest when with one man manned,
> My mine of precious stones, my empery,
> How blest am I in this discovering thee!

This passage is addressed to a woman who is compared to a continent, a mine, an empire. While this example of woman-as-nature repeats the theme of control—she is "safliest when with one man manned" —and emphasizes his possession of her, yet the tone of the poem is loving and playful.[11]

As a final example, the nineteenth-century German scholar J. J. Bachofen draws on the woman-nature association for his theory of history in which the higher civilization of patriarchy supersedes the earlier and inferior earthbound matriarchy. He explicitly links human motherhood with nature and associates both with a lower realm, contrasted with paternity and the heavens:

> The triumph of paternity [over maternity and matriarchy] brings with it the liberation of the spirit from the manifestation of nature, a sublimation of human existence over the laws of material life. . . . Triumphant paternity partakes of the heavenly light, while childbearing motherhood is bound up with the earth that bears all things.[12]

Note the similarity within the diversity of the examples. All have in common a metaphorical identification of woman as nature and of nature as woman, with both described as the site of bounty. The association works in these two interrelated directions: while cultural representations portray nature as metaphorically or literally mother, they also identify woman with nature. She is more associated with the carnal, the emotional, and the physical than is man, who is more associated with the cultural, the intellectual, and the spiritual. These associations hold true within the examples given even when the cultural projects with which men are linked—agriculture, mining, and the exploration of new continents—are metaphorically rendered as ones of sexual conquest. The bidirectionality of the woman-nature relation is one indication of its strength and of how closely intertwined are these two categories.[13] Furthermore, these examples reveal an emotionally charged relationship between the speaking subject and the woman/nature to which the quotation refers. These relationships presume a sense of both Mother Nature and women as fruitful or yielding for the benefit of humanity. In these and other examples later in the book, the emotional tone of the relation varies from being sometimes loving and respectful, to sometimes lustful, sometimes condescending and controlling, sometimes suspicious and fearful, and sometimes downright violently adversarial. I am fascinated by this diversity of emotional response to what is essentially the same relation. Much of what I explore in this book are psychosocial reasons for the ambivalence and intensity revealed in this response.

In regard to this ambivalence of tone—and to return to "Love Your Mother"—I find the picture accompanying the slogan on the posters, bumper stickers, and buttons to be itself significant. Its whole-earth image reveals the full circle of the planet, swirled in atmosphere, set alone in empty space. On the positive side, this representation highlights the oneness, beauty, and finiteness of the earth. However, it also shows the planet as a remote ball suspended in space in a way we never see the earth at first hand unless we are participants in a billion-dollar space project. This is an image of nature as separate and distant, as an isolated object without context. Despite the accompanying text's invocation of the loving and beloved mother, choosing this picture for the "Love Your Mother" slogan emphasizes for me the negative aspects of patriarchal motherhood: mother as idealized, the perfectly round globe-breast; mother as mysterious, shrouded in cloud; mother as ambivalent love-object from whom we seek to separate, left behind and abandoned in space.[14] In chapter 3, I investigate the ways in which mothering and motherhood function problematically in patriarchal culture and then lead to the Bad Mother motif, but the prior task is to examine how the equation of nature with mother becomes problematic itself, from both a feminist and an environmentalist point of view.

The problem, simply put, is that nature is also *not* our mother. While the planet is certainly life-giving, it is not a person who gave birth to us and/or reared us in a one-on-one family relationship. While the earth may well function as a self-regulating organism—as the Gaia hypothesis claims—it is not our personal mother. Ecotheologian Sallie McFague discusses the "is" and "is not" function of metaphors; they should both shock us (the "is not") and evoke recognition (the "is"). A metaphor, she writes, is not a definition but a likely account.[15] I do not deny that nature is like a mother in certain ways, but I want to argue that the "is not" aspect needs more emphasis. Although the "Love Your Mother" slogan and other examples of nature as the Good Mother seem at first glance to be positive and helpful images, from a feminist and environmentalist perspective, the complexities of their function can often undermine their appeal. Neither women nor nature benefit when the environment is described exclusively or unthinkingly in terms of the mother, even if she is loving. The rest of the chapter explores the why of this "is not."

ECOFEMINIST CRITIQUE

Despite the entanglement of notions of "nature" with those of "mother," the association seems curiously ignored outside of gender studies and ecofeminist circles. Although ecofeminism is a vibrant field that has seen huge growth in the last couple of decades, environmental thought tends to keep gender analysis on its periphery and to ghettoize ecofeminism as mainly of interest to radical feminists. Until recently, historians and environmental theorists spent little time discussing the role of gender in relation to nature, let alone engaging in sustained gender analysis. For example, Clarence Glacken, in his magisterial history of ideas of nature, *Traces on the Rhodian Shore* (1967), rarely focuses on references to nature as female. William Leiss's *The Domination of Nature* (1972) analyzes in a mere paragraph the significance of nature cast as female, in a discussion of Bacon's imagery of sexual aggression. Henry Nash Smith's *Virgin Land: The American West as Symbol and Myth* (1950) pays scant attention to the suggestion of gendered nature in its title metaphor. All three give brief indications that nature is at least sometimes imaged as female in the traditions they study, but they seem to take such associations for granted and do not subject them to critical study. They either fail to pick up on the references or dismiss them rather quickly as simply having to do with the primordial, the irrational, or the pagan.[16]

Before the widespread advent of feminist scholarship in the 1970s and 1980s, gender simply did not seem to be a major category of analysis in studies of nature. Nor do more contemporary works of environmental thought always attend seriously to issues of gender, unless their intent is explicitly ecofeminist or at least focused on women. In this latter category, Annette Kolodny's *The Land Before Her* (1984) and Vera Norwood's *Made From This Earth* (1993) both examine the history of American women's responses to nature (as landscape, frontier, or ecosystem) without either of them being ecofeminist works. Similarly, Kolodny's earlier book *The Lay of the Land* (1975)—written before the real development of ecofeminist thought, although pre-figuring its interests and some of the psychosocial analysis I develop here—traces "land-as-woman" as the central metaphor of the pastoral experience in American life and letters. But even the recent cutting-edge anthology *Uncommon Ground: Rethinking the Human Place in Nature* (1996) analyzes in the editor's extensive introductory essay eight different notions of nature as part of an argument that these ideas are social constructions—including nature as external reality, as Eden, as commodity, and as demonic other—without ever making mention of nature as female.[17]

Any such gender-blind analysis misses a key element of environmental imagery. A cursory study of popular culture—or even of television weather forecasting—reveals "Mother Nature" to be a major motif in conceptualizing nature. Because of this prevalence, gender analysis and ecofeminism can help us get to the heart of how society constructs concepts of nature and how gender serves as a central category in Western constructions of nature-culture relations. Ecofeminist scholarship documents the function of the woman-nature link and demonstrates how women in patriarchal contexts tend to suffer from it. This critique provides a preliminary approach to evaluating the motif of nature as Good Mother by showing that Mother Nature imagery carries more than merely metaphorical weight.

Sherry Ortner, an anthropologist, was one of the first to frame this problem. In a seminal 1974 article entitled "Is Female to Male as Nature is to Culture?" she argued that women are cross-culturally perceived to be closer to nature than men and that this perception accounts for women's universal subordination, since nature is itself universally devalued. Others—such as Colette Guillaumin, Dorothy Dinnerstein, Carolyn Merchant, Elizabeth Dodson Gray, Rosemary Radford Ruether, and Susan Griffin—responded and contributed to the debate to the point where critique of the woman-nature association is now well established by ecofeminist scholarship.[18]

I draw on this work to address the central question of my book: What is the meaning of Mother Nature imagery, and does it help out an environmental agenda or not? As the foundation of my analysis, I accept the basic ecofeminist argument, which strikes me as quite compelling and well supported by the literature: in patriarchal culture, when women are symbolically associated with nature or seen as having a particular affinity with nature that surpasses that of men, then women are seen as less fully human than men. Susan Griffin, for example, in her passionate and poetic book, *Woman and Nature: The Roaring Inside Her,* illustrates how this traditional association contributes to women's voicelessness and powerlessness by assigning woman the roles of passive and obedient reproducer and nurturer (in her chapter entitled "Cows"); obstinate and dull-witted drudge, bred for labor the breeders do not wish to do ("Mules"); and well-trained and well-groomed gratifier of her master ("The Show Horse"). One way to put this point reveals the connection between woman-as-nature and nature-as-mother: in patriarchal culture women are under-personified, and nature is over-personified. Women are perceived to merge with nature as servile resource, as part of the nonhuman surround and only semi-human. Nature, meanwhile, is perceived as female; as virgin or bountiful mother; as having personality, will, and the means to carry out her intentions. "We cannot believe," Dinnerstein notes, "how accidental, unconscious, unconcerned—i.e., unmotherly—nature really is; and we cannot believe how vulnerable, conscious, autonomously wishful—i.e., human—the early mother really was."[19]

The consequences for both women and nature can be noxious. Both are seen as an endless source of succor, who, if she fails to provide what we want, is cruelly withholding it, so justifying our exploitation or plunder. Love your mother, in other words, but feel free to rape her as well.[20] Women suffer because both men and women alike have trouble seeing women as fully human, autonomous subjects; instead they remain closer to objects. Women are perceived as a "natural resource, as an asset to be owned and harnessed, harvested and mined, with no fellow-feeling for her depletion and no responsibility for her conservation or replenishment."[21] Even when women are exalted as purer than men, as less bestial, and as the "guardians of culture and morals," Ortner points out that these seeming "inversions" merely place women above instead of below culture and that in both cases women remain excluded from the realm of culture.[22]

Although the notion of nature as mother is an evocative one, according to another pattern of interpretation nature is an inert, lifeless machine. Carolyn Merchant explains the historical confluence of these two notions in her persuasive reassessment of the rise of science in the sixteenth and seventeenth centuries. The Scientific Revolution brought about a change from organic to mechanistic models of nature. Prevailing images of the cosmos shifted from living female being to machine or inanimate, dead physical system. Nature is no longer seen as a "nurturing mother, sensitive, alive, and responsive to human action." It becomes instead a "disorderly and chaotic realm to be subdued and controlled" and a machine to be operated and managed. Yet, as Merchant explains, even when nature is no longer primarily the nurturing mother, metaphors used to describe nature remain largely female. The language of mechanism and the new experimental science is often that of sexual mastery, of enslavement and rape. Merchant cites numerous examples, such as Francis Bacon's promise in *The Masculine Birth of Time:* "I am come in very truth leading to you nature with all her children to bind her to your service and make her your slave." Baconian imagery of domination over nature includes references to mining as wresting hidden secrets and goods from nature's withholding womb and to how, through use of anvil and forge, nature can be "forced out of her natural state and squeezed and molded."[23] Similarly, cultural understandings of the female cast women's bodies, in the words of feminist theorist Adrienne Rich, as "both territory and machine, virgin wilderness to be exploited and assembly-line turning out life."[24]

Overall, it seems to me that the implications of these ecofeminist assessments are clear: As long as women are associated with nature within a cultural complex that perceives nature to be on the one hand semihuman, on the other hand mechanical, and in both cases legitimately exploitable, then women will be viewed as a resource, and both they and the environment will suffer. The woman-nature association, in its traditional form and in societies traditionally patriarchal, becomes both sexist and environmentally unsound.

ARE WOMEN CLOSER TO NATURE?

What, then, are we to do with Mother Nature imagery in general, and with the motif of the Good Mother in particular? If this imagery associates women with nature, does it have negative consequences for women and ultimately backfire for the environment? We can find an answer to this question by looking at a debate within ecofeminism as to whether women are, in fact, "closer to nature" than men. This debate arises directly from the "Love Your Mother" slogan itself. To the extent that the Good Mother motif claims nature to be the loving mother of humanity, it also implies that women (or at least mothers) are closer to nature or more easily in tune with it than men. Since nature supports all life, women, who similarly are the life-givers of the human species, would seem to have a greater affinity or a closer connection to the natural realm than men. The imagery further implies that it is a good thing for the planet that women have this special affinity. As a result of being closer to nature and being the species' child-bearers and child-rearers, women are claimed to also be more nurturant than men. They are programmed or "hard-wired," as it were, to nurture not only children but people in general and the environment as well, to be on the whole more peaceful and environmentally friendly than men.

These implications need closer examination. If every time someone waves a "Love Your Mother" banner, this act triggers and reinforces assumptions, held at least to some degree in the cultural imagination, that women care more, or more easily, about nature, then what effect do these assumptions have on women's (and men's) lives? And are they true? While much of my concern is with the import of imagery for the environment, ecofeminism—like social ecology and the environmental justice movement—also directs concern toward people's lives. What, then, are the implications of the Good Mother Nature motif, not just for the environment, but for contemporary women as well? We can get at this concern through the ecofeminist discussion over whether women are closer to nature than men.

Three options have been adopted by various feminists, environmentalists, and ecofeminists at different times, but only the last seems really viable to me as a way of decoding the Mother Nature imagery and avoiding some of its problems. The first option says that imagery of nature as the Good Mother is empowering for women and can also help the environment since women are, in fact, closer to nature. The second position claims that women are fully cultural beings who are not in any way closer to nature than men and that, accordingly, Mother Nature imagery is misleading, sexist, harmful, and should be rejected completely. The third position argues that the problem actually lies in a false hierarchical opposition between the categories of nature and culture themselves.[25]

Those in the first position tend to find "Love Your Mother" imagery to be positive for women. They see it as a contemporary way of rehabilitating the woman-nature association from the problems described above. This option agrees that women are, in fact, closer to nature but disagrees that the association must be disempowering. This choice within ecofeminism is sometimes called the "nature feminist" position; it often, but not invariably, entails involvement with feminist spirituality, Wicca, or goddess worship.[26] Here the problem lies not with the woman-nature association itself but with the patriarchal devaluation of both women and nature. Within an environmentalist, post-patriarchal value system in which nature and women were accorded high value—if (forgive my cynicism) such a vision be not merely utopian—we could reclaim the association and promote it as enriching and empowering. Imagery of nature as Good Mother may help to do exactly that. The respectful environmental intent of the imagery, coupled with its insistence on the goodness of the mother, may well begin to negate problems with the imagery identified in the earlier section of ecofeminist analysis. What, then, does it mean to say that women are on the whole more in tune with nature than men? Does this claim indeed rehabilitate the imagery?

Feminists and ecofeminists here connect women with nature as part of an overall theory of gender difference that tends to portray men as more aggressive and destructive than women, and women as more caring and peaceable than men. These differences are considered to be either innate or socialized. In a environmental context, such views blame the ecological crisis on male abusive greed and on a patriarchal order. It follows from this theory of gender difference that women are then the ones who can cure environmental ills. For example, Françoise d'Eaubonne, who coined the term "éco-féminisme" in 1974, argues that "the destruction of the planet is due to the profit motive inherent in male power" and that only women can bring about an ecological revolution.[27] Other writers, such as Ruether and Heller, lay major responsibility for environmental degradation at the feet of elite males.[28] Mary Daly, in a foreword to Andrée Collard's *Rape of the Wild*, refers to "the evil wrought by the patriarchal rapers of the Earth" and "the oneness of women's struggles to save our Selves and to save the planet." "*Rape of the Wild*," Daly asserts, "is a Call to women to protect our home."[29] And in an essay titled "Gaia

Women," Canadian environmental activist Elizabeth May insists that women are essentially different from men: "biologically and spiritually connected to the cosmos . . . more nurturing, more concerned with the flow and flux of life . . . much more *selfless* than men." "Consciously or not," she says, as women "we feel ourselves part of Gaia."[30]

These analyses assume men—at least elite men of the industrialized Western world—to be more alienated from nature than women and in some cases more immoral than women, in general as well as in terms of their participation in ecological destruction. I do not dispute that many of the decisions resulting in pollution, species extinction, and overuse of the earth's resources are made by elite white males at the level of large corporations, governments, and international organizations. But I am less certain that we can then conclude that women are innocent of causing damage to the environment, possessed of a concern and love for nature lacking in men, and more capable of effecting ecological healing. It seems somewhat of an oversimplification and even somewhat dangerous to assume that women are "by nature" or by socialization nurturant, benign beings who need only be given free rein for the world to become a better place.

As illustration of this danger, consider the cover art of *Ecofeminism*, a recent anthology of essays in the field. The colorful and attractive painting by Jane Evershed is entitled *Women Wiping Up the World* (see Figure 3). It pictures six black women working on a beautiful tropical beach reminiscent of South Africa, where the artist grew up. One dusts a palm tree, while another below her scrubs it with a wash cloth. Two women clean the beach, one in the surf with broom or rake, and another on her hands and knees with mop and bucket. A fifth woman waters with a hose the grass or garden farther up the beach. The final woman has climbed high up a ladder to scrub the sky, a sponge in one hand and a bucket in the other. What does such art suggest about the relationship between women and nature and about the role or responsibility of women in the environmental movement?

Multiple interpretations are possible, as with most art. The painting suggests that women are actively engaged together in a spirit of sisterhood to create a world of beauty. It implies that women are defining their own subjectivity and claiming for themselves a powerful identity as the real leaders of global environmentalism. But the

Figure 3. *Women Wiping Up the World*. Painting used with permission of
Jane Evershed, www.JaneEvershed.com. Featured on the cover of
Ecofeminism: Women, Animals, Nature, edited by Greta Gaard, 1993.

painting might also be taken to indicate that women are what Heller
calls the ecology movement's "janitorial martyrs." Here the women
in the picture appear as janitors, "wiping up the world" as women,
and especially women of color, have always been expected or paid or
forced to do. In conversation with the artist, I learned that she designed the image precisely as a whimsical challenge to this assumption that "wiping up work" is unimportant. But does the challenge
succeed outside ecofeminist circles, that is, outside the circle of those
already convinced the work is important? If the image can evoke
a sense of ecofeminists as Third World cleaning ladies, does it risk
strengthening stereotypes of women as second-class citizens? I am
concerned that such a strategy of picturing women as cleaners and
men as mess-makers could put women back in the traditional housekeeping role of tidying up after men who cannot be expected to do

it themselves. The strategy both lets men off the hook and hooks women as housekeeper, caregiver, and nurse. Evershed, it should be noted, shares this concern and addresses it in her overall body of work, which encompasses 120 pieces of art created over the past ten years, many of which support a vibrant environmentalist and feminist vision of social change.[31]

Another danger I see here is that of repeating in reverse the patriarchal tradition of making women into scapegoats for the existence of evil. In discussing the Bad Mother Nature motif in chapter 4, I will set it in the context of this historical association of woman with evil. The association blames women for the introduction of evil into the world and portrays women as of lower moral stature than men. The problematic repetition in reverse of this pattern of blame occurs, for example, among some feminists and ecofeminists who draw on archaeology and paleoanthropology to construct narratives of human prehistory. They portray early Old European societies as living in harmony with nature—as peaceful, socially egalitarian, goddess-worshipping, and matriarchal or matrifocal. In these feminist narratives, invaders from the northern or Asian steppes sweep in as conquerors, some four to six thousand years ago, and impose patriarchal "civilization" with its accouterments of warfare, class structure, and domination of nature. Such feminists use the vision of a woman-centered, nature-respecting way of life lasting for millennia as counterfoil to the sexism, warfare, hierarchy, and environmental destruction of modernity. The vision functions somewhere between history and myth, often invoked by Monique Wittig's famous phrase from *Les Guérillères:* "There was a time when you were not a slave, remember that. . . . Make an effort to remember. Or, failing that, invent."[32]

Such narratives serve well to expand the imagination to new ways of thinking and living, to disarm patriarchy of the validating claim that "it's always been this way," and to affirm woman's power and value. I agree that it is certainly valid and empowering for those who are oppressed to imagine a world in which they are not. Such vision and hope have always played a role in any movement to overcome oppression. Yet these controversial reconstructions of prehistory also present a new myth of the Fall. This version blames men or a patriarchal male order for the origins of evil in the world and for environmentally unsound attitudes to nature. Such stories of what Ruether calls "paradise lost and the fall into patriarchy" invert the terms of the scapegoating while preserving the structure of scapegoating itself. Here it is not a patriarchal order that blames women for the introduction of evil into the world but a feminist critique that blames men, or this patriarchal order, for the fall from Eden and the origin of evil. These stories suggest both the strength of our tendency to demonize the other and our need to guard against this danger. While men, or at least white men, have never before been the "other"—in the sense of being systematically placed, as a category of beings, in the position of subaltern on the moral, political, economic, and social levels— these feminist reconstruction narratives may accomplish or attempt just that. The narratives also function to let someone off the hook— this time women. As Ruether notes, they allow women "to identify themselves with a lost innocence and to fail to take responsibility for their own complicity in the evils they excoriate."[33]

In all these arguments, women are considered more peaceful and environmentally inclined than men, either because of innate differences arising from biology or because of social conditioning. However, neither the biological nor the social-conditioning arguments proffered for women's greater attunement to the environment strikes me as very convincing. On the biological level, although men do not menstruate, bear children, or breast-feed, they do share all other human biological processes (eating, sleeping, eliminating wastes, getting sick, dying); and, in their ejaculation of semen, men have their own direct experience of a tangible stuff of the reproduction of life. Furthermore, there are many women who do not bear children and even more who do not breast-feed. If these biological processes attune women to nature, are the women who never experience them out of tune? Emily Erwin Culpepper makes the same point in the context of feminist goddess spirituality. She notes how an overemphasis on the Goddess as mother overemphasizes the place of motherhood in women's lives; excludes women who are not mothers; and obscures the presence of lesbians, single women, and heterosexism.[34] All these same things can happen if we argue that women's biological motherhood attunes them more closely to nature than men.

In terms of the argument that women's social and psychological conditioning renders them closer to nature, such conditioning might well in some ways provide women with a greater sense of connection to the environment. Much sociological, psychological, and feminist research, for example, suggests that women are generally socialized to understand themselves more as nurturers and more in terms of relation and connection, whereas men's socialization emphasizes separation and autonomy.[35] However, as social systems change, women's socialized perspective of ecological sensitivity and life orientation could, in the words of ecofeminist Ynestra King, "be socialized right out of us, depending on our day-to-day lives."[36]

Moreover—and here is the real problem from a feminist perspective —the cost of this sense of connection is that women do not, to the same degree and with the same ease as men, perceive themselves as capable, powerful individuals able to bring about change and assert will. Using the terms of Catherine Keller's typology, the sense of the "connective self" that women's socialization helps to develop slides all too easily into an unhealthy sense of the "soluble self." The connective self—open to the world and realizing its relation to all other life—is the ideal, in that it is most supportive of sound behavior toward fellow humans and the environment, but it is not the sense of identity possessed by most women or men. According to Keller, we all first develop and have the potential to retain a connective sense of self; however, because of the patriarchal context in which we live, this connectivity is over-encouraged in women and suppressed in men. The result is women's soluble self: a "tendency to dissolve emotionally and devotionally into the other," a sense of having no self of one's own and of existing primarily for others. Also resulting is men's "separative self," representing an over-development of self, with excessively strict boundaries and objectification of the other.[37] Thus, although social conditioning might produce in women a stronger sense of connection to nature than that possessed by men, it might at the same time condemn women to a weaker sense of self. Although it might be environmentally sound, it is not necessarily good for women. Perpetuating the socialization that feeds perceptions of women's affinity with nature could be dangerously counterproductive to feminist goals. Ecofeminists do not always recognize these drawbacks to women's traditional sense of self.[38] Altering socialization to address these problems could erase any edge women gain in identifying with nature because of an outward-reaching self.

If imagery of nature as Good Mother is not, then, necessarily empowering for women, as this first position claimed, should we instead simply reject the imagery as sexist? Here, a second possible response is to stress that women are fully cultural beings and to disagree that they are in any way closer to nature than men, repudiating this claim as false and as sexist, biological reductionism. Both liberal feminists and socialist feminists, for example, reject any alignment of women with nature. They believe women's liberation can only be achieved by severing the woman-nature connection and by fully integrating women into the realms of culture and production.[39] Note that the choice between these two options of either claiming women are closer to nature or insisting they are not is partly one of strategy. Can we heal environmental damage and reclaim our connection with nature by asserting that yes, women *are* closer to nature, closer than men because we have never lost the knowledge of our deep connection with all other life? Or is the more important task that of staking women's full place in culture? Which strategy would most benefit women, as well as the environment? The question at this point becomes pragmatic.

A basic problem with this second approach, however, is that in its quest to empower women, it may slip into a denigration of nature. It tries to rescue women from their patriarchal devaluation as less than fully human by realigning them with the realm of culture. Implicit in this move is an acceptance of the devaluation of nature as inferior to culture. Women are elevated by removing them from the natural sphere. The move might be feminist, but is not environmentalist. This approach also misleads by implying that we could, at will and by ecofeminist fiat, rid ourselves of Mother Nature imagery. If women are cultural beings, then portraying the environment as mother makes no sense, and Mother Nature imagery should be abolished as sexist. But the task of simply banning the imagery seems impossible, since it is clearly alive and quite resonant in the culture. Left unaddressed by this strategy is the key question I want to examine of *why* the imagery resonates, of what feeds it and keeps it alive.

A final problem with this second approach applies equally to the first. Both the "woman-as-attuned-to-nature" argument and the "woman-as-cultural" option take at face value the question of whether women are closer to nature than men. The first approach answers yes, and the second, no. But the query misleads when reflected upon in light of environmental insight, and it seems to reduce here to a difference in definition—because, in fact, nobody is "closer to nature" than anyone else. Through inextricable implication in an environmental web of interconnection, all is already and equally "natural." None of us can be "further away" from nature, for there is nowhere we can go, nothing we can do to get away from our ecological embeddedness. All our actions and creations, even the most elaborate, sophisticated products of culture, are not totally apart from the environment that gives rise to them. The first, the nature feminist option, argues that women are more aware of this status than men, either because of their biology or their socialization. I have questioned those claims; but even to the extent that they are true, this greater consciousness still does not render any group—women, ecofeminists, or environmentalists—"closer to nature." The work of nature feminists is vital in celebrating our bodies, reminding us that we are a part of the earth, and infusing environmental consciousness into spirituality. Similarly, the work of the second group, those feminists who insist that women are "just as cultural" as men is invaluable in showing the damaging restrictions women suffer when identified with nature. In neither case, however, does the argument necessarily follow that women are "closer to nature," or that women and men together are "closer to culture." The argument is misleading, and when set up along these lines, it is unecological.

What option then remains? Neither a full embrace nor a complete rejection of Good Mother Nature imagery seems the right course. There is, however, a more helpful way to construe this debate. I take my cue here from the direction in which much ecofeminist thought has gone in this discussion over the affinity of women for nature. This third option repudiates, not the relation of woman to either culture or nature, but the dichotomy itself between culture and nature. Eco-philosopher Karen Warren, for example, makes the point that the question "Are women closer to nature than men?" is conceptually flawed. She and other ecofeminists reject the question as falsely based on a nature-culture dualism that they instead deny. In the first approach, nature feminists maintained this hierarchical dualism, merely reversing traditional patriarchal versions to name women "good/close to nature" and men "bad/further from nature." A hierarchy is equally set up by the second approach's insistence that women are just as cultural and distanced from nature as men. In this case, culture is set up over nature; for example, Ortner talks of culture's "transcendence" over and "subsumption" of nature.[40]

The third course of action instead questions the meaning and construction of the categories "nature" and "culture" themselves as well as the hierarchical dualism inherent in the traditional use of these terms.[41] This approach takes the ecofeminist project to be one of dismantling domination structures in the form of the dualistic "either/or" or the hierarchical "closer/further." I call this option that of "biodegrading" these structures: breaking down the "nature versus culture" dichotomies of the first two approaches into less ecologically harmful products.[42] This approach shifts the viewpoint of the first two and seeks to soften their oppositions by making their concepts of nature and culture less rigid or fixed and more biodegradable or environmentally sound. From this perspective, the real problem of patriarchy is its tendency to see the world in terms of binary oppositions arranged in a hierarchy: male over female, culture over nature (also white over black, abled over disabled, upper class over lower class, straight over gay, etc.). Patriarchal societies mandate a social order based on such hierarchical dualisms in which control or domination of the subordinate is justified as in the best interests of all concerned (even of women and nature, for such "wild" entities clearly need management). A key point here is that such a social order harms not only women and the earth but men as well, since these binaries ultimately disempower *all* parties involved and obscure the messy complexity of reality. As one of my former students says, "Binaries work only for computers."[43] This third approach wants to avoid repeating the pattern of hierarchical dualism and instead to break down or biodegrade these dualisms. I think we are on the right track when we thereby shift the terms of the debate away from the question of whether women are closer to nature than men. Ultimately, this question does not get us very far—or anywhere very interesting.

I apply this project of biodegrading to the Mother Nature imagery itself: decoding the images, breaking down the connection they imply between the environment and the female, peering into their roots. If it is not really accurate or helpful to claim that women are closer to nature or that nature and culture are two fully distinct entities, then where does the imagery that nature loves us like a mother and that mothers are naturally nurturant come from? If the imagery does not derive purely "from nature" or from a natural alignment of women with nature, then what are its deeper sources? To answer these questions, we need to look still closer at the woman-nature relationship. To the question, "Are women closer to nature than men?" I can claim that the question is flawed and that it is neither correct nor pragmatically helpful to think of nature and culture in dualistic and hierarchical terms. I could propose environmentally sound ways of conceptualizing nature and proclaim women's equality to men. But I do not thereby do away with the association of nature with woman, undermine its power, or resolve the problems with Mother Nature imagery. If unconscious roots are important, the analysis clearly has to go further.

Linda Teal Willoughby, for example, expresses reservations about the ecofeminist project of constructing alternative symbols and metaphors for the traditional "Mother Nature." She draws on the psychological theory of Carl Jung to point out that no symbol "can be inherently harmless or accomplish the task of dismantling hierarchical dualism [e.g., of culture over nature] without going through the process of withdrawing projections and breaking up identities."[44] The problem is not only or not so much in the symbol itself as in misguided endeavors to consciously create new symbols without attending to unconscious projection and content. Or, as ecofeminist Marti Kheel remarks, "The attempt by many ecophilosophers to graft a new image onto our current conception of nature fails to challenge the underlying structures and attitudes that have produced the image they seek to supplant."[45] The point is well taken. Efforts to overthrow one symbol and elevate another will not succeed if they attend only to the level of consciousness. The association of nature and the female is too strong and deeply rooted to be mutable by changes at the conscious level alone. To comprehend and alter attitudes, feelings, and images of nature, we must attend to unconscious processes, to Kheel's "underlying structures and attitudes."

Accordingly, we need to dig deeper into psychosocial causes of the woman-nature association and its ambiguous manifestations in imagery of Good Mother Nature. In the next chapter I turn to this task by focusing not so much on Mother Nature as on the "nature" of mothering itself.

THREE

Mothers and Mother Nature

*Here nature opens her broad lap to receive the perpetual accession of new
comers, and to supply them with food.*

　　—St. John de Crèvecoeur, Letters from an American Farmer, *1782*

If, as I argued in chapter 1, aspects of human relations—such as the
unconscious, ambivalence, and gender—shape relations to nature
and the expression of these relations in nature imagery, then a set of
questions emerges: What are the unconscious messages and evocations of popular nature imagery? What does it really mean to cast
nature as mother? Why and with what consequences is there so
much love, fear, and anger portrayed in Mother Nature relations?
How do culturally contingent meanings of motherhood influence this
nature imagery? How do early childhood experiences of the mother
shape the content and tone of the images? These questions become
important at this point because of the conclusion in the last chapter
that unconscious content and processes mean that nature as Good
Mother does not necessarily solve ecological or feminist problems.

In this chapter, then, I focus on the nature imagery's underlying
roots, on how its content is shaped by projections from unconscious
or semiconscious human relations to the mother. Here I have three
tasks: the chapter begins by opening up the question of what unconscious dynamics have to do with nature imagery and patterns of environmental degradation and by clarifying my usage of the term
unconscious; then I turn to an investigation of attitudes toward motherhood so deeply embedded in the culture as to be often invisible (or
unconscious); and finally, I return to the case study to bring all this
material to bear in an overall evaluation of the Good Mother motif.

THE UNCONSCIOUS AND THE ENVIRONMENT

Environmental theorists commonly advocate the need for changes in
consciousness, attitude, thought, models, belief, or worldview. They
depend on the assumption that conscious ideas more or less directly

shape action, and they are generally confident that people can, if they so desire, change the way they perceive human-nature relations in order to act in more ecologically sound ways. Accordingly, these theorists claim that environmentalist ideas—often borrowed from Asian, Native American, or alternative Western philosophical and religious traditions—can be adopted by Westerners as therapeutic to planetary ills. As just one example, comparative environmental philosophers J. Baird Callicott and Roger Ames engage this issue of the relation of idea to action in their edited volume, *Nature in Asian Traditions of Thought*. Their thesis is that Eastern cultures offer important conceptual resources to help cure Western ecological ills, although they acknowledge that "developing an appropriate philosophical orientation, alas, will not be a panacea for environmental ills." A good set of ideas will not cure all, since there is no one-on-one correlation between idea and action. Ecophilosopher Eugene C. Hargrove, in a foreword to their book, specifies further that "a world view, including its associated ethics and ideals, is, rather, only generally, and often only indirectly, related to conduct." But because there is *some* relation between idea and action, Callicott and Ames maintain optimism "about the power of ideas *eventually* to alter the course of history."[1]

I agree that these assumptions are generally true, but unless we look more deeply, I fear the project will not progress as far as it might. There are at least three problems. For one thing, this appropriation of environmentally friendly notions of nature raises the question of whether ideas and practices can be transplanted from one cultural context to another and still retain their resonance and meaning. While something is gained, surely much is also lost through attempts to incorporate into modern Western contexts—largely urban, broadly Judeo-Christian or secular—ecological lessons from Black Elk's Sun Dance, Buddhist gathas or "mindfulness verses," and the Chinese Taoist classic *Tao Te Ching*.[2] What may provide effective environmental protection in one society may lose that power when the text or tradition is transplanted into another. Secondly, the prospect of relatively well-to-do, white American environmentalists seeking to benefit from Third World, tribal, and Asian cultures raises questions of cultural imperialism, whether the appropriation is of natural resources, the population's labor, or the intellectual and cultural resources now sought. We need to be careful not to replicate the abusive "mining for resources" we are trying to repair. For example, whether and how Western environmental theorists can appropriate Native American concepts of nature is hotly debated: Paula Gunn Allen, a Laguna Pueblo/Sioux woman, argues that the "Indianization" of American culture occurred long ago, is the source of much—if not most—that is good in America, and should be still further embraced, as in the adoption of native concepts of nature. In contrast, Andy Smith, a Cherokee woman, sees continuing racism and genocide in New Age, environmentalist, and feminist interest in Native spirituality and attitudes toward nature.[3]

Of greatest concern to me, however, is whether this method of promoting new ideas in order to change behavior neglects the extent to which action does *not* follow from conscious thought and to which motivations are hidden, ambivalent, and elusive to control. I evoke here the notion of the heart of darkness and draw on both psychoanalytic theory and theological reflection to describe this disjuncture between intent and behavior, this shadow separating will from action. Psychoanalysts theorize this disjuncture in terms of the category of the *unconscious*. I am not wedded to a strict Freudian definition of the unconscious, nor is it necessary for the purposes of this book to debate the relative merits of Lacanian, Jungian, French feminist, or Kleinian interpretations of the unconscious and how it works. The crucial point for my analysis is that, in all cases, these psychologies posit that the human psyche has a dimension of depth, which I spoke of in Chapter 1 as one of the riddles of human identity.

The definition of the unconscious that I adopt is a general one common to all these forms of "depth psychology," namely, that there is a gap, a dividedness, or a discontinuity between conscious and unconscious, between what we can and cannot easily know about ourselves. Moreover, there is a constant interplay between conscious and unconscious levels of mental operation. The unconscious, however conceived, is a "site of causality": it influences behavior patterns, relationships, dreams, mistakes or slips of the tongue, artistic vision, and social productions. It even influences, I suggest, the social productions of pop culture that are intended for mass consumption, such as advertising and sloganeering. Emotion associated with desires, thoughts, or events that have been pushed into unconsciousness possesses great power to shape conscious representations, often in "wildly inappropriate ways."[4] Thus, popular images of nature can be intensely colored by the unconscious content projected onto them in the process of their cultural creation (chapter 5 will deal further with this process of unconscious projection).

This insight into how human behavior is shaped is not unique to psychoanalysis. As psychologist of religion William Meissner notes, psychoanalysis systematizes an insight that, "as Freud himself pointed out, poets and dramatists have always known," namely that "human beings are capable of living out meanings without being aware of them."[5] In reference to this less technical understanding, I have also been using the term *semiconscious* in this text. I employ the term more colloquially, in reference to meanings of nature imagery and attitudes toward nature that are not often publicly recognized or discussed either at the level of the individual or at the level of the culture, meanings and attitudes that we do not often admit to that are underlying, shadowy, or present but unacknowledged.

Some environmental thinkers do recognize this depth dimension and explore its implications for human relationship to nature. Ecopsychologists are a notable example. They often see a deeper or wider notion of self as a prime resource for environmental healing, for they claim that within the less conscious reaches of self we find and feel the connection to nature that modern industrial culture has repressed. Theodore Roszak, a central figure in this field, states, for example, that "the goal of ecopsychology is to awaken the inherent sense of environmental reciprocity that lies within the ecological unconscious."[6]

While I applaud this attention to the unconscious, and while this inherent sense of reciprocity may well lie there, the psychoanalytic ecopsychology I seek to develop teaches lessons that are perhaps less utopian about human ambivalence and about the centrality of love and hate. Thus, even when environmental thought incorporates a depth perspective, as in ecopsychology, it may dangerously downplay the reality of human destructiveness. For the depths contain not only loving and reparative impulses but also deep-rooted tendencies to destruction and disconnection (as Part II will explore).

A parallel point is made by Christian theology, which has likewise always been aware of, and even anguished by, this depth riddle of human experience. Theologians talk about it in terms of dividedness or irrationality, as in the "divided heart" or the "irrational will." This point strikes me as a curiously underdeveloped yet foundational one for ecotheology. St. Paul perhaps inaugurated this tradition of painful awareness in Christian thought with his tortured cry: "I cannot even understand my own actions. I do not do what I want to do but what I hate" (Romans 7:15). A strong theological tradition, then, runs from Paul through Augustine, Duns Scotus, Jacob Boehme, Luther, Pascal, Kierkegaard, and Dostoyevsky, all testifying to what theologian Paul Tillich calls "the unconscious, irrational will." This tradition is less obvious and acknowledged in theology than in psychoanalysis, for an alternate tradition within Christianity downplays or denies the unconscious to emphasize instead what Meissner calls a "more rationalistic, controlled, and idealistic view of human psychology." Tillich labels this alternate tradition the "philosophy of consciousness" and sees it as triumphing in the Scientific Revolution, the Enlightenment, and industrial society. He counts among its advocates Aquinas, Erasmus, Calvin, Zwingli, Descartes, and Hegel. Meissner even maintains that Christian theology has no real tradition of speaking about that which psychoanalysis calls the unconscious: "The psychology implicit in a theological anthropology is essentially a psychology of the ego and the superego, with their functions." Yet along with Tillich, I maintain that a notion of the unconscious has always existed in theology. Tillich even credits Freud with helping Christian theology to rediscover this tradition within itself: the "immense depth psychological material which we find in the religious literature of the last two thousand years."[7]

To give just a couple of examples beyond Paul, Augustine certainly had a deep sense of the complexity and mystery of the inner world, the unknowableness of our motivations, the "profound and permanent dislocation" and tension that characterize our inner self. He writes in his *Confessions:* "There is in me a lamentable darkness in which my latent possibilities are hidden from myself, so that my mind, questioning itself upon its own powers, feels that it cannot rightly trust its own report." On the problem of human motivation and the will, his biographer Peter Brown explains how Augustine becomes convinced that delight is the "mainspring of human action." However, the processes that prepare the heart to take delight are "unconscious and beyond [one's] control," such that conscious actions are "merely the final outgrowth of hidden processes . . . by which the 'heart' is 'stirred', is 'massaged and set' by the hand of God." Willing the good is thus a difficult proposition, as attested by Augustine's brilliantly equivocal prayer: "Give me chastity and continence, but not yet."[8]

Even Kant, taken by many as the arch-rationalist of the Enlightenment, has in his theological writings on "radical evil" a sense of our inscrutable deeps. In *Religion Within the Limits of Reason Alone* he writes, "Not even does a man's inner experience with regard to himself enable him to fathom the depths of his own heart as to obtain, through self-observation, quite certain knowledge of the basis of the maxims which he professes, or of their purity and stability."[9] This lineage of Christian theological writing, then, is painfully aware that we humans do not always know why we act as we do and that we cannot always act as we wish.

Here is the crux of the problem and the site of a key joint insight for ecotheology and ecopsychology: because of the influence of this "lamentable darkness," attested to by both psychoanalytic and theological discourse, *the ways people understand and respond to nature are not shaped exclusively by the rational will at the conscious level alone and are therefore not necessarily responsive to the adoption of new or better models of nature.* Environmental thought needs to effect change at a deeper level for real change in worldview and behavior to occur, for as Kierkegaard notes, an unconscious relationship is more powerful than a conscious one.[10] On this point William James, that great champion of the unseen and the nonrational, argues that rational consciousness "will fail to convince or convert you all the same, if your dumb intuitions are opposed to its conclusions. . . . The truth is that in the metaphysical and religious sphere, articulate reasons are cogent for us only when our inarticulate feelings of reality have already been impressed in favor of the same conclusion."[11] I am interested in our "dumb intuitions" and "inarticulate feelings" about nature as revealed in popular imagery and slogans. It is precisely in them that we find clues to why we do *not* love the earth, to what complicates this project of love, to how nature beneficent and benign becomes persecutory and vilified when tornadoes blow across the land. It is not easy to alter such habits of thought and action, for their deep roots complicate the translation of new imagery or ideas into sound practice.

Such is the problem, for example, when Arne Naess, ecophilosopher and founding figure of deep ecology, writes about "the supremacy
of environmental ontology and realism over environmental ethics."
He is claiming that with the right understanding of who we truly are,
ethics become unnecessary, since caring action flows naturally and
spontaneously from the realization that self and ecosphere are one.
"Just as we need not morals to make us breathe. . . . [so] if your 'self'
in the wide sense embraces another being, you need no moral exhortation to show care," Naess continues. "You care for yourself without
feeling any moral pressure to do it—provided you have not suc-
cumbed to a neurosis of some kind, developing self-destructive tendencies, or hating yourself."[12] But this last provision is quite a big one.
We *do* recognize ambivalences in ourselves or neuroses of various
kinds, and we find that we often act in self-destructive ways. We see
such self-destruction in addictions, eating disorders, suicide, and the
repetition of abuse, as victim or victimizer, by those who survive
childhood abuse. Surely this approach in environmental thought obscures the painful problem that behavior does not automatically follow from attitude and that we do not always act in our own or our
loved ones' best interests. In fact, we often act *contrary* to our conscious beliefs, values, and desires; or without being fully able to explain why; or without being fully aware that we are so acting. Or we
find ourselves unable to change ingrained behaviors and ideas, despite strong desire to change. This is what psychoanalysis describes
as the action of the unconscious, or what theology explains in terms
of the irrational will. As has long been recognized, to know the good
does not necessarily entail that one will do it. To a pronouncement
such as that by ecotheologian Sallie McFague in *Body of God* that
"Christians have a mandate to *love* the earth," we may agree, but
having a mandate to love does not mean that we will.[13] Despite the
intellectual knowledge that all life on earth is interrelated in bonds
of mutual dependence, and even despite the love of nature that many
people do feel or can be awakened to feel by books such as McFague's,
environmental destruction still moves forward. As T. S. Eliot writes,
"Between the idea / And the reality. . . . Between the conception /
And the creation. . . . Falls the Shadow."[14]

My argument, then, is for the need to expose shadowy unconscious
roots, emotional overtones, and half-hidden messages in the nature

imagery we use. Mother Nature imagery is shaped in ways of which we are often not fully aware by feelings about the human mother, linkages of nature with maternity, and gendered family relations. These unconscious gender dynamics can undermine environmentalist goals. Unless we examine these implicit messages—which can be quite opposite that of their conscious content—Good Mother Nature imagery will fail to work as intended.

THE NATURE OF MOTHERING

Since the "Love Your Mother" poster's text makes reference—through the "is" of its metaphor—to our actual mothers, we need to look next at this "mother-nature." What is the nature or experience of mothering, in its multiple meanings, and what are typical cultural constructions of "the mother" in recent American life? When posters speak of nature as mother and invite us to love that mother, they are inviting us at the same time to associate stereotypical mothering qualities with the environment. The slogan "Love Your Mother" suggests that we view the human-environment relationship through the lens of the child-mother relationship. But what are these qualities that are associated, consciously or unconsciously, with mothering? The question begs an ecofeminist response because of that scholarship's central point that female metaphors of nature are thoroughly infused with what Chaia Heller calls "the patriarchal values, desires, and definitions of women that saturate our media, religion, and education from the day we are born."[15] How then do these "patriarchal values, desires, and definitions" shape notions of mothering? What are the cultural expectations and realities of mother love—both of how mothers should love their children and of how children should love their mothers? And how do women actually experience mothering?

One argument holds that mothers are generally cherished and cherishing, and that the image of nature as nurturing mother serves as a constraint against human activities leading to environmental degradation. This argument assumes that we love our mothers more or less unambiguously and will similarly care for others perceived as mother. Merchant, for example, states that "one does not readily slay a mother, dig into her entrails for gold or mutilate her body." She argues that the older organic worldview of nature as nurturing mother —dominant in Western thought before the Scientific Revolution of the sixteenth and seventeenth centuries—acted as a powerful constraint against exploitation of nature, just as more recent mechanistic views of nature as inert matter actively encourage such exploitation. Harming Mother Nature by engaging in ecologically destructive activity would be "a breach of human ethical behavior."[16]

But is it true that we love our mothers in such a straightforward manner, entailing respect and protection from harm? The notion that mothers are to be cared for and cherished is certainly present in the culture. One recent financial services ad, for example, pictures a silver-haired woman working in her garden and displays the caption "Why 9 out of 10 of our clients say they would recommend their financial advisor to their mother."[17] We are so dependable, the ad implies, that you can even trust us with your precious mother. But it strikes me instead that mothers are *not* unambiguously loved, especially when one gets beyond platitudes to actual lived realities and to less-conscious emotional associations. At these levels, maternal relations are more often marked by ambivalence, as indeed are all human relations. But even more so than other relations, mothering is a particularly central locus of ambivalence in patriarchy.

Cultural notions about mothers and mothering are a complex mixture of genuine love, romantic idealizations, and veiled aggression. As a result, the role can be empowering, but it is also falsely idealized and devalued. With the impact of the women's movement since at least the 1960s, this role may be the one that has changed the most in American society as mothers now are told that they can have it all—career and family—or as economic pressures and changing family patterns force them to do it all—hold down jobs and raise children single-handedly. Either way, the rapid rise in mothers' participation in the workforce accentuates the conflicts in their role, both in terms of what the mother expects of herself and what society expects of her. As a mother who works full-time myself, I read society's message along the lines of "Be nurturing in the home and assertive in the marketplace; never let one job interfere with the other, even though they are both essentially full-time; and never whine about how tired you are. You are, after all, a mother, and as such we expect magic from you."

Clearly, mothering has been and is deeply satisfying for many women (most days, I count myself among them). Mothers are often truly loved and appreciated, and the childcare work they do can be highly regarded by spouses, families, and wider cultural circles. Nel Noddings, for example, in an extended analysis of the strengths and evils of traditional domestic life, argues that the "experience of mothering has been a source of great joy for many women, and . . . has given rise to opportunities for autonomy, creativity, and the sort of thinking that is generous and other-oriented."[18] However, the extent to which mothering is a liberating relationship and one that is genuinely valued is too often lost under the twin weight of mirror-related notions about mothering: an oppressive idealization and an equally crushing devaluation.

"Mother" in America, as in other societies shaped by traditionally patriarchal notions of the family, is understood first and foremost as the nurturer who loves us and takes care of us, no matter what. Traditional patriarchal visions of motherhood turn the Good Mother into the idealized mother: providing, caring, self-sacrificing, and inexhaustible. Mother is she who feeds and cleans and comforts and warms us, she who satisfies our wants and needs without any cost to us. This ideal mother embodies never-ending abundance and unconditional love.[19] She is somewhat captured by the notion of an "earth mother," evoking images of a large, maternal 1960s- to 1970s-era woman, who is loving and warm toward all and busy with gardening, baking, canning, and sewing (although the earth mother may also transgress feminine ideals in her negligent grooming habits by avoiding makeup and not shaving). The idealized mother is found in condescending eulogies on the joys of motherhood and in platitudes about motherhood and apple pie. In the nineteenth century, she is embodied in middle- and upper-class Victorian ideals of woman as the "Angel in the House."

This title of a poem by Coventry Patmore became an epithet in nineteenth-century life and twentieth-century feminist criticism for the "selfless paragon all women were exhorted to be, enveloped in family life and seeking no identity beyond the roles of daughter, wife, and mother."[20] The costs of the angel, sanctified yet imprisoned in the home, were famously counted by Virginia Woolf: "If there was chicken, she took the leg; if there was a draught she sat in it—in short she was so constituted that she never had a mind or wish of her own, but preferred to sympathize always with the minds and wishes of others."[21] (Note how the angel's practices recall the discussion in chapter 2 of women's soluble self.) Woolf struggled fiercely with the angel in the house, who, she said, "bothered me and wasted my time and so tormented me that at last I killed her."[22] The demand that women conform to the angel's model of the ideal mother imposes an impossible set of expectations and a limited definition of what woman can be. These costs, moreover, are not only to women. Deriving women's value from their role as mothers can lead them to use children negatively as, in Adrienne Rich's words, "a symbolic credential, a sentimental object, a badge of self-righteousness."[23]

Although women's roles have expanded today and men are taking on more childcare tasks, this patriarchal and idealized vision of motherhood is still alive and well. A recent British Airways advertising campaign provides a compelling example (see Figure 4). This full-page, black-and-white newspaper ad shows a woman tenderly cradling a baby in her arms. Superimposed over the baby's head, in color, is the face of a blissfully smiling older man, reclining in what is advertised as "the new Club World cradle seat. Lullaby not included." The mother's gaze is focused wholly on her child. Details of her hair and clothes and the baby's terry cloth diaper indicate a mom of mid-twentieth-century vintage, one undistracted by the hectic double shifts today's women often work with jobs and child rearing. The ad portrays what remains both a strong cultural understanding of the mother and a nostalgic, utopian fantasy: mother as idealized, old-fashioned nurturer, completely dedicated to our needs. The fantasy continues with another airline that puts itself in the role of mother through an ad picturing a close-up photo of a cute baby sucking its thumb. The ad's text asks: "When was the last time you were the center of attention and someone was around to see to all your needs?" and invites flyers to "let Northwest Airlines show you a little TLC." This fantasy may particularly apply to the older, white, affluent male pictured in the British Airways ad and addressed by it as the typical business traveler. Note also that the British Airway ad's metaphor equates mother with cradle and with airplane seat. Woman is made into thing, into the surround, into the comfort we crave or remember or fantasize as coming from the mother and as our rightful due.[24]

"Since idealization is based in illusion," Ann Dally notes in *Invent-*

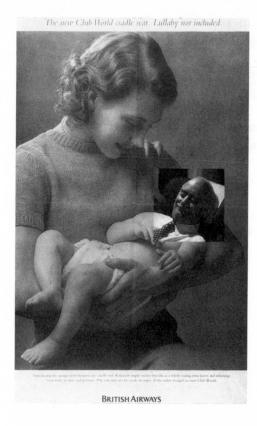

The new Club World cradle seat. Lullaby not included.

BRITISH AIRWAYS

Figure 4. *"Cradle Seat."* British Airways print advertisement. Appeared in the *Wall Street Journal,* 1996.

ing Motherhood, "there is always the danger of disillusion, and this tends to happen in idealized relationships."[25] Idealizations can mask and even encourage aggression; conscious idealization easily conceals unconscious devaluation. Thus, in public discourse the role of mother is not only valued but also defamed. Notions about mothering in the cultural imagination are in fact deeply divided: they both praise and punish women for the mothering they do. These notions accord mothers high status while relegating them to narrow and compulsory roles.

It is no new insight that Western culture, still shaped by patriarchy, fails to consistently hold mothers and mothering in high regard. Ecofeminist Greta Gaard, for one, sees a pattern of "white Western cultural devaluation of mothers."[26] Mothers are frequently neglected, patronized, and overworked. They are too often abandoned and left to raise their children without a father or sufficient and regular child support. Mothers on welfare are stigmatized and marginalized. Maternal housework and child rearing are unpaid, largely unrecognized by society, and usually credited with no value in economic calculations of nations' wealth. The Canadian national census did not include homemaking and childcare in its definition of "work" until 1996, after a protest campaign started by Carol Lees, a homemaker from Saskatoon, Saskatchewan. With wonderfully dry wit, Lees explains why she refused to complete the previous census form: "I was raising three children, they were young teens then, and I was not prepared to report that I had not worked."[27] Dally draws attention to the painful hypocrisy of this situation in her remarks on "the extent to which our society emphasizes the importance of the family, of mother love, mother-infant attachment and constant mother care, while at the same time making life increasingly difficult for mothers, doing little to help them beyond the physical health of babies and young children, and taking no steps to help mothers adapt to our fast changing world or to adapt that world to their needs and those of their children."[28] In a psychoanalytic study of this belittlement of women in motherhood, Coppélia Kahn reviews the work of leading gender theorists Jean Baker Miller, Adrienne Rich, Dorothy Dinnerstein, and Nancy Chodorow. "As a group," she summarizes, "they argue that the institution of motherhood is the root cause of the oppression of women and the sexual malaise experienced by men and women."[29] An even fiercer evaluation by feminist Shulamith Firestone attacks childbearing and child rearing as a "tyranny" women are forced to bear and from which they must be freed.[30]

   If these denunciations indicate that mothering has been both a primary site of women's social subordination and at the same time a vehicle for their idealization, we may look for explanations of this dichotomy in an underlying ambivalence toward mothers and mothering. Devaluation and idealization are twin strategies of the unconscious for dealing with ambivalence in relations, although both are problematic and ultimately unhealthy. Such maternal ambivalence seems to be held at both a cultural and an individual level and occurs in multiple forms. First, in the history of Western cultural portrayals of motherhood, mothers are often labeled as life-giving yet also life-taking. There is a powerful motif in such Western portrayals of woman as "bringer of death," a motif that is, in fact, linked to the association of woman with nature. It is precisely woman's "natural" fecundity, seen as mimicking or embodying the fecundity of Mother Nature, that allows her to create new human life. However, this power that women hold is also the root cause of all death, since to be born means that one will die. The story of Eve, which blames the primal mother for the introduction of death into the human realm, is a highly influential one in Western culture. To take two biblical texts as examples, the Book of Ecclesiasticus, also called Sirach, draws on the Eve story to make this point succinctly: "In woman was sin's beginning, and because of her we all die." In the Gospel of John, Jesus assures the Pharisee Nicodemus that being born from one's mother's womb leads only to death; for eternal life, one must be begotten from above, by God.[31]

Shakespeare also gives us powerful examples that demonize woman's natural fertility and indeed her very organs of reproduction. In *King Lear*, Lear wanders alone in the fields, raving, driven out and driven mad by his daughters:

> Down from the waist they are Centaurs,
> Though women all above:
> But to the girdle do the gods inherit,
> Beneath is all the fiend's.
> There's hell, there's darkness, there is the sulphurous pit,
> Burning, scalding, stench, consumption; fie, fie, fie!

In another of Shakespeare's plays, witches conjure apparitions who prophesy that "none of woman born / Shall harm Macbeth." Only Macduff, "from his mother's womb / Untimely ripped" by Cesarean section, proves capable of killing Macbeth. Not having passed through the "sulphurous pit" of the vagina, Macduff retains a potency all others lack. Bennett Simon comments on the *Lear* scene in a psychoanalytic study of tragic drama: "To be of woman born is to admit a dependency that is both the equivalent of death and a reminder of its reality."[32] Contemporary theorists read from such material an underlying resentment, envy, and fear of the female—either on the part of men or of men and women together—and a resultant tradition of mother-negation.[33]

These cultural portrayals with their split evaluation of mothers as source of life and as source of death relate to a second form of maternal ambivalence: evidence of male ambivalence about their dependence on women for bringing forth children. Western traditions contain examples of men's—or at least some men's—apparent resentment of this dependence and fantasies or claims of man as the true life-giving parent. "Mother-negation" here becomes a literal reality. Some well-known examples include Aeschylus's Apollo confidently asserting in the *Oresteia* that "the mother is no parent of that which is called her child, but only nurse of the new-planted seed that grows. The parent is he who mounts. . . . There can be a father without any mother." Jason, in Euripides's *Medea,* wants to remove women even further from the process of reproduction: "It would have been better far for men to have got their children in some other way, and women not to have existed. Then life would have been good." Paul's First Epistle to the Corinthians establishes a hierarchy of being—proceeding from God the Father, to Christ, to man/husband, to woman/wife—in part through appeal to the Genesis creation story in which "man was not made from woman, but woman from man." The theme of man-as-parent resurfaces in the recent Hollywood movie *Junior.* Here, finally, is the answer to Jason's 2,500-year-old plea as modern reproductive technology allows Arnold Schwarzenegger to bear his own child (although a woman's egg—stolen—is still necessary for the begetting).[34]

A third form of maternal ambivalence is women's own feelings about the experience of mothering: they report that it brings great fulfillment yet is hugely draining. Medea, who both loves and murders her children, claims she would "very much rather stand three times in the front of battle than bear one child."[35] Although the play is written by a male author, I think it captures an authentic insight into the experience and costs of bearing a child (especially in a time and place where childbirth carries substantial risk of death for the mother, the baby, or both). Toni Morrison's novel *Beloved* takes up the Medea theme of how a mother might feel justified in killing her child. As Morrison brilliantly dramatizes, the experience of mothering can be one of enormous cost to a woman. Because Sethe loves her child, she feels forced to kill her in order to protect her, an act which then literally haunts her and her family. The two stories testify to a mother's rage at being trapped within an unjust social system that deprives her of dignity and autonomy such that she concludes—whether rightly or wrongly—that she has no choice but to kill her own children. Other mothers' stories entwine themes of fiercely protective love for the baby made from her own body with those of rage toward the screaming, all-consuming creature clamped like a leech to her breast. Note, for example, Adrienne Rich's description of being a mother: "To be caught up in waves of love and hate, jealousy even of the child's childhood; hope and fear for its maturity; longing to be free of responsibility, tied by every fiber of one's being."[36]

Finally, as a fourth form of maternal ambivalence or explanation for it, psychoanalytic theory posits that we all carry the child's ambivalence toward its mother, for we were too dependent, too vulnerable toward a mother perceived as omnipotent, yet who never did—indeed cannot—deliver perfect care and satisfy all needs. The British object relations theorist D. W. Winnicott, writing at the same time as Klein, develops the concept of the "good enough mother." While the phrase is meant partly to reassure mothers that they need not be perfect in order to satisfy their baby's needs, it also places the burden for this satisfaction exclusively on women. (We can update and expand the concept to the "good enough parent," but such gender inclusiveness was beyond the cultural norms and expectations of Winnicott's mid-twentieth-century Great Britain.) The "good enough mother," expressed negatively, is the mother who always to some degree fails. I would venture to say that most, if not all, mothers—and indeed fathers—would agree that some degree of failure is the norm. Who can claim to live up perfectly to their ideals of parenting? From the point of view of the baby, Dinnerstein draws on Klein's work to describe how "we feel torn between two impulses" toward this perhaps good enough, but never perfect mother: "The impulse, on the one hand, to give free rein to the nursling's angry greed, its wild yearning to own, control, suck dry the source of good, its wish to avenge deprivation; and the impulse, on the other hand, to make reparation for these feelings, which threaten to destroy what is most precious and deeply needed."[37] Loving one's mother is thus a difficult task, and that love is often to some extent ambivalent.

Cultural representations, then, as well as the experiences of fathers, mothers, and children all point to deep ambivalence around the activities and expectations of mothering and being mothered within a patriarchal framework of woman-centered child rearing. These complex maternal relations elicit responses of either defaming the mother or regarding her as perfect precisely because these relations arouse such strong feelings of conflict. *My point here is that when we call nature "mother," we evoke all these associations and ambivalences, whether consciously or unconsciously, and bring them into play in the environmental arena.* As Rose notes, "Whatever 'mother' means to a given culture will metaphorically infect the meanings it attaches to mother earth."[38] Notions of nature take on the qualities ascribed to mother and become colored by experiences of mothering. From an ecofeminist perspective, the problems raised when nature is imaged as the Good Mother are several. Such imagery, especially when used exclusively or in idealized form, can lead to environmentally unsound understandings of nature, obviate the need for social action, and mask aggression toward both women and nature. A return to the "Love Your Mother" poster allows exploration of these three interrelated problems in more detail.

CASE STUDY REVISITED

If it is difficult for us to love our mothers, equally problematic is the way we expect our mothers to love us. This point is crucial for environmentalists using the "Love Your Mother" slogan, for we seem to want mothers to care for us in a way that we must never expect nature to care. *The last thing the environmental movement should do is encourage us to think of nature as an inexhaustible, self-sacrificing, all-nurturing mother.* Instead of leading to greater environmental soundness, the strategy of picturing nature as such a mother would have the exact opposite effect. If mother is defined as she who provides all our sustenance and makes all our waste disappear—as she whose job it is to feed us and change our diapers—then imaging nature in these terms promotes expectations that the environment can endlessly supply all resources and absorb all pollutants. Yet this is obviously just how we must *not* think of nature. Our ecological breakdown has arisen in part precisely from this attitude that nature is a storehouse of riches that will never empty and that we may use at will for any purpose we desire without incurring debt or obligation of replacement. Such is the myth of superabundance and the frontier ethic from the dominant modernist Western worldview in which nature, as a limitless supply chest, is valued to the extent that it can be physically transformed to suit human needs.[39]

Here, then, is the root of the problem with imagery of humans loving Mother Nature and of nature as a loving mother. Such notions become colored by ideal and unrealistic projections about motherhood, and nature then comes to be seen through this anthropomorphic lens. Both Gaard and Gray note that projecting idealized notions of motherhood onto the environment produces what Gray calls a convenient "illusion of knowledge" but that this process actually impedes authentic knowledge and relation by functioning "to hide and obscure the true identity of that which is projected upon."[40] These projections entail faulty and unhealthy understandings of nature, problematic for both women and the environment. Luce Irigaray makes this same point in her book *Sexes et parentés*. She observes that we act in the environment as if there were no cost attached to our use of natural resources, as if they existed purely for our use, and as if they would never be depleted. Our behavior can be explained in part, she suggests, by the fact that we assume the mother will, without charge and without limit, nourish and care for the child in particular and for the man and society in general.

A second problem related to such environmentally unsound understandings of nature is that idealized Mother Nature imagery can then obviate the need for social action and impede an environmentalist response. Images of nature as Good Mother tend to reinforce deeply ingrained presumptions that the environment exists to serve our needs and that we are not under an equal obligation to return this service. After all, it is children who need looking after, while mothers are supposed to look after themselves. From this perspective, Mother Nature is resilient, even tough; and while we should certainly love her, she does not require much else in the way of our care. Furthermore, we need not be overly concerned about her health. When nature appears as this ideal mother, ecological degradation appears as less of a problem. Such degradation seems even an impossibility—or a distant and remote possibility—since in this view, the bounty of nature never ends. The reality of ecological ills is obscured, and the need for environmental protection and activism can come to seem less immediately pressing. As a cross-cultural example, the Hindu philosopher and ecofeminist Lina Gupta reports that many Hindus in

India revere the Ganges River as a goddess so holy, powerful, and pure that she is traditionally considered unaffected by the massive polluting of her waters. Seeing the river as imbued by divine presence makes environmental protection seem less necessary in the popular and religious imagination of India.[41]

Even when environmental destruction is perceived as a problem, portrayals of nature as the Good Mother who suffers from our abuse can prompt an ineffectual romantic response of rescuing the "damsel in distress." Chaia Heller illustrates the way such imagery can go awry in an article entitled "For the Love of Nature: Ecology and the Cult of the Romantic." She cites an affirmation marketed together with a button bearing a variant of our slogan. The button says "Love Our Mother," and the affirmation reads: "I hold in my mind a picture of perfection for Mother Earth. I know this perfect picture creates positive energy from my thought, which allows my vision to be manifested in the world." Heller criticizes such language for its idealized romanticism. She argues, I think correctly, that through such idealizations of nature, "the romantic expresses his love through 'perfect thoughts' rather than through authentic knowledge or action."[42] In the example of this affirmation, the "Love Our Mother" slogan is evoked for no explicit environmental activism other than the dubiously effective "power of positive thinking."

Finally, the romantic idealization of Mother Nature imagery is problematic in that it masks aggression. As discussed, idealizations stem from underlying ambivalence, and the environmental movement provides disturbing examples of how reference to nature as Good Mother hides aggression toward both women and nature. "Romantic ecology," Heller suggests, "often veils a theme of animosity toward woman under a silk cloak of idealism, protection, and a promise of self-restraint." As example, she quotes another green slogan, advertised as a sticker in the journal *Earth First!* that is a second variation on the "Love Your Mother" theme. The sticker orders: "Love Your Mother, Don't Become One." By addressing its message to women—since only women can be mothers—the sticker implies that they are especially responsible for the problems of overpopulation and environmental degradation as well as for the solution to these problems. This somewhat misogynist assignment of blame comes, paradoxically, from "the same men who romantically express love for 'Mother Earth.'"[43]

The oft-heard notion of "Gaia" further demonstrates this point. Scientist James Lovelock chose this name of the ancient Greek Earth Goddess to describe his hypothesis of the planet as a self-regulating, organic unity. But Gaia imagery conveys far more than this. It draws freely on maternal idealizations, as in this description from Kirkpatrick Sale's book on bioregionalism, *Dwellers in the Land:* "A vibrant globe of green and blue and grey binding together in a holy, deep-breasted synchrony . . . a pulsing body . . . Gaia, the earth mother."[44] Whenever we find notions of nature idealized to the extent of this "holy, deep-breasted synchrony," we should not be surprised—but should, indeed, expect—to also find the opposite. Thus, Gaia imagery also reveals, in its merging of woman and nature, the projection of aggression onto both that can be cloaked by such idealizations. In this boldly sexualized and demonized portrayal of the planet, Lovelock claims that Gaia neither needs our care nor is harmed by our abuse: "It seems very unlikely that anything we do will threaten Gaia. . . . The damsel in distress [that the environmentalist] expected to rescue appears as a buxom and robust man-eating mother."[45] Nature is here again deep-breasted, but far from being a nurturant caretaker, she turns on her children and devours them in the tradition of mother as bringer of death.

This problem of veiled aggression has another aspect. Idealized Mother Nature imagery serves to reinforce narrow and oppressive ideals of the feminine. Notions of nature as the Good Mother both draw on and underscore patriarchal understandings of what women should be. The more exclusively and unthinkingly nature is referenced as mother—she who provides and sustains all life—the more support is given to the notion that women are the sole nurturers and that they must be exclusively nurturing. As Linda Vance remarks about the Mother Nature image, "On a general, cultural level, it is a reminder that [women's] primary role is as caretakers and providers, and that our only source of power is to threaten to become angry and withhold our bounty."[46] In fact, if the metaphor of Mother Nature is crafted, as Heller argues, "within a patriarchal ideology that 'justifies' women's compulsory heterosexuality, motherhood, and submissiveness," then it is difficult, although not impossible, for Mother Nature imagery to avoid recalling and recapitulating these compulsory roles of women as submissive, heterosexual mothers.[47]

One implication of this analysis of the Good Mother is a disagreement with Merchant. While I find her work on the organic and mechanistic models of nature and on their cultural contexts in the sixteenth and seventeenth centuries very rich, I disagree with her interpretation of the psychosocial function of these images. Because the Mother Nature image seems to me so fraught and ambivalent, I do not share Merchant's conclusion that it functioned as a constraint against environmental abuse. Or rather, I doubt that this image functioned simply, unambiguously, to constrain human action into habits of environmentally sound care. I think its function was and is more complicated. Feelings for mothers are too complex for the mother-nature relation to function unequivocally as an environmental prod. The sense of nature as Good Mother can work in intricate ways both to inhibit and to fuel actions that are environmentally unsound. If ecological integrity was better preserved in earlier times, I suspect it was due more to lower population pressures and lack of technological capabilities than to any clear-cut control exerted by notions of earth as nurturing mother. Regardless of whatever associations might exist historically and presently between mother and nature, there is no "Mother Nature" wanting to nurture and care for us, no "Mother Earth" who loves us. We need to "biodegrade" these weighty projections and try to clearly see the earth as earth and not as the mother we have imagined it to be. Surely now, as Gaard says, "it is time for humans to stop behaving like children."[48]

My overall point, then, is that environmental degradation is not necessarily checked, despite the best intentions of the sloganeers, when nature is associated in any exclusive or literal manner with the Good Mother. The difficulty stems from the way Mother Nature imagery evokes ambivalent feelings toward mothers—feelings not only of love but also of hate. Furthermore, nature as the Good Mother sets up mutually reinforcing expectations for mother and for nature: notions of both as the beneficent and ever-bountiful nurturer whose "natural" role is to serve others' needs. In an environmental context, the "Love Your Mother" slogan keeps these expectations intact. Given such ambivalence and idealization—felt toward both mother and nature and tying them together in complex ways—imagery of nature as Good Mother can lead to insensitivity to the needs and vulnerabilities both of women and of the environment.

The slogan, in short, does not work as intended. Imperatives to "Love Your Mother" too easily backfire because they draw on and are shaped by ideals of mothering that hide ambivalence and aggression and allow them to fester. Instead of achieving the desired result of encouraging environmental soundness, the slogan can have almost the opposite effect of maintaining exploitative patterns toward both mothers and nature.

This conclusion, however, raises a big question. If the value of this Mother Nature imagery is so ambiguous, why does it remain popular and pervasive, even among some ecofeminists? In Part II, I try to clarify how and why Mother Nature imagery persists and to shed light on the ambivalence underlying the imagery. We will see here that Mother Nature appears not only as the idealized Good Mother but also as the demonized Bad Mother—dangerous, threatening, and in need of human control. This second motif is less discussed than that of the Good Mother but is equally prevalent in the nature imagery of popular culture. Lovelock's comment about Gaia as "man-eating mother" is not an isolated one. Nature imaged as the perfect, loving mother turns with great ease into the man-eater.

The next part explores why.

Part Two:
Nature as Bad Mother

FOUR

"She Will Try to Drown You"

If Mother Nature has proved one thing, it is that she can be a real bitch.

—*Letter to the Editor,* Time *magazine*

Thunder crashes, and lightning forks the sky. A car drives in a pelting rainstorm, sloshing through thick mud on a soaked and rutted road. Quick shots of crashing waves and lashing rains follow, as an unseen woman intones, in a deep and throaty voice: "She will try to drown you." A New Age-sounding track plays in the background, accompanied by wordless female vocals. The car still drives, in the midst now of a blizzard of snow and ice. Deep drifts block its path, but the car plows through. The woman's voice warns: "She will try to freeze you." Scenes flash of a blistering sun and a parched landscape. The car, looking hazy through the heat, speeds along the scorched, cracked earth. Same voice: "She will try to burn you." A hurricane now rages. Fierce winds whip at the car and push it diagonally across the road: "She will try to blow you away." Finally, the weather clears. The car drives down a rugged highway in a mountain setting. It leaps over a rise in the road—jumping for joy? defiant even of nature's law of gravity?—and the voice triumphantly exults: "But she will not succeed." The car lands safely to ride off into a pass in the mountains, having survived it all, pristine and unharmed. The woman then announces the victor in this life-or-death battle, like the winner at the end of a boxing match: "The Nissan Pathfinder."

THE THREATENING MOTHER:
CASE STUDY OF TWO COMMERCIALS

This scenario, played out repeatedly on network television in the fall of 1994, was a thirty-second commercial for Nissan's Pathfinder sport-utility vehicle (SUV). The ad's fascinating language and imagery tell us at least four things. First, nature is female and mother. Although the term "Mother Nature" is never used in the commercial, that is the ad's name, as I discovered when the people at Nissan kindly sent me a video copy of the ad.[1] But even without knowing the official name, audiences have little or no trouble identifying the "she" of the text as Mother Nature. Second, this female intends us grave harm: nature is dangerous, cruel, and torturous as she attempts to drown, freeze, burn, and blow us away. Third, nature's threat can be neutralized, and humans can emerge unscathed. And finally, this control and ultimate conquest of nature comes about through the power of human technology. From Nissan's point of view, of course, the purpose of the ad is to suggest that the Pathfinder does the job with particular finesse and that viewers would be well served by buying one soon.

With images like this commercial, we may well start to wonder whether there is an "or else" implicit in the "Love Your Mother" poster. Chapter 3 revealed some of the ambiguities of the slogan, but here these ambiguities emerge full-blown in the motif of nature as Bad Mother. Love your mother, the images suggest, or else she will turn on you, get you, hurt you. Be nice to your mother to ensure that you are protected against her mean and persecuting side. Obey nature's rules, as Lovelock warned about Gaia, for she is "ruthless in her destruction of those who transgress."[2] Nature here is capricious and fitful, easily transformed from beloved and loving into hated and hateful.

One emotion that animates this commercial is fear, not only of nature but also of the mother's rage or of the anger in general of a woman who has been crossed. The commercial implies that the recipe for neutralizing this dangerous fit of pique is sexualized control by the male over the unruly female. Thus the hand viewers see on the car's steering wheel—our only glimpse of human presence—is solidly male. The narrator's voice is a sultry female purr, devoid of anger, hinting that she, at least, has been tamed. Her exultant tone on her last line, "But she will not succeed," reassures that this female is not united in sisterhood with Mother Nature but is on the side of the viewer, of the human, of the male. I think the intended implication is that all females—including the one currently launching the attack—can and will soon be brought under control. Indeed, I suspect that the narrator of this commercial has to be female in order for the ad to convince its audience that rampageous females, and Mother Nature in particular, can be controlled and that the Pathfinder is just the thing to do the job right. The commercial has a subtext of sexual conquest, emphasized by the quite sexy background music in which the singer's wordless vocals could just as easily be described as moans. Male conquers female—or turns her howls of rage into purring pleasure; culture, cast as male, conquers nature, cast as female. Women viewers can participate in this fantasy equally well, either agreeing that the mother's rage needs to be tamed (as children themselves of sometimes scary mothers) or identifying with the satiated, well-pleased woman who has accepted her place in the male-ordered world.[3]

If the Pathfinder commercial is a prime example of nature as Bad Mother, an earlier commercial most famously captures the threat of the transformation from Good Mother to Bad. This threat was the imagistic heart of one of the most popular advertising campaigns in recent decades. Chiffon margarine used the slogan "It's not nice to fool Mother Nature" to suggest that their margarine tastes so much like butter that Mother Nature herself would be fooled (see Figure 5). A thirty-second television commercial built around this slogan aired in 1977. It opens with a woman, "Mother Nature," seated in a rocking chair and recounting the fairy tale of Goldilocks to a group of animals (a raccoon, a deer, and a cougar). She is middle-aged, attractive in a matronly way, dressed in flowing white robes, and has a crown of daisies in her short dark hair.

Mother Nature: *Then Goldilocks said, "Who's been eating my porridge?"*

A male voiceover, cheery and affectionate, interrupts her.

Voiceover: *Mother Nature, was this on the porridge?*

Mother Nature: [She tastes from a tub proffered by an unseen hand.] *Yes, lots of my delicious butter.*

Voiceover: *That's Chiffon margarine, not butter.*

Mother Nature: *Margarine! Oh, no! It's too sweet, too creamy!*

Voiceover: *Chiffon's so delicious, it fooled even you, Mother Nature.*

Mother Nature: *Oh, it's not nice to fool Mother Nature!*

Figure 5. *"It's not nice to fool Mother Nature."* Still from Chiffon margarine
television commercial, 1977.

On the last two words, her voice drops from its previous loving tones
into a deep and angry register. She stands up and casts her arms
wide, unleashing peals of thunder and flashes of lightning. We see
the raccoon hide its eyes behind its paws. The closing jingle then plays
over an image of the margarine package in front of leafy branches
blowing in a gentle breeze: *"If you think it's butter but it's not, it's Chiffon!"*

The phrase "It's not nice to fool Mother Nature" implies not only
that humans can fool nature by making a "butter" just as good as
hers, but also that nature is hurt or angered by being made such a
fool. Human attempts to imitate or improve upon her bounty may
well rouse her displeasure, signaled at the end of the commercial—as
in the case of the Pathfinder—through thunder and lightning. By the
1980s, "It's not nice to fool Mother Nature" had become one of the
most recognized commercial lines, and it remains so today, often no
longer even connected in people's minds with Chiffon margarine.[4]
Clearly, this imagery has broad resonance, or what the advertising
industry calls "associative appeal."

The Chiffon commercial, however, is more ambiguous than the Nissan ad, for it is not clear how a tub of margarine can control the rampage of nature it might provoke. In the Chiffon commercial, humans seem to get away with their foolery, like naughty children caught in a prank at mother's expense that makes her bluster but is not wicked enough to incite real punishment. The commercial's mood is light-hearted and comical, and it contains the threat it evokes of nature's destructive power by limiting signs of ire to those few seconds of atmospheric disturbance. The imagery of the final shot, as the jingle is sung, immediately reassures us that mother is not really angry, that she was only bluffing, that she has already gotten over her pique. In this last image, the befooling trickster margarine sits securely in the forefront, and nature is once again a peaceful background of swaying branches, as on a warm summer day. The packaging of the margarine in this last shot features prominent pictures of daisies. They are, in fact, the *same* daisies that Mother Nature wore in her hair. Chiffon thus naughtily dupes Mother Nature not only into thinking the margarine is butter but also into unwittingly becoming spokeswoman and symbol for the product that itself adopts—or co-opts—her symbols. Here is the paradox—by no means uncommon—of a product of human technology purposefully manufactured and marketed to appear as natural as possible. The commercial conveys the message that although Chiffon's deliciousness comes not from Mother Nature, it still partakes of the simple goodness the ad associates with the "natural." It tastes just like nature's butter, and it is backed by and decked out in nature imagery.

The Nissan ad takes the ambiguity of its predecessor in the opposite direction. Here the mood is epic or even tragic, although ultimately triumphant. Nature is fully realized as the dangerous killer only hinted at in Chiffon's portrayal. Considering the two commercials together raises the possibility that Mother Nature is so angry in the Nissan ad precisely because of the indignities she has had to suffer, as in the Chiffon ad. Has a change occurred in the cultural imagination such that we no longer expect Mother Nature to let us off lightly? Do we assume less easily today that we can get away with making her a fool? Do we in fact now fear we have given her good cause to punish us and seek her revenge? In this reading, anxiety over nature's retaliation—a danger perceived comically in Chiffon's commercial—impels us to develop new technologies, such as the Pathfinder, which promises to conquer nature in any of her angry moods. The genre changes, then, from comedy to tragedy, and we end up with a vision of escalating warfare between humans and nature. Every time we challenge or best or wound her, she becomes more wrathful and dangerous, requiring us to invent new technological superiority that both promises to subdue nature's enmity and yet rouses it to a fiercer pitch. Running all the slogans together produces a narrative: "Love your mother/Mother Nature, but do not try to fool her, lest she try to drown you. She will not succeed, however, if you are protected by the armor and weaponry of the right technology."

While this narrative sounds like the plot of a fairy tale or action-adventure movie, it is, quite literally, one popular way human-nature relations are cast. I am not trying to mock this portrayal, but indeed to take it very seriously. The mother-nature link taps into a wellspring of images and emotions that are not only loving in reference to the Good Mother but also aggressive in relation to the persecuting mother. The environmental movement rarely invokes this picture of nature as female adversary, but it exists nonetheless as one powerful strand in the complex and ambivalent relationship to the environment portrayed in popular culture. For our task of biodegrading the imagery to proceed, we must dig into the roots of this ambivalence and its full-blown negative expression as the Bad Mother.

"AND YE SHALL BE AS GODS": FANTASIES OF ASEITY, A THEOLOGICAL ANALYSIS

As a first approach, we may set such imagery in the context of historical depictions of woman or of the feminine in Western culture and religion, which often furnishes the prescriptive norms for the feminine ideal. One strand in this complex portrayal of the female depicts woman not only as the bringer of death, as discussed in chapter 3, but also as morally inferior to men and as dangerously wicked. Scholars have written about this motif of "woman-as-evil"; and feminist psychologists, theologians, ethicists, and theorists provide much-needed accounts of the scapegoating and misogyny at work in the notions of moral development, evil, and original sin that vilify women by means both subtle and explicit. These scholars also show how the association of woman with the bad is part of a broader cluster linking her with nature, the body, and sexuality—all of which carry an ambiguous moral status that turns all too often into the other, the inferior, or the dangerous.[5] Since delving into this rich material would take us too far astray, I will simply illustrate with a few paradigmatic examples the argument that one reason for the popularity of Bad Mother Nature is that she resonates, consciously or unconsciously, with this long tradition of woman's association with badness. The tradition feeds the contemporary nature imagery, and the images draw power and cultural legitimacy from the "woman-as-evil" tradition.

This misogynist history dates back to such famous figures as Eve and Pandora. Christianity has been particularly influential in this history and has at times—although by no means always—placed special blame for original sin and the fall from grace onto Eve and, through her, onto all women. The New Testament epistle First Timothy, possibly written by the Apostle Paul, explains why "a woman must listen in silence and be completely submissive" (2: 11) with this justification: "For Adam was created first, Eve afterward; moreover, it was not Adam who was deceived but the woman. It was she who was led astray and fell into sin" (2: 13–14). The early-third-century church father Tertullian is particularly harsh on this point in his notorious condemnation of all women as the "Devil's gateway" because of Eve's act: "Do you not know that each of you is Eve? The sentence of God on this sex of yours lives in this age: the guilt must of necessity live too. *You* are the Devil's gateway. *You* are the unsealer of that forbidden tree. *You* are the first deserter of the divine Law. *You* are she who persuaded him whom the Devil was not valiant enough to attack. *You* destroyed so easily God's image man. On account of your desert, that is death, even the Son of God had to die."[6]

The ancient Greek story of Pandora, as told by the poet Hesiod, imputes blame in even stronger terms. Pandora is triply evil, created as punishment for man. She is herself evil, fashioned by the gods with "the mind of a bitch and the character of a thief." She is the bringer of all evils—including hard work, painful diseases, and death—which she scatters among men from her jar (later a box). She is also the mother of "the ruinous tribes of women," Hesiod recounts, "for from her is the race of the female sex . . . a great affliction, who live with mortal men."[7]

The European witch-hunts of the late fifteenth to mid-eighteenth centuries drew on traditions of woman as especially prone to evil, to association with the devil, and to the lustful sexuality so often seen, since Augustine, as root and paradigm of all sin. In ninety to ninety-five percent of the witchcraft cases, those accused were women. They were seen as sexually dangerous because they supposedly copulated with Satan and destroyed the fertility of men, women, animals, and the fields. As the *Malleus Maleficarum*, the main witch-hunting manual of the time proclaimed: "All witchcraft comes from carnal lust, which is in women insatiable." Recalling last chapter's discussion of ambivalent portrayals of the mother, the *Malleus* adds that when women are good, they are very good, but when bad, "they indulge the worst possible vices."[8]

In the twentieth century, these theological notions of woman's evil or sinfulness emerge transformed into psychological language of woman's moral deficiency. Freud, for example, elaborates a theory explaining why women "show less sense of justice than men." He claims that the conscience, as part of the super-ego, fails to develop in girls as completely as in boys because of differences in their passage through the Oedipus complex. Hence, women's "super-ego is never so inexorable, so impersonal, so independent of its emotional origins as we require it to be in men." Freud believes his theory accounts for "character traits which critics of every epoch have brought up against women—that they show less sense of justice than men . . . that they are more often influenced in their judgements by feelings of affection or hostility." He writes that "for women the level of what is ethically normal is different from what it is in men," although he seems sufficiently aware of the sexism of his theory to be somewhat chagrined about presenting it. One commentator, tongue in cheek, draws the connection between Freud's theory and theology: from this distinction between the sexes "arises the unfortunate fact of woman's weak moral nature, demonstrated, as everyone knows, by the action of Eve, who at one stroke lost us our birthright and brought about the need for psychoanalysts."[9]

But something more besides misogyny and sexism is at work in imagery showing nature as mastered or in need of such taming. Scholars doing gender analysis in theology, ethics, and psychology reveal this long tradition of "woman as evil"; and on the basis of their scholarship, it seems fairly clear that the tradition provides a backdrop against which the angry Mother Nature ads of Nissan and Chiffon make a certain cultural sense. The tradition, in other words, serves to legitimate the commercials. But this gender analysis does not, on its own, fully account for the depth of ambivalence toward nature displayed in such images. Nature is not even always cast as mother in this imagery; sometimes, instead of being our active female aggressor, the environment is simply our subdued, genderless other. Something more besides gender is at work here. Accordingly, I want to take the argument further and propose the following interpretation: *Negative imagery of nature as hostile other and of humans as its/her master assuages the anxiety aroused by ambivalence toward nature through a fantasy that casts humans as gods.* More specifically, these media images co-opt for humans the perceived *aseity,* or independence, of the Western monotheistic God. At this point, Christian theology and ecotheology again become particularly useful in the analysis.

Let me explain. The control of nature—or to go further, its domination as conquered adversary—can be a powerful and attractive fantasy. It is the fantasy of freedom from the limitation, vulnerability, and ultimately death entailed by our human status as beings-in-nature. We are, perhaps not unreasonably, ambivalent about this status. This ambivalence encompasses heartfelt desires to be free from an enemy feared and disdained, as well as equally sincere desires to mend and preserve a beloved home. Two recent newspaper advertisements illustrate this ambivalence and the fantasy of humans as gods.

The first ad, for Texas Instruments, pictures a man standing beside his truck with a laptop computer open on the hood (see Figure 6). The truck is precariously parked, clinging to a rocky mountain face; yet the man works calmly, confidently. Note the main text:

> There is a voice inside you that questions status quo.
> And yearns to abandon the ways of traditional thinking.
> It urges you not to be controlled by your environment. But rather,
> *let the environment adapt to you.*
> The voice inside whispers for you to start doing extraordinary things.

In another ad, this one for General Motors, a man gallops bareback on a horse across an open desert, clutching a briefcase (see Figure 7). Beside them is written:

Figure 6. *"Let the environment adapt to you."* Texas Instruments print advertisement. Appeared in the *Wall Street Journal,* 1996.

It's 1894. You've got a job interview. Tomorrow. 140 miles away. Giddyup.

There was a time when people couldn't chase their dreams any further than a good horse could carry them.

When men and women who wanted to see the world spent days just getting to the next town.

Driving changed all that.

It frees us from the constraints of place. We go where we want, when we want. And if we hit a red light, we know more surely than we know most things in life, it will soon turn green.

These ads reveal a deep, perhaps only semiconscious, ambivalence toward nature. They complain about "the constraints of place" and rebelliously, arrogantly, urge that you "let the environment adapt to you." Yet their photography celebrates the beauty of nature, the endless open vistas of mountain and desert, the power and speed of a gal-

Figure 7. *"Giddyup."* General Motors print advertisement. Appeared in the *Wall Street Journal,* 1996.

loping horse—ridden without bridle or saddle. These are all used as images of freedom. Most fundamentally, then, the ads seem to reveal an envy of nature. Nature both represents and withholds freedom. The ads promise that technology grants both freedom *from* nature and the freedom *of* nature. They illustrate how we rely on technology to deny the limits we perceive nature to impose on us. At the same time, technology is to provide us with the limitlessness—the openness of possibility, the room to maneuver—that we perceive as inherent to these wilderness landscapes. This love/hate relationship has us admiring and celebrating nature, while at the same time deriding and rejecting it. Because of this ambivalence many—perhaps most of us—are moved to environmentalism only when and if our well-being seems threatened by a sick or diminished natural environment.

We start to see the connection between ambivalence and the fantasy that technology allows godlike mastery over the natural constraints that provoke the ambivalence. Andy Fisher recounts this story illustrating the presumption that technology grants humans

Figure 8. *"Decisions, decisions."* TOLES © The Buffalo News. Reprinted with permission of UNIVERSAL PRESS SYNDICATE. All rights reserved.

greater rights of place and privilege than other creatures. "Of the many ethical dilemmas I faced as an environmental engineer," Fisher writes, "one stands out in particular":

> A sand and gravel company wanted to expand its quarrying into an area that was home to a regionally endangered species of butterfly. The conflict between butterflies and gravel disturbed me profoundly, especially when I was told (jokingly) to step on any of those butterflies should I happen to see one. . . . No longer an engineer, I am now an ecopsychologist: I think about butterflies and why we might want to step on them . . . or not.[10]

A cartoon strip reprinted in Fisher's article illustrates the point further (see Figure 8). The cartoon shows a man watching a television broadcast as it reports: *"Worldwatch Institute says we need to stop consuming the planet immediately. Or we lose it. It's as simple as that."* After a frame of silent reflection, we get the punch line of the cartoon. A balloon appears over the man, who has not moved: *"Decisions, decisions,"* he thinks. A tiny cartoon-within-a-cartoon is tucked into the bottom of this last frame. It represents, perhaps, "the little voice inside our head" and a deeper, second level of response, less conscious and acknowledged than the first. Here, still slouched in his armchair by the TV, he asks: *"How much longer am I, personally, going to need it?"*[11]

The cartoonist, Tom Toles, no doubt created the strip to mock such arrogant self-centeredness. In so doing, he might arguably be exaggerating his portrayal of modern man, master of technology, as only marginally concerned about ecological collapse and half-convinced it will not affect him. Yet environmental theorists tell us that this por-trait is not so far off. While the attitude seems callous, I think it masks an even deeper third level of response, this one full of feeling—and of fear. Here the callousness is bravado that covers up and wards off—but also betrays—an underlying anxiety of helplessness and despair. Thus, the most hidden, unspoken response in the cartoon is either: "How much longer am I going to live (in this increasingly poisoned world)?" or "How soon will technology allow me to live without it?" in the fantasy of escape from nature or of complete mastery over it.

To invoke the language of Christian theology, this fantasy is one of aseity. Despite the fact that Coleridge, the nineteenth-century English Romantic poet, referred to aseity, not unfairly, as an "obscure and abysmal subject," I find this medieval scholastic term quite useful here. It derives from the Latin *a se*, meaning "from oneself." Aseity describes the nature of the Western monotheistic God as self-derived or self-originated. God is claimed to be without dependence on any other being for either origination or continuing existence. The doc-trine thus refers to God's absolute self-sufficiency, autonomy, and in-dependence from the creation.[12] Thus, were the world to blow up to-morrow in a giant asteroid smash, God would not be changed or harmed. By applying this term to the media images, we see that not only do the images portray ambivalence about nature, and not only do they use technology to assuage the anxiety of this ambivalence, but these advertisements and cartoon seek to resolve the ambivalence by casting humans as godlike beings, independent of *their* environ-ment. Freud, in fact, made a similar point in 1930 when he wrote that through advances in science and technology, which function like "auxiliary organs" that we put on, "man has, as it were, become a kind of prosthetic God," now able to fulfill his fairy-tale wishes.[13] If our wish is for godlike control and independence of the creation, we seem to get it through these media images, which co-opt for humans the perceived aseity of God. The imagery incorporates assumptions of God's power over nature and freedom from nature, both granted here to humans. This imagery seems to further suppose that nature has, or at least had, some of these same powers itself: nature is the realm of freedom, autonomous and self-sufficient, independent of any other being. It is a god or goddess too, although a rival one that we want to topple and overtake.

In the Pathfinder commercial, this goal is realized. The vehicle displays a quality not unlike the perceived aseity of God. Control and ultimate conquest of nature come about through the power of human technology—here in the form of an SUV—that confers godlike independence from the grip of natural creation, once independent itself but now subdued by humans. If technology indeed makes us gods, we need no longer chafe under the dominion of nature or fear destruction from her threats. From this perspective, we can read the Chiffon commercial in a new light as well. Human aseity or independence comes not only from the protective armor of the SUV that outwits nature's storms, but it comes also from the scientific triumph of the margarine as we make our own fruits of the field better than can Mother Nature herself. The Chiffon ad promises to free humans from implication in nature through products of technology that imitate but supersede their natural counterparts. Twenty-five years after the ad first appeared, the technologies that now make possible genetically modified organisms, both plant and animal, take the promise even further.

A final ad leads to the inevitable culmination of this trend and provides the strongest evidence of the aseity fantasy. Given the analysis so far, it should come as no surprise that auto companies actually promote the association of their product with the divine. (It is interesting to note how auto companies seem leading players, indeed self-cast warriors, in the battle against nature. Their ads do not hesitate to give free rein to the fear and anger behind the aseity fantasy. We may speculate here about the special role of the car in American myth, as the vehicle *par excellence* of the individualistic freedom so central to that myth.) In a splendid example of SUV advertising, Toyota sets this slogan above a shot of their Land Cruiser parked in a southwestern desert setting (see Figure 9): *In primitive times, it would've been a god.* The ad's copy explains that the Land Cruiser "has the qualities man has revered and respected for thousands of years. The power to tame the forces of nature. The prowess to navigate almost any terrain. . . . an interior so roomy, it can inspire awe in up to seven adults at once. . . . For us mortals, it's the ultimate."

In very small print at the bottom—along with contact information (1-800-GO-TOYOTA) and a warning to always buckle up—is a nod to environmentalists and property owners: "Toyota reminds you to

Figure 9. *"In primitive times, it would've been a god."* Toyota Land Cruiser print advertisement. Appeared in *Bon Appétit* magazine, 1997.

Tread Lightly! on public and private land." How reassuring that while the Land Cruiser has the power to tame the forces of nature, it will proceed with caution while doing so! We see here the conflicted response to nature: conquer it, but protect it at the same time. Toyota's slogan in the bottom right completes the ad's triumphant and self-satisfied tone: *"I love what you do for me."* While the ad modestly (or ironically) still calls us "mortals," since it is we who have created the divine Land Cruiser, we may rightfully infer our own status as divine. At the turn of the millennium, humans and cars together have attained the godly ability to tame nature, at least in the imaginative world of the advertisement. The ad worships the technology that allows us to fantasize our own godlike independence from nature.

This fantasy of aseity springs from an ambivalence that is partly justified (to the extent that natural disasters do kill and that nature reminds us of our vulnerability and mortality) but is also largely exaggerated. We exaggerate this ambivalence and fantasize our aseity out of fear of mortality; out of envy of nature's goods (openness, power, beauty); out of resentment at being made to feel helpless, imperiled, and bested; and in retaliation for a sense of Mother Nature as unresponsive to our infantile wishes for an inexhaustible source of care and love, there just for us. The victorious technologies of Nissan, Texas Instruments, General Motors, Chiffon, Toyota, and other products make us feel strong and adult; they reassure us with their satisfying promises to quell nature's fits of rage.

This fantasy, finally, is a form of human badness (a category I will develop in the next section). From the point of view of environmentalism, the freedom fantasy of aseity is clearly a dangerous one. It works against ecological knowledge that nature does not exist to cater to human desire and that we are deeply dependent on the health of the environment for our own healthful existence. The fantasy constitutes a violation of ecological knowledge about the integrity and interrelation of all parts of the global ecosystem. Undermined also by the fantasy is any motivation for environmental protection, for who aids an adversary bent on their destruction? From the theological perspective, the fantasy of aseity is equally suspect. In traditional Christian terms, it renders those who succumb to it guilty of the sin of pride. By claiming one of God's qualities for humans or for the products of human technology, people in effect claim divinity. Theologians find this problematic for exactly the same reason as do environ-mentalists: it entails a denial of human finitude, of our physicality and embodiment; it claims that humans in this world are to enjoy godlike exemption from the natural constraints of life and death. The fantasy of aseity ends up as an idolatry of technology that is deeply worri-some to theologian and environmentalist alike.

The popularity of the Bad Mother Nature images reveals the chal-lenge to the environmental task. The images portray, on the one hand, nature as the wickedest of mothers, abusive toward her inno-cent human offspring. On the other hand, they portray, not the in-nocence, but the crafty ambivalence of that offspring toward the mother or the other from whom they long to be free and against whom they rebel. While the popularity of this nature imagery makes the environmental task seem daunting—perhaps even somewhat hopeless—I actually find the imagery to be extraordinarily helpful in clarifying the shape of that task and how to reach its goals. On this point, the next section will take us deeper into the wilderness within the human heart and into a heart-of-darkness environmentalism.

HUMAN BADNESS AND
ENVIRONMENTAL DISCOURSE

Bad Mother Nature imagery reveals something important about the problem of environmental destruction and even about the problem of human badness in general. The imagery becomes, in fact, a key to unlocking patterns of human-nature relations. The popularity of this imagery tells us that environmentalists' attempts to protect nature by invoking the image of mother will likely not be sufficient for these efforts to succeed. There is a depth of rage and hatred at work in im-ages of humans conquering and controlling nature, in media fantasies of aseity in which consumers break free from its intolerable dominion. Environmental discourse needs to take more seriously this "negative" passion toward nature, this problem of what we may call "human badness." Psychoanalytic ecopsychology and Christian ecotheology are together of assistance in this project. Psychological and theologi-cal analyses of human badness, when applied in the environmental arena, flesh out the heart-of-darkness environmentalism laid out in chapter 1 that makes sense of the Bad Mother imagery.

Let me offer some brief definitions to clarify the point. *Aggression,* etymologically, means "to step toward" (*ad gradior*). Within certain bounds, such aggression can be positive. It can fuel curiosity and exploration and be an impetus for action. When it is excessive, however, "stepping toward" becomes a destructive "stepping over the edge," a stepping beyond proper limits or boundaries. Christian theology talks about this excess as evil (etymologically, a "going up or over proper limits") and locates our tendency to such excess in original sin, both in the Augustinian tradition and in twentieth-century Protestant neo-orthodoxy. Psychoanalysis, on the other hand, talks about this excess as destructiveness and locates our tendency to such excess in the death drive (in Freud) or in our passions of hate and envy (in object relations theorist Melanie Klein's elaboration and revision of Freud's theory). I use the term "badness" to label such excess because it is a generic term, not specific to any one discipline.

Clearly these different disciplines vary in how they describe badness. The classical Christian tradition conceives sin as rebellion against God and God's will. More specifically, Augustine understands sin in terms of a perversion or vitiation of the will, fed by concupiscence or the inordinateness of desire, such that we tend to turn away from the higher good (God) toward lower goods (the "delights" of this world). For Augustine this condition characterizes all humanity as the sinfulness inherited from Adam and Eve's "original" sin. As a result, sin is inevitable but, paradoxically, not necessary. Reinhold Niebuhr reasserts an Augustinian notion of original sin in twentieth-century American neo-orthodox theology. Influenced also by Kierkegaard and existentialism, he analyzes sin mainly in terms of pride as man's "unwillingness to acknowledge his dependence [on God], to accept his finiteness and to admit his insecurity."[14] (Note that the fantasy of aseity in the media images involved exactly this refusal to "accept finiteness.") At roughly the same time, Freud theorizes badness in terms of the controversial idea of an inborn destructive "death drive" (translated more or less interchangeably as "death instinct"), a drive toward the "death" or reduction of tension internal to the individual that manifests outwardly as antisocial destructiveness or aggression. Melanie Klein reworks Freud's more biologically based model into interpersonal terms so that for Kleinians, the death drive refers to strong and innate passions of destructive hate, envy, aggression, and rage, which are present even in the baby at the breast.[15]

Despite their differences, both the theological and the psychoanalytical discourses make the claim that to be human is to grapple with tendencies to both the good and the bad. Underlying ideas of original sin and the death drive is an analysis of the central human task as one of dealing with feelings of loss, breach, and separation.[16] This task is difficult, and that difficulty is not infrequently expressed or manifested in acts of badness. Badness—whether defined theologically as sinfulness or evil, or psychologically as aggression or destructiveness —seems a central and inevitable aspect of being human. I intend by this claim to detour debates about whether badness is inborn and innate to the human condition, or whether it is acquired in response to experiences (themselves inevitable) of frustration and lack in one's environment. I simply suggest that both history and the painful reflections of personal experience tell us that we act in hurtful ways, that we sin, that we fall short of our ethical ideals. Whether inborn or acquired, this tendency seems to some degree an inseparable part of being human.

Here lies, I think, another of the great contributions of a heart-of-darkness ecotheology and ecopsychology to environmental discourse: *humans are creatures who are prone to badness.* From this perspective, environmental degradation is a major contemporary form of human badness and one that is even, arguably, the greatest individual and societal "sin" whose consequences now threaten humanity and the planet as a whole. Some might object that it is not so much sin and evil as it is stupidity and ignorance that causes people to pollute and damage the environment. But right knowledge does not guarantee right behavior. We can know the good and not do it; indeed, this happens all the time.

The problem is more fundamental than mere ignorance. The difficulty seems, in fact, twofold. The human heart is dark both in the sense that our motivations and feelings are partly hidden to us and in the sense that we often struggle with propensities to hurtfulness that seem woven into the fabric of being human. The darkness is thus both the unknowable that we cannot easily see and the unspeakable that we do not want to face. On the first point, as discussed in the last chapter, the problem is that we are influenced in myriad ways, both subtle and gross, by unconscious factors of which we are only dimly aware. But the problem is even more severe. The dividedness is not only between what we can and cannot easily know about our-selves, but also between desire to do the right thing and desire to take the easy way out, between selflessness and selfishness. This ambiva-lence is further complicated by the difficulty of deciding what consti-tutes the "right."

We arrive here at the heart of the problem of evil. "The fact that modern man has been able to preserve such a good opinion of him-self," writes Niebuhr, "despite all the obvious refutations of his opti-mism, particularly in his own history, leads to the conclusion that there is a very stubborn source of resistance in man to the acceptance of the most obvious and irrefutable evidence about his moral quali-ties." The "heart of darkness" is how I have been naming this source of resistance. It is the complex intertwining of the very real mysteries of our deepest motivation and intent with our self-deceptive attempts to hide from ourselves and others our baser side. As Niebuhr adds, "The final sin of man, said Luther truly, is his unwillingness to con-cede that he is a sinner."[17] Sometimes the darkness goes unknown precisely because looking upon it is too grim. "To the depths of ter-ror, too dark to hear, to see," intones the Chorus of *Oedipus Rex* on the tragic destiny of the blinded king.[18] The darkness is both real and exacerbated by our own ability to repress and evade the truth. We do not want to know—because the knowledge is painful and humiliating—how hurtful we can be, in thought if not in deed, in fantasy or desire if not in action or omission of action.

Such discourses about badness help biodegrade imagery of Bad Mother Nature and heal environmental destruction by granting a clearer picture of the situation facing us. Both the psychoanalytic and the theological discourses are anti-optimist in their lessons about the strength of the negative passions, which they view as ubiquitous and deep-seated.[19] They share a somewhat tragic view of the limitations on the good we can hope to accomplish in this world and of the fra-gility of the moral balance we attempt to maintain. This view exists as a countertrend to the more generally optimistic notions of person-hood in modern Western culture, an optimism that seems adopted by much current environmental thought. Both Enlightenment and Romantic notions of personhood emphasize the goodness of the hu-man being, deriving such goodness either from the human ability to reason or from humanity's harmony with a vision of nature as noble.[20]

In contrast, the traditions I highlight within theology and psycho-analysis emphasize instead the depth and persistence of human bad-ness. In a theological and ethical context, Niebuhr termed this ap-proach "Christian realism"—a sober, even pessimistic assessment of the limits on human goodness and on political attempts to achieve so-cial justice.[21] Similarly, Freudian and Kleinian psychoanalytic thought stresses the centrality of hate and destructiveness in intrapsychic and interpersonal relations. Contemporary feminist writers such as theo-logian Kathleen Sands agree as well; Sands criticizes both main-stream and feminist Christian thought for failing to take seriously the problem of evil and the inescapably tragic character of life. Similarly, Cynthia Burrack, writing from the intersection of feminism, psycho-analysis, and social theory, maintains that most feminist and psycho-social theorists ignore the ubiquity of the "disagreeable" or "negative" passions of rage and hatred.[22] If these negative passions are a central element of human experience—as these diverse theological, psycho-analytic, and feminist thinkers all argue—then such passions inevi-tably play a role in human experience with nature. Following the lead of these theorists, I suggest that environmental discourse needs to place more emphasis on badness. Such an emphasis provides this discourse with "environmental realism" (to adapt Niebuhr's term) and better enables it to account for ambivalence and ambiguity in nature imagery, for callousness and reluctance to change in patterns of interaction with nature.

It seems to me, in other words, that it is not enough for the envi-ronmental movement to urge us to think of nature as a loving mother, or as Gaia, or as the home God has made us, and to urge that we all act in ways that are environmentally sound. Environmental thought tends to rely too much on such attempts to encourage loving im-pulses, without adequately addressing the reality of ambivalent, hate-ful, and destructive ones.[23] The task of environmental thought is not to say people should not feel this ambivalence, which although true, does not get us very far. The task must be to accept that this is in-deed a part of how many of us do feel at some level, and to ac-count for how and why we feel this way and what then to do about it. These ambivalent and even hateful feelings may be hidden, denied, or masked over with idealizations—and may also be completely ab-sent for those people most environmentally aware—but the nature imagery reveals such feelings clearly at work in the cultural imagination (as in advertising images that both revel in nature's freedom and reveal desires to master its constraints).

In one example of how environmental thought can downplay destructiveness, ecotheologian Sallie McFague writes: "We are members of the universe and citizens of planet earth. Again, were that reality to sink into human consciousness all over the world, not only war among human beings but ecological destruction would have little support in reality. This is not to say that they would disappear, but those who continue such practices would be living a lie, that is, living in a way not in keeping with reality as currently understood."[24] But human sin and destructiveness are realities too, ones surely as deeply understood, if not more so, than the reality of our ecological membership. Theology knows this reality of sin deeply, and ecological theologians, along with other environmental humanists, struggle with the interpretation of this knowledge.

Rosemary Radford Ruether poses the question I take to be crucial here: "Are our ways of naming evil usable in helping us to understand this destructive capacity [of humans], or have they actually been an element in promoting this destructiveness and allowing us to turn a blind eye to it?" Her answer is that the legacy of the classical Christian understanding of sin is mixed. It offers a powerful analysis of the divided self, the inheritance of sinful systems, and the evil of unjust relations. It also leads, however, to a denigration of sexuality and bodies, of this life and this earth (in its evaluation of mortality as the "fruit of sin"); and it scapegoats women for sin and death.[25] While I agree with much, if not all, of Ruether's critique, I want to dwell, nevertheless, on the usefulness for environmental thought of a strong emphasis on human badness such as that provided by the concepts of the death drive and original sin.

Such an emphasis strikes as dangerous critics who fear that talking about wickedness can serve to validate and encourage it. This debate on theories of human evil is often cast pragmatically in terms of which notion of personhood best grounds sound action. It is a perennial debate, occurring within both Christian thought and psychoanalysis. Both Pelagian arguments against Augustine (Pelagius was the leader of a rival theological position later labeled heretical) and arguments by some psychoanalytic object relations theorists against

Freud maintain that models of self that stress human badness prevent our acting to better ourselves or society by implying we are bound by nature to be sinful or destructive. Critics worry that such notions of personhood deflect attention from attempts to change the socialization of aggression, leading instead to passive acceptance of its inevitability. One could excuse one's wrongdoing, in other words, by simply saying "The devil made me do it!" and then continue merrily on one's wicked way. These opposing views rest on differences in judgment as to the extent of our capacities for self-knowledge and self-control and as to the severity of the problem of human badness.[26]

While I am aware of the dangers these arguments point out, I am more persuaded that their opposite is true. I admit that I urge my two-year-old to behave by trying to remind him that he is a good boy and not by insisting to him that he is a wicked sinner. But when he rages, nonetheless, as two-year-olds sometimes do (and mine went through a long phase of thinking he was a *Tyrannosaurus rex*), I find a strong theory of human badness, Kleinian or Augustinian, to hold descriptive power for what he is doing and why. Does such theory obviate responsibility for bad behavior? Is the theory merely another version of the socialization of aggression? Does the risk it poses of encouraging bad behavior outweigh the gain in explanatory power the theory provides?

I agree that a strong view of badness or a tragic perspective *can* be used as an excuse for bad behavior, but I do not generally buy that as an excuse. Freud, similarly, never intends his theory of the death drive as justification for such horrors as world wars, but instead as a psychoanalytic explanation for human violence and as a theoretical tool against it. A strong view of human badness, in other words, is not *pre*scriptive, but *de*scriptive. Such theory serves not to excuse or justify destructive behavior, but instead grants the theoretical insight to more adequately understand and counteract the reality of human violence. Less sanguine models of self, far from ratifying destructiveness, help us understand why relations to each other and to nature can be so fraught and ambivalent. They provide a powerful and clear-sighted view of the depth of our problem. By so doing, a strong theory of badness protects against self-deluding utopianism and what Luther called "the pretension of righteousness" in evaluating problems of environmental destruction and our prospects for change.[27] The pragmatic value of thus coming to terms with our evil, as Fred Alford notes, is that it "may help to make us more moral," for to recognize "the intensity of our desires, as well as the ugliness of our greed, hatred, and envy . . . at least establishes the possibility that they might become the subject of conscious influence and choice."[28]

In fact, overly rosy views of the human condition strike me as far more dangerous, for downplaying the reality of human destructiveness gives it the opportunity to escape notice, and that which is denied or repressed has passed beyond conscious control. I fear that ignoring the extent of ambivalence in human relations to nature would guarantee the failure of the environmental movement, just as it would guarantee the failure of any movement for justice and the betterment of life. Without such knowledge of why we do bad, we might never get to what would make it better. Melanie Klein has exactly this danger in mind when she writes:

> The repeated attempts that have been made to improve humanity—in particular to make it more peaceable—have failed, because nobody has understood the full depth and vigor of the instincts of aggression innate in each individual. Such efforts do not seek to do more than encourage the positive, well-wishing impulses of the person while denying or suppressing his aggressive ones. And so they have been doomed to failure from the beginning.[29]

Much environmental thought can be seen as one of those attempts to improve humanity to which Klein refers: well-intentioned, but doomed to failure because they fail to consider the depth of our aggression, in this case, against the environment. So too does Reinhold Niebuhr have this danger in mind when he argues for realism in theology. Environmental thought will not succeed in its task of earth healing until it grapples with this problem of the persistence of human badness.

If discourses about badness aid environmental thought by clarifying the picture and the depth of the problem, they also clear a path for action. Both theological and psychoanalytic discourses inform a heart-of-darkness environmentalism on how best to deal with the consequences of badness, how to mitigate tendencies to hurtful patterns of imagery and behavior. They warn that we hide at our own peril from these darker realities of human life and agree that we should start, not by emphasizing and encouraging our lovingness, but by acknowledging our destructiveness. We can work toward a better world by acknowledging badness and integrating it with love, containing hateful impulses within a context of care and concern that points toward real possibilities for environmental repair (Part III will develop these points).

In religious language, we need to start, as does Christian liturgy, with confession. Furthermore, this "confession" is not simply to specific acts of moral failure, but to an underlying aspect or orientation of the human condition out of which we act badly (Augustine's own *Confessions* stands as prime example of this approach). Or as Kant says in his philosophical interpretation of sin, "In the moral development of the predisposition to good implanted in us, we cannot start from an innocence natural to us but must begin with the assumption of a wickedness of the will . . . and since this propensity [to evil] is inextirpable, we must begin with the incessant counteraction against it."[30] Environmentalists need to take seriously the influence of this "wickedness"—this heart of darkness—for it interferes with the success of their program like a shadow obscures a path and makes one stumble. "Between the conception / And the creation," to recall Eliot (who quotes Conrad's *Heart of Darkness* in his poem), "Falls the Shadow."[31]

One last point remains to be addressed. While such environmental realism or heart-of-darkness environmentalism clarifies the gravity of the situation and how this situation may be addressed, this clearer picture is still muddied without an important corrective from feminist theory. Feminist researchers point out that women and men often experience and express badness differently and that men commit more violent crimes (such as murder and sexual assault) than do women. Earlier psychoanalysts and theologians tended either to present gender-blind theories of human badness or at their worst, as noted earlier, to suspect women of moral inferiority and a special inclination toward the bad. In revising such theory, feminist researchers ask: Is women's sin, aggression, or moral development different from that of men? Have categories of sin, aggression, evil, and morality traditionally been defined in terms of male experience? How do these categories change when considered from the perspective of women's experience?

Work by feminist scholars in theology on the meaning of sin,[32] in philosophy on the phenomenology of evil,[33] and in psychology on aggression[34] and moral development[35] all now supports, in various ways, the notion that there are gender differences in the expression and perceived meaning of badness. I disagreed in chapter 2 with the argument made by some feminists for women's greater peaceableness. The more compelling argument, it seems to me, is that women and men are both "bad," although in different ways. The research cited above starts to spell out some of these differences, at the same time that it finds both women and men to have a capacity for the bad. The research suggests that in the case of women, badness more often has to do with excessive self-sacrifice and insufficient development of self; anger is experienced as a loss of control instead of as a means of exerting control; evil is more often understood as disruption or denial of relationship than as a violation of rules.

The implications of these differences are still just beginning to be explored. If women's sin is more often that of self-abnegation, might women's aggression more often turn against the self than does that of men, as in the eating disorders, poor body image, and body slashing found predominantly among girls and women? Might men's aggression typically be more public and women's more private? I am especially intrigued by the implications of this research for possible differences in how men and women perceive Mother Nature and in how they interact with the environment. Are there gender variations in responses to nature imagery and patterns of environmental behavior?

I confess that beyond the suggestions I have pointed to so far, I do not yet know what these possible differences might be. However, one further idea comes from Annette Kolodny's research in *The Land Before Her.* She finds in the frontier records of American women (1620–1860) the fantasy of taming the wilderness into a domestic garden that the women cultivate as a sanctuary for home and family. She contrasts this fantasy with a male pattern that emphasizes the conquering hero who possesses and masters the virgin continent.[36] All of these notions taken together suggest that, to at least some degree, women may have an easier time embracing ecological concepts of interconnection and interdependence and thus may more readily perceive environmental destruction as a form of human self-abuse. If, however, self-damage or neglecting to care sufficiently for one's self is more typical of women's badness, then seeing the planet as an extension of one's self would not save women from committing environmental abuse, especially when this planetary self is identified as a "mother." If human mothers tend to forego their own needs, what is their likely response toward claims about the needs of Mother Nature?

My present humanistic study has not included social science interview or survey data on such gender differences (although I see it as a fruitful area for ecofeminist research and hope that future studies—mine or others'—may fill in these gaps). However we approach these questions, we should heed feminist theorist Naomi Goldenberg's warning that "any future inquiry into the differences between the aggressiveness of men and that of women must avoid the common feminist propensity to idealize women."[37] The challenge is to strike a realistic balance that neither portrays women as the passive and constant victims of all-pervasive male violence nor ignores women's disproportional suffering from domestic abuse and entrenched rape culture. Such a gendered theory of badness helps point toward possibilities for earth healing.

Part III will elaborate on these issues of healing Mother Nature, but we have not yet finished dealing with her as our persecutor. If the argument above is correct, then a strong theory of human destructiveness should be able to shed further light on the meaning and function of Bad Mother Nature imagery and point to a way beyond it, toward more irenic relations. In the next chapter, I test this hypothesis and take on the challenge of fleshing out a heart-of-darkness environmentalism through the use of Kleinian psychoanalytic theory.

FIVE

Splitting Mother Nature

*Gaia, as I see her, is no doting mother tolerant of our misdemeanors, nor is she
some fragile and delicate damsel in danger from brutal mankind. She is stern
and tough, always keeping the world warm and comfortable for those who
obey her rules, but ruthless in her destruction of those who transgress.*

—James Lovelock, *The Ages of Gaia*

In the pre-ecological era of 1936, psychoanalyst Melanie Klein reflected on how ambivalence toward the mother is linked to ambivalence toward nature: "The manifold gifts of nature are equated with
whatever we have received in the early days from our mother. But
she has not always been satisfactory. We often felt her to be ungen-
erous and to be frustrating us; this aspect of our feelings towards her
is also revived in our relation to nature which often is unwilling to
give."[1] Klein makes two important points here: she draws an equation between nature and mother; and she speaks about the dissatis-
faction we feel toward both, the sense that nature can be a Bad
Mother who is withholding and cold. In this chapter, I present an explanation of Bad Mother Nature imagery and its role in patterns of
environmental abuse by conjoining and developing Klein's points. For
this work, I draw on Klein and two more recent writers who interpret
and expand her work: feminist psychoanalytic theorist Dorothy Dinnerstein and social theorist C. Fred Alford, both of whom demon-
strate the explanatory power of Klein's theory, not just at the level of
individual psychology, but at the larger social level as well.[2]

Klein is an important twentieth-century thinker, influential not
only in psychoanalytic practice and theory but also, increasingly,
in such areas as social theory, religious studies, and gender studies. While she saw herself as a Freudian, Klein developed several of
Freud's concepts in new ways that became foundational for object relations theory, the direction in which much psychoanalytic theory
has gone since Freud. She was, for example, one of the first psycho-

analysts to work with children, and her theory focuses more than does classical Freudian psychoanalysis on the mental life of the child —especially the infant and even the newborn—on the role of the mother in that internal life and on a generally interpersonal model of human relations.

The argument I develop in this chapter is that a Kleinian analysis is particularly fruitful for the study of Bad Mother Nature, precisely because such a large part of Klein's theory concerns the ambivalence experienced by infants toward their mothers. Perhaps more than any other theorist, Klein delves deeply and boldly into the passions of hate and rage that surround the figure of mother. In the opening quote above, Klein herself suggests the relevance of this point for humans' relationship to nature, but she does not elaborate the point. This chapter takes up that task by developing a Kleinian object relations ecopsychology. I draw on Kleinian ideas to explain how fear, hate, and aggressive rage are felt from infancy and first projected onto and against the mother. These passions feed into societal images of nature as a mother who, if not currently wrathful, could easily become so. Committing violence against this mother then feels satisfying and even necessary to us, as the Bad Mother Nature imagery attests.

A PSYCHOANALYTIC PERSPECTIVE

To put these ideas to the test of interpreting and biodegrading popular nature imagery, we need a little background first on object relations theory. Since I do not expect most of my ecofeminist or religion and ecology audience to have much familiarity with Klein, bear with me on a quick tour through her key concepts.

For Klein, love and hate are the central passions of life. These passions have their starting point in infancy, in what psychoanalysts call our "object relations." "Objects" refer to others with whom we interact. An object can be a person or thing (whole object), or an attribute of a person or thing (part object). Objects are both external (e.g., the actual human mother) and fantasized internal representations of that external object (e.g., the maternal object). Psychoanalytic object relations theory is about this interplay of self and others, of internal and external worlds. It focuses on relations within the self and of self to others, and on how these relations are mutually constitutive. Klein's work stresses in particular the complexity of the internal world and the centrality of the relation to the mother.[3]

An important concept here is that of "phantasy." The "ph-" spelling distinguishes the Kleinian usage, which is particularly broad, from the Freudian sense of the term. For Freud, "fantasy" is a conscious mental process of compensation for frustrated desire and an alternative to direct gratification. Klein, however, enlarges both the concept and its significance by understanding phantasy as the basic substance of all unconscious mental life. For her, phantasy is elaborate and continuously active in each individual. As the forerunner of symbolism and imagination, phantasy "emanates from within and imagines what is without," such that it shapes and can distort our experience of the external world, even as it is shaped by such experience. Phantasy is where the external and internal worlds interplay in something like a continuously running unconscious movie offering commentary on our object relations.[4]

Furthermore, in a point crucial for my analysis, groups can share phantasies and use them to construct social reality. As Alford notes in a usage that I generally follow, there is no "sharp distinction between internally generated phantasies and collective beliefs learned during processes often called socialization or acculturation."[5] The psychological dynamics of the individual blend here with the psychosocial dynamics of the group or society. When I discuss Alfred's work later in this chapter, I will show how this socialization function of "group phantasy" is especially crucial for the role nature imagery plays in popular culture.

Also central to Klein's work is her reinterpretation of Freud's notion of the death drive, or death instinct, as a force in fundamental conflict with the life drive.[6] Drives are for her not the Freudian "energy arising from specific body tensions" but passions involving others, passions of love (the life drive) and of hate (the death drive). Drives are thus relationships.[7] Her research and clinical work with children led her to conclude that humans are beset by feelings of anxiety from the very beginning of life. As infants, we are terrified of being destroyed by the hate we feel operating inside of us as a dangerous force. This force of hate is what she calls the death drive. All mental development is started off by this "primary anxiety" over feelings of threat to the developing ego as well as from the trauma of birth and the frustration of the baby's bodily needs.[8] This early experience of anxiety in terms of passions of hate, phantasies of persecution, and attempts to surmount the anxiety constitutes what Klein calls the *paranoid-schizoid position*.[9] It predominates, typically, for the first three to four months of the baby's life.

"Positions" are not only or primarily developmental stages, but they exist throughout life as patterns of organization for object relations. Positions are ways of organizing individual psychic reality, one-on-one relations, group dynamics, and cultural life. We never entirely give up the paranoid-schizoid position, for it persists and re-emerges later in childhood and in adult life in cases where the personality is not well integrated, in mental illness, and during times of stress. Furthermore, the influence of the paranoid-schizoid shows up at the cultural level as well: in the dysfunction of prevalent gender arrangements (as Dinnerstein argues), and in group life (according to Alford). Here again, the psychological blends with the psychosocial in Kleinian theory. This important point about the persistence and widespread function of the positions, coupled with the concept of group phantasy, is what allows me to derive a cultural analysis of Mother Nature imagery from a psychological narrative about child development.

The paranoid-schizoid position is followed, at around six months of age, by the *depressive position*. Here the infant begins to realize that the good and bad split objects are really one (e.g., the good and bad breast are parts of the same mother). This realization causes feelings of guilt, fear, and anxiety as we mourn that we have damaged in violent phantasy the mother whom we love and upon whom we depend. Through what Klein calls *reparation* (discussed more next chapter), we use loving, restorative phantasies and actions to repair and re-create the whole object.[10]

One last important concept is that of the ego's defense mechanisms against anxiety.[11] Two of the most relevant defense mechanisms for our purposes are *splitting* and *projection*. Through phantasy, the infant splits both objects and ego in an attempt to protect itself against the hate and destructiveness of the death drive. Splitting results in idealized and demonized versions of an object, starting with the infant's first object, the breast. Klein explains that "the breast, inasmuch as it is gratifying, is loved and felt to be 'good'; insofar as it is a source of frustration, it is hated and felt to be 'bad'."[12] "The result of splitting," she tells us, "is a dispersal of the destructive impulse which is felt as the source of danger." This defense protects the goodness of the object by exaggerating this goodness (through idealization) and isolating it from the object's perceived badness (then demonized) and from the baby's own destructiveness. As the ego splits the object, a corresponding split occurs within the ego. Its "bad parts"—aggressive and violent impulses, derived from the death drive and roused in maternal relations—are split off, allowing the ego to disown the parts of itself that are perceived as dangerous.[13]

The baby then tries to rid itself of this danger and badness through projection. It projects the split-off hate outward onto objects that will hold the hostility, such as the split bad breast and bad mother. The baby expresses this projection in phantasies of sadistic oral aggression against the mother's breast and body.[14] But because the terrifying parts of itself are now identified with that bad breast and mother (through what Klein calls "projective identification"), the infant not only attacks the phantasied bad mother but also experiences this object, filled with its own hatred, as attacking itself. The infant comes to attribute all negative experiences to this evil mother. Such paranoid phantasy further provokes the infant to violent aggression, both real and phantasied, in retaliation against the mother.[15] These defenses of splitting and projection are all paranoid-schizoid ways of dealing with the anxiety roused by hate. Their purpose is to protect the self and good objects by keeping them away from the persecuting objects. Such objects are phantasied as bad both because they have been devalued through splitting and because they are infused with the infant's own hate and aggression through projection. Phantasy thus magnifies ambivalence many times over, creating sharply demonized and idealized objects that come to bear little relation to the actual objects.

What makes Klein's work so fruitful for environmental thought is how these dynamics, first played out with the mother, seem to play out in similar ways with nature. In other words, *the way that passion and phantasy split the human mother into good and bad parts is close to the way that passion and phantasy make nature into a Good and Bad Mother.* Relations to nature in the cultural imagination repeat elements of both the paranoid-schizoid and the depressive positions. Popular images of

Bad Mother Nature—as in the Pathfinder commercial—replicate aspects of the paranoid-schizoid position, especially in the violent aggression the advertisement directs against the mother and imagines her directing back at us. Moreover, in images of nature as wounded mother, we may start to see elements of the depressive position. How is it that infantile relations with the mother re-emerge in the ways that popular culture images Mother Nature? How do the positions, which Klein originally theorized as individual processes, relate to notions about nature current in the culture as a whole? And what does this psychosocial analysis imply about the inevitability of environmental destruction and our hopes for a sustainable future?

THE BAD MOTHER

When I see ads like those of the Nissan Pathfinder and Chiffon margarine, I think of Klein's concept of the paranoid-schizoid. The type of mother portrayed in those popular advertising visions of Mother Nature is very much like what Klein describes as the infant's experience of the mother in the paranoid-schizoid position. This Bad Mother appears in nature imagery as part of a two-sided warfare between humans and the environment in which Mother Nature is either conquered by humans or is trying to conquer us. She is either our deservedly vanquished victim, the target of assaults both subtle and blatant, or our hostile persecutor, launching dangerous attacks of her own. In both cases, she is enemy. The Pathfinder and Chiffon commercials combine these two sets of images, but their overall message is one of humans triumphing over nature.

It is interesting to recall, in this context, Merchant's argument that the older organic worldview of nature as nurturing mother acted as an environmental constraint; one does not readily slay or mutilate the mother or dig into her body, Merchant claimed.[16] According to Klein, however, the infant's unconscious internal world is rife with exactly these phantasies, in which "the child attacks its mother's breast, and the means it employs are its teeth and jaws." She continues:

In its urethral and anal phantasies it seeks to destroy the inside of the mother's body, and uses its urine and faeces for this purpose. In this second group of phantasies the excrements are regarded as burning and corroding substances, wild animals, weapons of all kinds, etc.; and the child enters a phase in

which it directs every instrument of its sadism to the one purpose of destroying its mother's body and what is contained
in it.[17]

Klein describes the child's mental life in the paranoid-schizoid position as one of extreme and violent passions that are explicitly directed
toward the goal of harming the mother. Her analysis of a time popu-
larly imagined as pure, innocent, and free of evil no doubt strikes
some readers as extreme, but popular nature imagery pictures humans launching just such attacks against the mother-figure of nature.

Let me cite more examples. While in the Nissan and Chiffon ads
nature is depicted as legitimately bested, the relation of the human
subject to the environment in such imagery can be even more complex. Consider three cases where speakers use imagery of humans
threatening nature in order to criticize and decry such paranoid-
schizoid attacks. Smohalla, a Native American of the Columbia Basin
Tribes, spoke out famously against European-American attitudes to
the land around 1885. While it is anachronistic to call Smohalla an
"environmentalist" in a contemporary sense of the term, I cite him
here because he is widely quoted by Merchant and others who argue
that casting nature as Mother functions as an environmental re-
straint. As leader of a small group of Native Americans resisting settlement and treaty, Smohalla asked a white negotiator with horror,
"You ask me to plough the ground? Shall I take a knife and tear my
mother's bosom? . . . You ask me to dig for stone! Shall I dig under
her skin for her bones? . . . You ask me to cut grass and make hay and
sell it, and be rich like white men. But how dare I cut off my mother's
hair?"[18]

More recently and with equal imagistic verve, Jim Morrison, vo-
calist and songwriter for the sixties rock group, The Doors, inquires
in their 1967 song "When the Music's Over": "What have they done
to the earth? / What have they done to our fair sister?" His answer is
graphically violent, spoken over chaotic and disintegrating guitar riffs
and drum beat:

> Ravaged and plundered
> and ripped her and bit her.
> Stuck her with knives
> in the side of the dawn

and tied her with fences
and dragged her down.[19]

In the same era, the 1969 "Battle for People's Park" in Berkeley at the University of California saw "sod brothers" seeking to reclaim a plot of land for garden and communal use. They waged their battle with leaflets, handbills, and speeches featuring language about the university as literal "motherfucker":

> The earth is our Mother.
> The University put a fence around
> the land—our Mother.
> The University must stop
> fucking with our land.
> The University must stop
> being a motherfucker.[20]

The rhetoric of all three speakers strongly criticizes, yet at the same time imagistically repeats, attacks on Mother Nature. (Morrison does refer to the earth as "sister," but I take him here to be drawing on 1960s counterculture egalitarian language of "sister/brother" in order to make an environmentalist point about solidarity with the plight of "Mother Earth.") Their language about the hurt people do to Mother Nature is no less violent than that Klein uses in reference to the human mother, and it employs equally sadistic imagery. Klein, Smohalla, and Morrison (a strange ménage à trois, certainly) all paint pictures of biting, ripping, stabbing, cutting, digging into, and disemboweling the mother's body. The People's Park defenders add imagery of rape. Phantasies of attack against Mother Nature appear, then, even in environmentalist relations to nature, if only in opposition to the dominant culture and in critique of its abuses.

In terms of the converse imagery of nature threatening and attacking us, the Pathfinder commercial dramatically illustrates the phantasy of nature intent on humans' harm. So too do everyday references to the "wrath of Mother Nature." A Boston television news anchor, for example, repeated that phrase twice when reporting on a major rainstorm on Memorial Day (May 1996). Strong winds had downed trees in a local cemetery and knocked over headstones. Those interviewed for the story were particularly troubled that the storm had happened on Memorial Day, when people traditionally honor the dead and visit burial sites. Does such timing stimulate phantasies of the environment as a devouring mother, a figure of death and destruction? Does it elicit visions of nature gloating over her power to birth and kill us all, visions that draw on the infant's legacy of fearful vulnerability and that make nature, before which we are also vulnerable, seem even more motherly?

Another example comes from ecofeminist Greta Gaard, who describes a newspaper cartoon that appeared in 1989, shortly after the United States was hit by both a major earthquake in San Francisco and a hurricane in Charleston: "The cartoon depicts a buxom, almost Valkyrie-like woman towering above the cities of San Francisco and Charleston, whose buildings are quaking, swaying, or crushed. On her dress is the word 'Nature,' and her voice-bubble says, ' . . . just in case you've forgotten how insignificant you really are.'"[21] Yet another illustration of nature as persecutory mother shows up in this tagline of a Boston subway ad for running shoes: "Through rain, sleet, snow, and whatever else that Mother throws at you." Finally, a newspaper ad for golf rainwear features the caption, *"Impress* your foursome. *Tick off* Mother Nature."* Here nature appears not only as the spoil-sport of the golfers' fun but also as the butt of their joke as they beat her at her game and revel in thwarting her attempts to soak them.[22]

This notion of nature as Bad Mother—whether attacked or attacking—appears almost everywhere in the popular realm and mass media: TV commercials, rock music, the news, cartoons, print advertisements. If object relations theory helps to explain the origin of this villainous mother image through the concept of the paranoid-schizoid position, does it also help explain how this persecutory mother gets linked up with nature? A psychoanalytic interpretation suggests that the close metaphorical relation, and even conflation, that binds mother and nature together—and that then portrays nature as either good or bad mother—has its deepest roots in the earliest stage of infantile development. Dorothy Dinnerstein delves brilliantly into these issues, tracing the association of woman and nature back to the parenting arrangements of infancy to explain how mother comes to play the role of "representative of nature." Given that women provide all or most of the care for children and especially for infants, mother is the most important part not only of the baby's emotional world but also of its physical world. It is not universally true that the biological mother has sole responsibility for the care of her children; however, in cases where the community, extended families, adopted families, or professional childcare providers perform "mothering" tasks, it is still usually women who look after, or are expected to look after, children, especially babies. Although these expectations are changing in contemporary American culture and generally throughout the Western industrial world, they remain largely intact. Mother plays this caregiver role at a time when a baby is not yet able to tell the difference between a person and the impersonal environment. As a result, the baby does not at first perceive the mother as a separate, fully human being with her own subjectivity. She instead appears as unbounded, as a "global, inchoate, all-embracing presence," as "half human, half nature."[23]

Furthermore, Dinnerstein writes, "Because the early mother's boundaries are so indistinct, the nonhuman surround with which she merges takes on some of her own quasi-personal quality." The baby confuses and conflates categories of "mother" and "nature" since both are experienced as the amorphous physical environment. As mother becomes this surround, nature becomes mother-like. We assign maternal sentience to nature, and the environment's impersonality to mother. Since the mother's body is the infant's first ambience, her body becomes "a kind of archetypal primary landscape" to which later understandings of land are then related.[24] Claire Kahane expresses this process well: "Because the mother-woman is experienced as part of Nature itself before we learn her boundaries, she traditionally embodies the mysterious not-me world, with its unknown forces. Hers is the body, awesome and powerful, which is both our habitat and our prison, and while an infant gradually becomes conscious of a limited Other, the mother remains imaginatively linked to the realm of Nature, figuring the forces of life and death."[25]

The relationship between these early childhood experiences of mothering and the sense of nature as mother is not strictly causal. Nor is the association invented anew for each generation. The infant's relation to its mother reinforces this association, but it is also reinforced by long-standing cultural tradition. Indeed, the two factors reproduce one another. Patterns of parenting that hold women responsible for childcare ensure that we hold tight to the childhood belief that our first, magic parent was a semihuman force of nature, as well as to the idea that nature is our semihuman mother. These beliefs become entrenched as deep cultural truths that then favor the continuance of traditional mothering arrangements, which seem to take on the status of unshakable cultural logic: women should look after children because they are "naturally" more suited to parenting than men.

Mother and nature become imaginatively linked by these means, but even more is at work in the phantasy of early infantile relations. The sexual arrangement of women providing early childcare not only lessens our sense of mother's full sentience and contributes to the woman-nature association, but it also makes mothers into the main targets for the ambivalence and anxiety of the paranoid-schizoid position. Notions of mother (and of Mother Nature) are thus rooted in the paranoid-schizoid position and bear its marks. In the extreme and shifting passions of this position, the baby experiences the caretaker as protective and nurturing (barring abuse) but also as frustrating, since its needs are inevitably not always met. The baby's feelings of frustration intensify the persecutory anxiety and hostility aroused by the death drive in this position. In phantasy, the caretaker becomes all-powerful and all-good but also capricious and malevolent. The baby loves and desires but also hates and fears this caregiver. Because the mother typically fulfills the function, she is targeted in infantile phantasy as both the source of all frustration and as the main object on which to project hate.

Women's disproportional share of childcare saddles them with a greater share of this anxiety roused in infant relations. As a result, mother is rarely a "clean" parent like the father. She instead assumes what Dinnerstein calls an "ambivalent role as ultimate source of good and evil," especially for boys and men—for whom this ambivalence is not mitigated through identification with the mother—but also for girls and women.[26] Mothers bear the burden of being too powerful and mysterious because we were too completely dependent on them. As we saw, to defend against the anxiety of this phantasied omnipotent and fickle mother, the infant splits her into two parts: one loved and idealized as all-good, the other hated and devalued as all-bad. The badness of the Bad Mother is intensified when the infant projects its own hate onto her, perceiving her then as even more hateful. She becomes in phantasy both murderously malevolent—so reinforcing the need for attacks against her—and the omnipotent source of goodness.

The key point is that these intense and early experiences of hate and love, of fear and need, have an enduring legacy. They lay a psychosocial foundation that turns nature into mother and mother into both protector and persecutor, not just for the individual but also in the wider social realm. The Good Mother/Bad Mother split then continues to exert influence in adult life and in the cultural imagination, to the detriment of both women and the environment. We see the cultural influence in portrayals that dichotomize woman as either virginal saint or whore and in the other forms of ambivalence toward the mother discussed in chapters 3 and 4. The psychoanalytic interpretation added here reinforces that sociohistorical one. Because the baby conflates mother and the nonhuman surround, the paranoid-schizoid anxieties that cast mother as this prime figure of ambivalence project easily onto nature. The result is portrayals of the environment as either a beneficent or a threatening female force. Merchant commented on the association of these two sets of dichotomies in the context of sixteenth- and seventeenth-century Europe: "The images of both nature and woman were two-sided. The virgin nymph offered peace and serenity, the earth mother nurture and fertility, but nature also brought plagues, famines, and tempests. Similarly, woman was both virgin and witch: the Renaissance courtly lover placed her on a pedestal; the inquisitor burned her at the stake."[27]

Note that the same structure of ambivalence underlies and connects the images of nature and of women; we romanticize and demonize both in similar terms. A Kleinian perspective finds the deepest root of this common ambivalence in the maternal object. In other words, both female imagery and nature imagery mirror the splitting of the original mother into idealized and demonized aspects. I have argued all along that one way the popular imagination constructs notions of nature is through the lens of notions about mothering. From the perspective of psychoanalytic theory, we can now say more specifically that popular culture focuses images of nature through the paranoid-schizoid lens of the split maternal object. This Good Mother/Bad Mother split animates imagery of nature and of woman.

An interesting implication here is that if men shared parenting tasks more equally with women, individuals and society might harbor less antagonism toward women. Imagery about nature might even become less violent. Indeed, traditional childcare expectations and arrangements are slowly changing as the women's movement and the influx of women into the workforce have made "shared" or "equal" parenting by men more common. On an anecdotal level, I and the majority of my professional women friends already have such shared parenting arrangements; we expected them in our marriages almost as a matter of course. Although I received the maternity leave, my husband and I have split equally all of the childcare for our son since then (sometimes quite insistently—as in "I changed the last diaper; it's your turn now"). The men's movement influences this phenomenon as well. In 1993 (the last year for which figures are available), at least 1.9 million men in America were "stay at home dads" (what the literature refers to as SAHDs or PCGFs—primary caregiving fathers). In 2001, the Sixth Annual At-Home Dads' Convention met outside Chicago at Oakton Community College to "celebrate the joy and magic of at-home fatherhood" with shouted affirmations like "Who are you? *Proud dads.* What time is it? *It's DAD time!*" and seminar topics like "The Anatomy of a Working Mom's Brain."[28]

In relation to such shared parenting, Dinnerstein maintains that "the universal exploitation of women is rooted in our attitudes toward very early parental figures, and will go on until these figures are male as well as female." As long as it is mothers who look after babies and children, women will bear the brunt of infants' conflictual paranoid-schizoid feelings toward the early caretaker, with the result that women's subjectivity will appear more ambiguous than that of men and the association of mother with nature will be reinforced. Baby's ambivalence exists no matter the gender of the caretaker, but this ambivalence would be borne by mothers *and* fathers if they shared equally in child rearing. Woman would not become nature and nature would not become Good and Bad Mother to the extent that they do now. Both Dinnerstein and Keller suggest that equal parenting by mothers and fathers could change social and psychological conditioning so that instead of producing—to recall Keller's categories from chapter 2—a female soluble self and a male separative self, we could raise both girls and boys with a more connective sense of self. Presumably at least some of our culture's sexism and misogyny would then fade, as well as some of its antagonism against nature, because although men and women would still be different from each other, they would be more similar than they are now, more connective, and, through their recognition of interconnection, more ecologically minded.[29]

WHY POPULAR CULTURE
ATTACKS MOTHER NATURE

Aside from the problems for women, there are problems here for nature too. From the Kleinian point of view, passions of love and hate and the unconscious phantasy in which these passions play shape our understanding of reality. The world is like a screen onto which we project unconscious phantasies. We have seen that potent phantasies about the mother—both idealized and demonic—project onto the environment. There they play to at least some degree convincingly, since certain legitimate metaphorical ties do exist between nature and mother. These ties are reinforced—or one may even say exploited—by paranoid-schizoid phantasy that helps create the figures of Good and Bad Mother Nature. The intense and polarized passions of this position contribute to the emotional intensity and popular resonance of the Mother Nature imagery.

However, this world built out of phantasy also interacts with the givens of the external environment. From the environmental perspective, precisely here lies the problem, for some phantasies clearly do not play well on the screen of nature. As Alford puts it, while passion and phantasy shape how we view reality, "obviously some phantasies just won't play, as the external world cannot be given just any meaning at all."[30] From an environmentalist point of view, he is certainly correct that "the external world cannot successfully—that is, in the interests of human survival—be interpreted as an ever-giving mother whose fruits require no labor."[31] For the fruits are not ever-abundant, and those that remain become spoilt by our greed and misuse. In other words, ecological degradation occurs; and then, or with an earthquake or flood, the ever-giving mother suddenly becomes all-taking.

This Bad Mother, whether attacking us or suffering our attacks, is just as problematic for nature as is the Good Mother. Such negative nature imagery draws on phantasy about the persecuting mother

that distorts the perception of reality. These adversarial images mis-
perceive nature by personifying and demonizing it, by overstating its
threat and exaggerating the need for human control. The ecological
problem is clear: these phantasies license war. They rationalize the
conquest of nature as necessary for our survival, given that she "can
be a real bitch."[32] Viewing nature in these terms justifies—and even
requires—our counterattack against her. Images featuring this evil
Mother Nature may, then, both reflect and fuel a harmful intensity
of rage and anxiety centered around the mother, both human and
natural.

If this imagery is so problematic, why is it so common? One reason
is that the imagery is not a simple matter of conscious choice but
resonates and appeals at a largely unconscious level. The imagery
also thrives because it serves as a culturally sanctioned outlet for
paranoid-schizoid ambivalence about the mother. Alford's development of Kleinian theory helps explain this key point about how a theory originally focused on individual psychology can be applied to the
wider cultural sphere and provides another angle on how nature becomes mother, and especially the Bad Mother. He argues that phantasy occurs not only at the level of the individual, but at the level of
the society as well. This point is crucial for my analysis, since the
nature imagery under investigation, while produced by individuals,
is reproduced and consumed at the cultural level. Alford asks why
groups and cultures, unlike individuals, typically "exaggerate the
goodness and badness of the abstractions" with which they deal. He
makes the claim that groups are less forgiving than individuals and
more marked by the paranoid-schizoid passions of rage and hate. For
Alford, the morality of groups, more so than that of individuals, tends
to remain stuck in the paranoid-schizoid position. Such morality
"rarely transcends *lex talionis*"—the law of retaliation and of "an eye
for an eye." Accordingly, groups usually fail to attain the reparative
morality of the depressive position, a morality based on "love and
concern for the object for its own sake" and on deep identification
with the other (a point I explore next chapter).[33]

Alford explains this failure by building on Klein's ideas to construct a theory of the large group. He argues that cultures serve as
"containers" for individuals' paranoid-schizoid anxieties. Collective
beliefs—such as popular notions that nature is in some sense a mother

to us—give "shared content and cultural form" to the anxieties and phantasies of a society's individual members. The group defends individuals against such anxieties by transforming them from private concerns into shared ones and by interpreting them in socially acceptable ways. We are allowed and even encouraged by the group to split off and project our hate onto an "other" that is communally constructed and sanctioned for this role. A group idealizes itself and devalues or even demonizes the other as a threat to its own goodness. Thus the countless versions of "us versus them" at work in group thinking: business versus labor, conservatives versus liberals, the free world versus communism, the saved versus the damned, and even nature versus culture or humanity versus nature.[34] This "good guys" versus "bad guys" dynamic is one sign that splitting and projection from the paranoid-schizoid position are at work. It demonstrates both how individual phantasies and anxieties become psychosocial ones, and how Kleinian analysis provides interpretive power at both the individual and social levels.

Such us-versus-them thinking abounds in nature imagery. John McPhee's *The Control of Nature* quotes an informational film put out by the U.S. Army Corps of Engineers that uses exactly this language to describe the fight against Mother Nature in the case of flood control along the Mississippi and management of the river's course:

> This nation has a large and powerful adversary. Our opponent could cause the United States to lose nearly all her seaborne commerce, to lose her standing as first among trading nations. . . . We are fighting Mother Nature. . . . It's a battle we have to fight day by day, year by year; the health of our economy depends on victory.[35]

This example brings to mind again the harmful consequences for women of the Mother Nature association. Language and imagery that seek the control of nature often express this goal in terms of control of the female; the two seem intimately bound together. My point, however, is not a condemnation of those who hold or utter such views of human-nature relations. In terms of the settlement patterns and established economy of the area, this control of the Mississippi is indeed necessary. Phantasy distorts reality, but it does not necessarily imply falsity. Natural events such as floods and earthquakes do cause great damage by killing people and destroying homes and businesses. For such reasons, theology traditionally labeled these events "natural evil." Although the people of rich industrialized nations have more power and control over nature than ever before, it can still evoke our fear. No one caught in a blizzard or tornado doubts the reality of this danger. My concern is with the images and metaphors and narratives we use to describe such dangers. My interest is in how we construct human-nature relations as a pitched battle of "us versus her," with "her" cast as menacing mother figure, as sadistic killer, as man-eating bitch. This Bad Mother, I argue, is a cultural phantasy, operating out of the paranoid-schizoid position.

Alford says that as members of groups we act badly and get stuck in the talion morality of the paranoid-schizoid position because, in a certain limited sense, this position *works* for the group. In the case of cultural imagery about nature, I suspect the stance prevails for the same reason. As we saw, splitting and projection protect the ego and the maternal object from the infant's own aggression by creating an idealized Good Mother, who is invulnerable to harm, and a demonized Bad Mother, who provides a safe repository and target for the infant's aggression. Splitting nature in the cultural realm into images of Good and Bad Mother works similarly as a defense against paranoid-schizoid anxiety. The defense's effectiveness, against our fears both of nature and of the bad maternal object, serves to reinforce our tendency to split these objects. Individual anxiety *is* reduced when we can project our hate and fear into an "other" that the group agrees is dangerous or inferior. Membership—whether the group be as small as a gang or as large as the American public—thus confers protection against the individual's paranoid-schizoid anxieties. It is in this sense, Alford says, that the defenses of splitting and idealization-devaluation "can be quite functional for group life," albeit at the cost of emotional growth and the rule of talion morality.[36]

Recasting one of Alford's examples (which is about Nazis in his account) illustrates this point: in effect the group says to its members, "You may defend yourself from your internal persecutors, such as the persecuting mother, by naming her Mother Nature, which our culture agrees needs to be controlled, used, and battled for human victory."[37] The nonhuman environment serves well in this function

Figure 10. *"Control Your Mother."* Chevy Blazer print advertisement.
Appeared in *USA Today,* 1996.

because we actually do fear it, as we fear our internal persecutors. Splitting nature is a defense against this anxiety that allows us to interact with that which we fear. Furthermore, by mirroring our split maternal object, the splitting of nature acts as a defense against the bad human mother by licensing attack and control of Bad Mother Nature.

We see this fear of nature in people's justifiably nervous response to fierce storms. As one woman said after Hurricane Fran wreaked devastation on her community in 1996, "We're so sophisticated in this age of technology and science, but Mother Nature comes through and we're back to 400 B.C."[38] Her comment is telling: nature can make us feel helpless and vulnerable, as if back in the cradle, whether the cradle of civilization or of babyhood. Nature can reduce us to a sense of infancy wherein we feel in grave danger from the perceived attacks of the mother. Technology, on the other hand, makes us feel powerful, strong, and adult. We cast nature as mother when nature casts us back into our childhood, and we portray her as bad because we resent being infantalized, bested, and controlled.

Of course, the strategy of choice from the paranoid-schizoid war manual to undo the scary feeling of being controlled is to reverse the vector of persecution and try to control the controller. Accordingly, the following advertising campaign seems inevitable. One of the American auto manufacturers based a recent promotion on a transformation of the "Love Your Mother" poster (see Figure 10). A full-color newspaper ad pictures the Chevy Blazer, a sport-utility vehicle similar to the Pathfinder, aglow in handsome profile. Next to it is a slogan that reads like reassurance of safety and promise of retaliation against an unruly other whose bad temper we have too long endured. *"Control your Mother,"* it says, in both offer and order. Smaller copy elaborates: the Blazer "helps you control just about anything Mother Nature throws your way." This is the perfect revenge phantasy in which humans get back at nature—and at the mother—for her annihilative attempts at our murder, her punitive attempts at our control. Both Pathfinder and Blazer vanquish nature. These images reassure. They provide a safe other on which to project aggression, as well as a satisfying sense of conquest over the dangers of nature and over the internal persecutors for which such dangers stand as cultural substitutes.

Nature's threat is thus both real and exaggerated; our ambivalence both justified and inflated. The ambivalence is real to the degree that nature represents or reminds us of our human vulnerability and mortality. But it is exacerbated by paranoid-schizoid phantasy about the human mother that is projected onto the environment because of anxieties about nature and especially about the mother, with which nature is merged. I am suggesting that when nature appears so ferocious in popular imagery such as these auto advertisements, the ferocity is largely our own.

If the paranoid-schizoid stance is so easily adopted in relation to nature, if phantasies of control over a threatening mother feel so right, can groups hope to rise above this stance? Alford suggests that powerful obstacles block the passage of groups into reparative morality. Besides the paranoid-schizoid stance's effectiveness in combating anxiety, the position tends to prevail because the group generally lacks two important conditions and opportunities available at the individual level to move into the depressive position. First of all, the group lacks a concrete and present other. Its other tends instead to be abstract or distantly located. The result is insufficient intimacy and depth of relationship for emotional learning to take place and for the depressive position to develop. Nature, in this regard, is one of the great "others" of Western religion and culture. We have seen that it often functions as an abstract and objectified concept, and many in our urbanized and heavily populated world have little contact with wilderness.

Secondly, the group gets stuck in the paranoid-schizoid stance because the other group is unlikely to return love for hate, as parents do. Without this reassurance of love to mitigate depressive anxiety, the depressive position cannot be maintained, and we fall back into attacks and phantasies of persecution. Nature certainly does not respond with love to our abuse, and it often seems not to respond at all. This perceived lack of love may enrage us as much as the perception of abuse, for emotional security is as important a need as is physical security. The two are closely related: Klein notes that "the satisfaction of our self-preservative needs and the gratification of our desire for love are forever linked up with each other, because they are first derived from one and the same source," namely, the mother.[39] Floods and hurricanes pose dangers and represent "nature's wrath," but perhaps equally harsh is the apparent unresponsiveness, the givenness of nature. The Bad Mother, after all, not only devours but also withholds. Scientist and writer Richard Feynman once said, "Let's face it, nature is absurd, so accept nature as she is."[40] The choice of the word *absurd* is interesting in this context, for its definition as "irrational and ridiculous" derives from an etymological meaning of "completely deaf." Do we feel that nature is deaf to our calls and neglectful of our needs? Do we hear echoed in Feynman's statement the plaintive whine of children who feel ignored by their mothers? Freud, for one, says of nature that "[she] rises up against us, majestic, cruel, and inexorable."[41] In this light, the Pathfinder commercial seems to embody the sulky phantasy of ignoring nature back. The vehicle remains ultimately untouched by nature's violent buffeting, unresponsive, taunting her for her inability to get her own way.

These, then, are the challenges to group morality and the difficulties we face in weaning ourselves from imagery of nature as Bad Mother. They are also the challenges facing any future environmental agenda. So far, I have suggested that the Good and Bad Mother imagery is physically given from realities of the environment as well as psychologically and socially constructed from phantasies of the split maternal object. One explanation for the energy and appeal of this imagery is its relationship in the unconscious to these two powerful phantasies, first generated in early maternal relations but with lifelong and culture-wide influence: the phantasy of the never-ending abundance provided by the Good Mother, and that of the threat posed by the Bad Mother that requires aggressive counterattack. From this perspective, the ferocious assaults, false idealizations, and aspersive devaluations of contemporary Mother Nature imagery as well as the realities of ecological damage are all evidence of a paranoid-schizoid cultural stance toward nature. The environment becomes a screen onto which these anxieties are projected, and popular culture becomes the theater or arena in which they are played out.[42]

But what about the image of nature as the mother we have wounded and now long to heal: does it suggest reparative morality at work? Does it represent a solution to the group tendency to get stuck in the talion morality of the paranoid-schizoid position? My argument would not be complete and would certainly be all too grim without careful attention to these possibilities for hope and healing. Part III draws again on Christian (eco)theology and on psychoanalysis to highlight this final motif of nature as the Hurt Mother. On this point, Dinnerstein writes that feminism (and environmentalism, too, I would add) "is a living movement . . . only insofar as it embodies . . . optimism that has faced the possibility of failure, and felt through (come to terms with, and put in its proper place) the silent hatred of Mother Earth which breathes side by side with our love for her, and which, like the hate we feel for our human mothers, poisons our attachment to life."[43]

It is to this work of reparation and reconciliation that I now turn.

Part Three:
Nature as Hurt Mother

SIX

"Our Mother Needs Our Help"

The way to love anything is to realize that it might be lost.

—G. K. Chesterton

"We only have one planet. We only get one chance. Our mother needs our help!"

This rousing plea echoes with fear and loss and a keen edge of desperation, yet it also resounds with the righteous determination and bright hope of a knight—medieval or Jedi, cavalry or cowboy—riding to the rescue. Such imagery has become a major motif within the Mother Nature genre. It both expresses and seeks to motivate an increasing cultural desire to help the Hurt Mother. We know more now than ever before—although scientific knowledge is still fragmentary —about the intricate web of interrelated ecosystems making up the ecology of this earth. Unprecedented too is our awareness of how we are damaging these ecosystems and of the global reach and consequences of such degradation. The environmental movement represents a growing consensus that human activity is harming the planet and that we must cease and repair this harm. Embodying the conviction is imagery of nature as our mother whom we have foolishly injured and now seek to restore.

GREEN KNIGHTS: CASE STUDY OF
A PUBLIC SERVICE ANNOUNCEMENT

Earth Communications Office (ECO), author of the opening quote, is one group using Hurt Mother imagery. From their base in Los Angeles, they draw on the entertainment and communications industries to work for environmental education and protection. The high public profile of Hollywood stars no doubt helps their mission; among their board members and conference participants are Michael Keaton, Woody Harrelson, Arnold Schwarzenegger, Shirley MacLaine, and Glenn Close. One of their endeavors is a series of annual public service announcements, screened primarily in theaters as movie trail-

125

ers. The intent of these pieces is to "inspire and motivate the general public on environmental issues." They offer "messages of positive reinforcement to tell viewers that their efforts to save our planet are already making a difference."[1]

"Mother" is ECO's 1995 release. The two-minute piece, dubbed "extraordinarily successful" by ECO, played in 20,000 movie theaters, as well as on CNN International, in retail stores, on airplanes, and at universities and military bases. Overall, more than 100 million people have viewed it worldwide. Among numerous awards, "Mother" won Gold Prize in the communications industry CINDY Awards and was the only non-network public service announcement to be nominated for an Emmy. A narrative of the piece cannot hope to recreate the big-screen effect of its sumptuous photography and production values or its careful pairing of image with spoken word. Nevertheless, the script, with images indicated in brackets, conveys a sense of ECO's self-described "most powerful environmental trailer."[2]

It opens with a scene of burnished sky, accompanied by ethereal New Age music. Written text appears: "*It is not a thing.*" Then, "*It is alive.*" We see a shot of one of the earth's poles from space as a male voiceover begins in a professional narrative tone:

> *Long ago, before the first human was born, before the first tree began reaching for the sun, her life began* [movement-filled shots of sky, desert winds, clouds, water].

The music begins to swell, and a string section comes in.

> *She breathes* [ocean wave cresting] *and grows* [lush forest foliage]. *Her blood rushes through her veins* [gushing stream].

The tempo of the music becomes lively now, with the addition of drums and then voices.

> *She can speak her mind* [bubbling lava field]. *And she can feel pain* [burnt landscape]. *She can feed us when we're hungry* [wheat field]. *She can heal us when we're sick* [hot springs]. *She has the power to give us energy* [Niagara Falls] *and the power to make us smile* [lion cubs playing].

The lilting voices break into an up-tempo world music song. The narrator continues, now personalizing the opening text:

She is not a thing. She is the Earth, and there's a reason we call her mother [moving bird's-eye view over gorgeous wilderness landscapes of open water and mountain].

Shots of animals in the wild then accompany the narrator's litany of facts:

Every day, nineteen more of the Earth's species disappear forever [quick views of a big cat, tree frog, panda, gorilla].

But there is hope. With your help, whales have begun to return [killer whale breaches]. *The bald eagle is off the endangered list* [eagle lands]. *And one million acres of rainforest were protected, forever* [monkey swings through trees].

We only have one planet.

The music is suddenly, dramatically, cut. We see a slow-motion shot of a whale fin slicing through the water and sinking out of sight.

We only get one chance.
Our mother needs our help.
Do something, anything.

The upbeat world music then returns and slowly fades. We are left with the final text, written in stark white on black: *"You have the power."*

This public service announcement portrays Mother Nature as an organic unity in many senses alive, similar to Lovelock's vision of Gaia. It presents her, however, in glamorous Hollywood style and with a New Age twist of personal empowerment. The trailer focuses on the theme of nature as a mother who "needs our help" since she suffers from damage that we have inflicted. It also focuses on the degree to which humans have the power to mend her and are now exercising that power. While highlighting this theme of the Hurt Mother and our ability to restore her, the piece also draws on the two other motifs we have explored. Indeed, it exemplifies the interrelation of all three themes and shows how easily one can turn into or include the others. Thus, ECO's Mother Nature is not only Hurt, but also Good in that she feeds and heals all creatures, gives us energy and makes us smile. Furthermore, she becomes the Bad Mother—if only for a moment—through the image of the lava field and the rather ominous line, "she can speak her mind." Like Pele, the Hawaiian fire goddess who rules the volcanoes, this Mother Nature makes known her anger or disappointment or desire for revenge by unleashing destructive sprays of molten lava. ECO's promotional material hints, too, at this switch from Good to Bad Mother. The trailer, ECO writes, "reminds people that Mother Earth has the ability to be our caretaker and provider, *provided we take care of her in return.*" The warning repeats, in milder form, Lovelock's earlier comment that Gaia keeps "the world warm and comfortable for those who obey her rules, but [is] ruthless in her destruction of those who transgress."[3]

Sentiments of concern over the wounded mother who is in need of healing are, of course, not the exclusive creation of a contemporary ecological consciousness. While recalling the warning about the dangers of ahistoricity in chapter 2, I want to make the point again that despite radically different social contexts, similar motifs emerge in Mother Nature imagery over the centuries. Part of the power of the metaphor is its apparently timeless appeal to what is perceived by many societies as a "natural" connection between mothers and the natural environment. To mention only a few older examples of the Hurt Mother motif, strictures against mining both in ancient Rome (by Pliny, Ovid, and Seneca) and in the Renaissance expressed concern that mining violates Mother Earth by stripping precious metals from her womb in a process that despoils the earth's surface and fuels human avarice and war. "When will be the end of thus exhausting the earth?" asked Pliny in worried lament.[4]

Smohalla, previously quoted, inveighed against the injury to the earth caused by white American land practices in nineteenth-century America. Making skillful use of maternal metaphor to contrast the impact of his people's traditional root gathering, Smohalla told a visiting cavalry officer: "We no more harm the earth than would an infant's fingers harm its mother's breast. But the white man tears up large tracts of land, runs deep ditches, cuts down forests, and changes the whole face of the earth. . . . Every honest man knows in his heart that this is all wrong." And from the dustbowl crisis of the 1930s, American painter Alexandre Hogue created powerful art that despairs over the damage of land erosion (see Figure 11). His oil painting, *Mother Earth Laid Bare*, shows a woman's naked body outlined in the

Figure 11. *Erosion N. 2. Mother Earth Laid Bare,* 1936. Alexandre Hogue, American 1898–1994. Oil on canvas. Museum purchase. The Philbrook Museum of Art, Tulsa, Oklahoma. 1946.4.

barren ground, stripped of all topsoil. Hogue describes her as "raped by the plow and laid bare."[5]

Today, as exemplified by the ECO public service announcement, imagery flourishes in the popular culture from this long-standing tradition of nature as suffering from the pressures of population, technology, and disrespectful practice. Reflecting the present-day environmental agenda, the imagery features humans as her/its healers. Turner Broadcasting has a successful children's cartoon series called *Captain Planet and the Planeteers* and *The New Adventures of Captain Planet* in which five children from around the world work with the environmental superhero Captain Planet to aid Gaia, "the spirit of the Earth" and "archetypal mother."[6] Other examples of the motif from recent book titles in ecotheology include Pratney, *Healing the Land;* Young, *Healing the Earth;* Pitcher, *Listen to the Crying of the Earth;* Rowthorn, *Caring for Creation;* and Oelschlaeger, *Caring for Creation.* One fascinating illustration is Matthew Fox's *The Coming of the Cosmic*

Christ: The Healing of Mother Earth and the Birth of a Global Renaissance. Fox, a censured Catholic priest, is a major advocate of a form of eco-theology called nature-based creation spirituality. He views both degradation of the environment and efforts toward its protection through an explicitly religious lens. His detailed and intensely emotional language portrays nature as a divine "Cosmic Christ." We have "maternal blood on our hands," he writes, "the blood of Mother Earth crucified." She is "deeply wounded. . . . Yet, like Jesus, she rises from her tomb every day." "Is Mother Earth today not hungry and thirsty, a stranger and naked, sick and imprisoned? Then Jesus is Mother Earth. . . . " Our work must be to "redeem" this mother. More than just practical necessity, the project is an exercise in spiritual devotion.[7]

Some ecofeminists use healing imagery as well. The subtitle to Ruether's *Gaia and God* is *An Ecofeminist Theology of Earth Healing*, and she uses this trope in chapters entitled "Healing the World" and "Creating a Healed World." Her more recent book, *Women Healing Earth*, an anthology of Third World women's ecofeminist writings, continues with the same language. One of the authors, Aruna Gnanadason, cites an elegiac refrain highlighted also by Fox: "Our mother is dying." The phrase, she says, is "a tragic reflection of the present ecological crisis—and out of this cry women have drawn strength. . . . 'When sister earth suffers, women suffer too' is a commonly used expression."[8]

Love, appreciation, concern, and remorse infuse all of this imagery, and its intent is explicitly environmental. ECO, for example, created "Mother" in order to inspire people to "do something, anything," in protection of wild nature. My question is whether this invocation of the Hurt Mother succeeds in encouraging ecological care. Is this motif finally the answer to environmental concerns? Or is it, like much of the other imagery examined in this book, more often counterproductive to environmental and feminist goals, despite its intent? In "Love, Guilt, and Reparation," Melanie Klein writes that "the struggle with nature is therefore partly felt to be a struggle to *preserve nature*, because it expresses also the wish to make reparation to her (mother)."[9]

Environmental science and cosmology teach us today that the entire universe and all life on earth is a unified whole of complex interdependent relationships. The harm we do to one part—even such a remote part as the ozone layer over Antarctica—we now know we do to the whole, including to ourselves. The phantasy of the loving Good Mother or the persecuting Bad Mother still plays well on the screen of nature, but more and more, nature appears as the Hurt Mother: poisoned, trampled, raped, penetrated, killed. We are now sufficiently aware of the damage we have done to feel guilt, remorse, and fear that we have harmed beyond repair that which we love and which we know, more than ever before, that we are dependent upon. Klein teaches that such mourning and pining for the lost object stimulate reparation phantasies in the child and, in later life situations, in the adult. Are we as a society in the process of mourning the damage we have done to nature and beginning to make reparation, both meta-phorical and actual, to the environment? I pursue the question in this chapter by developing a relational and reparative model of self that draws together strands of (eco)theology, (eco)psychology, and (eco)feminism developed elsewhere in the book. In an environmental context, this notion of the relational self provides both hope for real healing and a means to evaluate when the healing imagery is false.

THE RELATIONAL SELF: TOWARD A THEORY
OF ENVIRONMENTAL RIGHT RELATION

To be human is to be in relationship. We are constituted and shaped by our relations with others that occur both in external reality and in inner psychic life. One way to express this idea is through the fa-mous pronouncement of object relations theorist D. W. Winnicott that "there is no such thing as a baby."[10] He means by this that babies exist only when looked after by someone else, in dependent attachment to a caretaker (in his construction, to a mother). A baby without such a context dies or fails to thrive from lack of physical and emotional care. Despite the individualist focus of much Western philosophy and American ideology, this relationality is generally recognized as true at all stages of life. "No man is an island," goes John Donne's fa-mous saying. People are embedded in communities that may include family, friends, work, worship, school, volunteer and club groups, neighborhood, and more. Although such ties are often the source of our deepest pain and disappointment, few choose lives of complete solitude. We seem to need and want one another.

The environmentalist point here is that we also need nature. To paraphrase Winnicott, "There is no such thing as a human." We exist always and only in a human-environment relationship. We are as dependent on nature as we are on each other. Without air to breathe, food to eat, clean water to drink, and the sun to provide energy and warmth, human beings could not exist. Indeed, there would be no life at all.

A relational model of self defines us by these networks of human and nonhuman relations.[11] I argue for such a model by stressing the fundamentally relational character of human experience but at the same time by emphasizing the role of ambivalence in such relations. From this perspective, ambivalence seems to entail a tension between tendencies toward unnecessary, hurtful disconnection (what I have called badness) and opposing tendencies toward healing and reconnection. We both want and do not want connection. As D. H. Lawrence puts it, "We cannot bear connection. That is our malady. We *must* break away, and be isolate. We call that being freed, being individual. Beyond a certain point, which we have reached, it is suicide."[12] This "suicide" of disconnection may be from parts of oneself, from other people, from nature, from one's God, or from one's ultimate concern or highest ideal. Disconnection from the environment, for example, happens in the aseity fantasy of human independence from the constraints of the natural world. Badness thus occurs in relationship and entails its disruption or distortion. (Some disconnections do seem necessary, although the deliberations over which are so and when bring us to the core of ethical debates. Does not the resistance of evil at times demand that we make hurtful disconnections? Is a battered woman justified in killing her husband as he sleeps? Is it a moral act for a sniper to kill a terrorist who threatens hostages but who might have been convinced to release them? Is there any nice way to tell a Nazi, a rapist, a murderer, no?)

But my point here in Part III is that badness is not the final word on the human condition. A relational vision of what it means to be human focuses on the interplay and conflict between desires, on the one hand, for breaking connection, for destruction and death; and desires, on the other hand, for reciprocity, union, and life. To be human is to struggle with these passions of love and of hate, these impulses to repair and to destroy. Such dynamics of ambivalence seem at the core of human experience and characterize all relations, including human relations to nature. The moral challenge, as illustrated in the example of the Hurt Mother imagery, is to nurture relation, to tolerate its ambivalences, to curb tendencies to destructive separation, and to repair breaches. The task of ethics is, as E. M. Forster writes in the epigraph of his novel *Howard's End:* "Only connect. . . . " These connections—or reconnections—are, in a psychological context, to a fuller sense of self; in an ethical context, to each other; in a theological context, to one's God; and in an environmental context, to nature.

Environmental healing thus involves restoring relationship. Accordingly, a relational model of selfhood serves particularly well as underpinning to a heart of darkness environmental ethic. I have been inspired here by the many feminist theologians, ecofeminists, and ecophilosophers who emphasize relationality.[13] Much of their work argues that relation is the primary category of existence and that badness consists most fundamentally in disruption of relationship. Their efforts, then, are to create theories and practices of right relation in the social and the environmental arenas. I find hope in this reparative vision of the relational model of self in its sense that it is possible to establish or reestablish connections, to heal, and to love. Ecophilosopher Holmes Ralston suggests that "nature is a generative process to which we want to relate ourselves and by this to find relationships to other creatures."[14] Nature invites, permits, even requires, an appreciation of relationality.

To relate is thus to connect, but *relate* also means "to narrate." A narration is a tale told by one to another. It is a story that binds together teller and listener at the same time that it weaves together ideas, histories, themes, or images. Narratives serve a connective function of holding together both communities of discourse and communities of people. I have claimed that theology and psychoanalysis are two prime narratives in Western culture that offer stories about separation and (re)connection, about humans as relational beings tending toward badness but with a capacity for the good and for caring relationship. Both narratives trace dynamics of love and loss, whole remade from parts, return from fall, repair of breach. In the language of theology, sin is counterbalanced by grace and reconciliation; in the language of psychoanalysis, the death drive is counterbalanced by the life drive, hate by love and reparation. Freud, for one, sees the life and death drives as setting up a primordial struggle and "vacillating rhythm" in the life of the individual.[15] These theological and psychoanalytic narrations of relation provide categories useful for testing the authenticity of the urge to reconnect and heal that is manifested in the Hurt Mother imagery. The narrations yield criteria for working toward right relation and earth healing in a heart of darkness environmental ethic.

What, then, do the Christian (eco)theological and psychoanalytic discourses teach about relation and healing? As I noted in the Introduction, William James concludes in *The Varieties of Religious Experience* that the "common nucleus" of all religions is a two-part feeling of something being *"wrong about us* as we naturally stand" and of our salvation coming through "proper connection with the higher powers."[16] Religion in general, in this view, is about the longing for relation, connection, and healing. Contemporary Christian ecotheology, for example, draws upon a biblical tradition in which the arc of history is understood as one of human and cosmic redemption. This eschatological trajectory is variously conceived as entailing the salvation of all or of only the elect, as requiring human action or as purely God's gracious work, as pointing to a distant end time or as already here. All accounts agree, however, that sin separates humans from God and that reconciliation signifies a restoration of unity between God and humanity (and in some accounts between God and nature) where previously there had been estrangement and conflict.

Just as crucially, reconciliation must occur among fellow humans as well. "Whatsoever you do to the least of my brothers, so you do unto me," Jesus teaches in Matthew 25:40. Yahweh holds Israel responsible for the protection of widows and orphans; God requires just relations among God's people. Evil or sin lies in the denial, or as Ruether says, the violation of relationship. "The central issue of 'sin,'" she proposes, "is the misuse of freedom to exploit other humans and the earth and thus to violate the basic relations that sustain life."[17] Because matrices of relationship are the inevitable context in which we live, sin or badness is also inevitable but—as noted before —paradoxically not necessary. Relationality furnishes the occasion for sin or badness but not its cause. Furthermore, at least in the Hebrew Bible, Ruether finds an ethic of "redemptive eco-justice" in the "intimate unity between justice and right relations to nature."[18] For example, the sabbatical laws make it a religious duty to allow animals and cultivated land to rest at regular intervals. God will not otherwise ensure prosperity and may even revoke the gift of the land.

Within the secular context of psychoanalytic object relations theory, reparation and integration take the place of justice and redemption in a model of right relations. In Klein's schema of infant development, the paranoid-schizoid position that gives rise to phantasies of the Good and Bad Mother is followed by the depressive position, wherein concern over the Hurt Mother predominates. When the infant passes into this depressive position, it comes to fear that its sadistic phantasies have destroyed the good object in particular and goodness in general. The baby feels guilt, remorse, sorrow, and fear of loss; in Klein's words it "mourns" or "pines" for the loved object. The task in this position is to overcome grief and fear by finding a way out of this conflict.[19] The baby accomplishes the task through what Kleinians call reparation.[20] Here, the infant makes amends for the damage done in phantasy to the mother's body. Mourning awakens in the baby "the over-riding urge to repair, preserve or revive the loved injured object." Because of the omnipotent character of phantasy, the baby believes that the harm it has imagined has really taken place. A new set of phantasies about "putting the bits together again" helps reduce depressive anxiety. The baby also overcomes the depressive position "through being loved and through the enjoyment and comfort [it] has in relation to people." By these means, it acquires belief in "the predominance of its own life instinct over its own death instinct."[21] As the child matures and on into adulthood, reparative phantasies lead to creativity, sympathy, empathy, gratitude, and genuine love. These processes continue all life long, since the depressive position and its anxieties of guilty love are easily reawakened by experiences of loss or threat of loss.[22] My point here is that the baby's task in reparation is also the present task of humanity, faced with a potential crisis of ecological degradation: how to mobilize feelings of guilt and loss into concrete actions of repair.

Reparation contributes to integration, which undoes splitting by bringing good and bad part objects together again as whole objects. Integration unites passions of hate with love, aggressive impulses with loving impulses, the death instinct with the life instinct. As Klein explains, the child comes to recognize "that there are potentially dangerous parts of his self"; but instead of splitting or projecting these parts filled with its hate and envy, he or she is more able to accept them because "these emotions become bearable and diminish" when "they are mitigated with love."[23] The personality is much enriched by these processes. They enable lost parts of the ego to be reincorporated, producing a greater sense of wholeness, hope, security, happiness, and control. This is an important insight in Klein's theory. It shows that hate, envy, and aggression are ferocious only when split off, projected, or otherwise denied. When integrated, these passions come into closer contact with love and gratitude, and their severity is tempered. Integration in this way renders "destructive impulses less powerful" and is a key element in moral development.[24] It enables us to tolerate ambivalence and ambiguity, to accept ourselves and others as complex wholes with parts both good and bad.

I suspect that this same process applies in the environmental arena. The sustained capacity to feel both love and hate toward nature means that the destructive excesses of these passions can be tamed. Nature then no longer becomes the vicious persecutor or the idealized goddess, with all the negative consequences those projections entail. The further point for environmentalism is that the ubiquity or deep-seatedness of badness is not, in itself, an impossible impediment to ecologically sound behavior. Indeed, according to the Kleinians, it is precisely our aggressive phantasies that fuel reparation and integration by leading to guilt and remorse. Without badness, there would be no love. Like Christian notions of the "fortunate fall" in which Adam and Eve's transgression is just the first act in a blessed history, without sin there is no salvation. The challenge, then, is not to eradicate human badness—an impossible task anyway—but to acknowledge and experience it in relation to caring. When aggression is set in its proper context as a part of the human condition, healing occurs. Hate is lessened by feelings of guilt and balanced with love.

If these relational and reparative models of self hold true, then imagery about healing the Hurt Mother may be all about trying to make up for having acted out the ambivalence traced in Part II. When the motifs of Good, Bad, and Hurt Mother are considered together in this context, they suggest three linked modes of relation to nature. The first mode is the prelapsarian, preoedipal, mystical, unadulterated pleasure of union with the beloved mother/nature (the Good Mother). Second is the lashing out against such relation in angry rejection of the union as suffocating (the Bad Mother). Third, then, is the guilty, remorseful attempt to reestablish the connection and heal the lash's scars (the Hurt Mother). Unfortunately, as we saw in the last chapter, the depressive position is difficult for groups to maintain. As a result, nature imagery can *seem* reparative without actually *being* so. Kleinians explain this point by distinguishing true reparation from "manic" or "mock" reparation, which has characteristics of denial, control, and contempt and is actually a defense against anxieties about having ruined the sources of good.[25] There is, in other words, no sure way to enact a widespread reparative morality. The problem of how best to motivate large-scale environmental conservation and protection remains a difficult one, with no easy answers.

EARTH HEALING AND THE ENVIRONMENTAL MOVEMENT: FOUR CRITERIA

The Hurt Nature imagery provides excellent material illustrating these struggles toward reparation and integration as well as strong evidence of how a relational model of self can, despite the difficulties, act as a guide to earth healing. The imagery, however, is by no means a unified whole, nor is it always successful. While it embodies our real capacity for relatedness, it also exposes the perils of self-delusion and self-righteousness (the dangers of mock reparation). In using the imagery, we may fall prey to a narrative of endangerment and rescue by painting the environmental movement as a white (or green) knight set to rescue the damsel in distress that is Mother Nature.[26]

The theological and psychoanalytic narratives of opposites or ambivalences held together in creative tension that have been discussed above provide criteria for evaluating the images of Hurt Nature that environmentalists promote. In this evaluation, I will use the Kleinian term "reparation," not in a strictly psychoanalytic sense, but more generally to refer to the impulse to restore right relations, an impulse equally attested to in the discourse of Christian theology. The four criteria that follow point not only to how to evaluate the Hurt Nature imagery but also to how we might strengthen the reparative impulse toward the earth.

DOES THE IMAGERY AVOID IDEALIZATIONS AND DEMONIZATIONS?

First, to questions of whether imagery is reparative and of what would make it more so, we need to determine if it displays the integration described by Klein. Does the imagery avoid idealizations and demonizations, both in its portrayals of nature and of human groups in relation to nature? Or does it continue with splitting and deny the problem of badness? As an example of these issues, I received in the mail a promotional pamphlet from a school called the Sophia Center at Holy Names College. It offers programs that draw on "the new science, women's wisdom, teachings of indigenous people, and Western Christianity in dialogue with other classical traditions." Students specialize in Earth Wisdom, Art Wisdom, or Spirit Wisdom. (We are perhaps not surprised to learn that their campus is nestled in the Oakland Hills of Northern California.) The description of the Earth Wisdom concentration of the master's degree in Spirituality invites potential students to "celebrate your interconnectedness with earth and every species" through program options of "eco-justice and sustainable communities or ecofeminism."[27] I appreciate their desire for celebration. We are indeed all connected to one another, to the earth, and to other species through complex ecosystems, shared genetic material, food chains, and subtle bonds of kinship, friendship, and empathy. Developing and celebrating feelings of spiritual connection is a path that can lead to environmentally sound patterns of action and belief. However, the Sophia Center's accent on the positive strikes me as incomplete. Before we celebrate our interconnectedness, or along with it, we should plumb the reality and motivations of our *dis*connections, for therein lies the real problem.

Hanna Segal writes that manic reparation aims "to repair the object in such a way that guilt and loss are never experienced."[28] Yet we need to recognize our guilt, mourn our losses, and face up to the persistence of human badness. In psychoanalytic terms, we need reparation and integration. Recall that from the Kleinian perspective, a paranoid-schizoid manner of protecting an object is to split and idealize one part as all-good and to project aggression onto the other part, demonized as all-bad. Integration requires instead that aggression not be split off, projected, and denied, but rather acknowledged. Integration involves withdrawing projections and learning to accept reality. The Kleinian expression of the goal both of development and of psychotherapy is this capacity to differentiate psychic reality from external reality, to see the world in less phantastic terms for what it is, relatively free of how phantasy perceives and misperceives it to be.

If in Klein's terms this criterion calls for integration, in the terms of Christian theology we need repentance and what Reinhold Niebuhr calls realism. We need to acknowledge "the reality of a stubborn evil that persists in human will, behavior, and social structures." Such realism recognizes and atones for wrong-doing. Niebuhr has this need in mind when he writes that "the modern naturalist, whether romantic or rationalistic, has an easy conscience because he believes that he has not strayed very far from, and can easily return to, the innocency of nature." But, as Niebuhr warns, "every effort to return by a too simple route to the harmony and harmlessness of nature inevitably results in daemonic politics in which human ambitions and lusts defy the restraints of both nature and reason."[29]

This effort to reconnect with nature by "a too simple route" seems characteristic of much New Age spirituality, of which the brochure stands as example. The New Age movement, broadly defined, is an eclectic, syncretistic movement focused on development of human potential through spirituality or the expansion of consciousness. It concentrates on positive messages of personal empowerment. (The home page of ECO's Web site features but two short sentences, all in uppercase: "YOU HAVE THE POWER. USE IT.") It also banishes talk of sin—or counters it, as in Matthew Fox's *Original Blessing: A Primer in Creation Spirituality.* Fox uses the term "original blessing" in contrast with "original sin" to assert the essential goodness of all creation and to explain fallenness as a secondary reality, experienced, for example, in modern alienation from nature. He compares a creation-centered spirituality that celebrates our natural self with a false Christian fall-redemption theology that contributes to the matricide of Mother Earth.[30] But as Gabriel Fackre comments in a Niebuhrian response to the New Age movement, "The elimination of original sin as a chapter in the human story is itself a form of delusion that invites misreading our imperial inclinations and our capacity for self-deception." The story of the Fall is a powerful cautionary tale against these self-deluding and self-regarding tendencies; against our pride, complacency, and private agendas; against the ambiguities, corruptions, and tragedies of history.[31]

By this first criterion, environmental groups become problematic if they represent nature in ideal terms as harmonious, beneficent, and nurturant or if they demonize developers, loggers, or industrialists as evil. The resistance of such splitting is an important means to reparation, as is viewing one's opponents as part of a moral whole. In theological terms, Kathleen Sands writes of this means as *compassion:* "opposition that is not benumbed to the enemy, negation that dares to understand."[32] Accordingly, environmentalists and developers meet this criterion when working to see each other as sharing the same ultimate goal of human welfare and global sustainability. Community-based conservation, for example, represents one such effort in contemporary environmental activism to avoid demonization. This growing movement seeks to build consensus among community stakeholders and environmentalists in order to conserve local biodiversity while also addressing a region's human needs. The movement is meeting with significant success, especially in rural areas.[33]

In a literary mode, Annie Dillard provides splendid models of nature writing that avoids idealization. In *Pilgrim at Tinker Creek,* referring to the ubiquity of parasitism, she asks, "Is this what it's like . . . a little blood here, a chomp there, and still we live, trampling the grass? Must everything whole be nibbled? Here was a new light on the intricate texture of things in the world, the actual plot of the present moment in time after the Fall: the way we the living are nibbled and nibbling—not held aloft on a cloud in the air but bumbling pitted and scarred and broken through a frayed and beautiful land."[34] Such a vision presents the interconnectedness of all but recognizes also the violence and chaos of nature and of our place in it.

IS THE IMAGERY CONCERNED WITH THE
ENVIRONMENT OR WITH HUMAN SELF-INTEREST?

As a second criterion, is the concern expressed in the imagery really for environmental degradation, or is the concern more for consequences to human health and prosperity? In other words, do we seek to repair nature or merely to avoid suffering from the damage we inflict? Alford explains the distinction as having "to do with the nature of the phantasies involved, particularly whether they serve merely to defend . . . against paranoid-schizoid and depressive anxiety or whether they also express a genuine concern for the object qua object."[35] Ecotheologian Fox's reverence toward Mother Earth, for example, does not prevent him from appealing to human self-interest. After listing ecological disaster spots around the world, he warns that "if this continues, eventually we and our children will pay the price. If we persist in poisoning the 'mother of all,' then we will ultimately poison ourselves."[36]

Continuing the theme, a bookmark from the Jane Evershed Collection features a charming house surrounded by lush tropical gardens, all rendered in bright greens, blues, and golds (see Figure 12). The caption above labels the setting, with dramatic irony: "Proposed toxic waste site." The text below sets forth the lesson that "when we poison Mother Earth, we poison ourselves."[37] A third example draws the point even finer. Accompanying the videotape of "Mother" sent by ECO was an information sheet entitled "The Environment and Public Health." It announces, in bold and centered letters:

It is our health, not the earth's that is really at stake!

I assume that ECO merely seeks to motivate an environmentalist stance, but this proclamation seems rather shockingly at odds with the loving solicitude of their video.

All these uses of the Hurt Mother motif raise the question: Is the real problem here poisoning Mother Earth or poisoning ourselves? Obviously, the point of the imagery is that the two fates are inextricably related. In the words of an early ecological slogan, "There is no free lunch." A healthy and thriving human future cannot happen in a polluted and degraded natural environment. But what if we *could* poison Mother Earth without harming ourselves? Would we do it? Would we lose our motive for environmentalism? The NIMBY phenomenon ("not in my backyard") proves us less likely to tolerate garbage incinerators or toxic waste dumps in our own neighborhood than in someone else's. If the poison goes elsewhere, if it enters the system of another, we seem less inclined to protest.

One suspects that the problem perceived by many is precisely that we *do* get poisoned when we poison the earth and that we should therefore desist. The argument makes sense, and I do not deny that appeals to human self-interest can and often do work as shrewd motivators of behavior. Concern for both nature's welfare and our own can certainly be combined without falling into a problematic stance of mock reparation. It is legitimate to undertake environmental pro-

Figure 12. *"When we poison Mother Earth, we poison ourselves."* Bookmark from the Jane Evershed Collection www.JaneEvershed.com. Used with permission of the artist.

tection for our own sake or for that of future generations as well as for the sake of the earth. From a purely pragmatic stance, then, it may not matter so much *why* one engages in reparative acts.

An interesting question in this regard is whether the environmental movement could better harness the power of the free market economy in order to foster human behavior that is sustainable. For example, a highly effective motivator for the business community is the argument that ecologically unsustainable practices cost more money than sustainable ones. The pro-development sector claims that the economy cannot afford costly environmental protections; however, billions of dollars are already lost annually in America due to decreased worker productivity caused by illnesses (asthma, respiratory infections, cancers) triggered by pollution. In this context, is a self-interested profit motive sufficient for environmental protection? If "self-interest" expands here to include the global human community and economy (a word which, like *ecology*, derives from the Greek *oikos*, "house," and signifies the management of one's household), with the understanding that a healthy environment is necessary for long-term economic health, then such self-interest may well be sufficient and may be the best way to motivate people, given my presumption of human badness.

However, if all one really cares about is personal well-being, narrowly defined, then talk about healing Mother Nature becomes duplicitous and is merely a sentimental smoke screen. At some point along the line—although this line can never be cut-and-dried—appeals based on narrow self-interest collapse as a basis for environmentalism. The stance becomes a front for a largely non-environmentalist agenda, often hidden or denied. I by no means attribute such an agenda to Fox, Evershed, or ECO, but many big companies' green advertisements and ecofriendly policies do raise such suspicions. Are their claims genuine or merely designed to win customers' good will by seeming so? While we never fully escape an agenda of self-interest, and while in a wider sense self-interest may be sufficient, as the sole motivation for ecological care, narrow self-interest is an insufficient motive for maintaining a long-term reparative approach toward nature. Without Alford's "genuine concern for the object qua object," we end up asking, with the cartoon character in chapter 4, "How much longer am I, personally, going to need it?" We end up trying to figure out ways to distance ourselves from the damage we inflict, to get away with as much as we can, to defer problems to future generations or faraway communities.

A third criterion asks whether the Hurt Mother imagery is actually effective. Does it influence people's behavior and attitudes in the direction of greater ecological sensitivity? A possible criticism here is that phantasies of repairing the damaged object—whether such reparation be real or mock—involve internal, psychic reality. Yet to have a practical effect, environmental protection must obviously entail action in external reality.[38] Reparative phantasies of healing the mother might seem to be on the level of positive thinking: nice, well-intentioned, but dubiously effective. If all the imagery does is encourage us to feel sorry for Mother Nature and wish her well, what use is it?

This question raises the more general one of whether environmentalism itself is becoming so watered down that it is losing its effectiveness. Nowadays, the environmental movement has made broad inroads into even the highest levels of government and business. Former vice president Al Gore wrote the best-seller *Earth in the Balance,* and multinational corporations routinely proclaim their ecological commitments. The 1992 United Nations Conference on Environment and Development (UNCED) in Rio de Janeiro saw the governments of the world for the first time publicly and jointly recognizing the dangers of environmental destruction and agreeing to act. But as Wolfgang Sachs comments in relation to UNCED, "After nearly everybody— heads of states and heads of corporations, believers in technology and believers in growth—has turned environmentalist, the conflicts in the future will not centre on who is or who is not an environmentalist, but on who stands for what kind of environmentalism." Has the contemporary green movement lost its critical edge as it has gone mainstream and global? Has environmentalism abandoned its grassroots oppositional message and become an elite movement of human domination of nature, infected with economic notions of nature as "a commercial asset in danger" and an "aggregate of ever-scarce resources which have to be strictly managed"?[39] In other words, has an ecological worldview become pervasive or only a certain degree of ineffectual public lip service? And does Mother Nature imagery just further serve this agenda?

I recently received an email from a listserv to which I subscribe for women working in religion, ethics, and the sciences. A member had posted this message:

> Because we are in such an important time in our history, I would like to invite you to join me in a group mediation every Monday evening from 8:00 P.M. to 8:10 P.M. (EST). By joining together in a meditation for world peace and calm harmony everywhere, we will be joining forces as a powerful thought-form for the future. I invite you to follow your own guidance and intuition about what feels right to offer as a meditation for the healing, harmony, and joy of the planet, for the leaders and citizens of all countries, and for Mother Earth herself as she goes through her changes.
>
> This group meditation will be on-going through January, 2013. . . . Let's join together as map-makers and dream weavers of the future.[40]

In Part I, I discussed instances of ineffectual romanticization in im-agery of nature as the Good Mother. I am not going to undertake here to judge whether this group meditation for Mother Earth has a re-parative effect or not, although I admit I have my doubts and al-though a number of people asked to be removed from the list after this message was posted.

Klein, however, makes clear that real reparation involves not only internal phantasy but also action in external reality. In the child, these actions may be hugs and kisses, loving games, or art projects. In the adult and in culture as a whole, Kleinians view all creative and productive endeavors as, at some level, the work of reparation, which gives "expression to [our] constructive tendencies."[41] On a related point, Ruether writes that the truth of metaphors lies in the test of relationship: Do the metaphors "bear the fruits of compassion or of enmity?"[42] James's pragmatic method of truth-testing directs us simi-larly to listen for the "cries of the wounded." We can test the truth of the Hurt Mother Nature metaphor, then, by looking for its effects— not just in the psychic reality of phantasy and imagery or in the power of positive thinking, but in the external reality of concrete environmental action. Here, reparation shows itself in sustained commitment to environmental protection. Evidence of the reparative effectiveness of nature images and of environmental groups accumulates over time to the extent that these groups and images actually help diminish ecological damage to the planet and its populations.

One means of encouraging this active effectiveness is the inspiration of reparative leaders. Alford mentions as examples Gandhi and Martin Luther King. In an environmental context, we may think of marine biologist Rachel Carson, who catalyzed the contemporary environmental movement with her 1962 publication of *Silent Spring*. Carson spoke out against the dangers of insecticides and herbicides in one of the first books to predict and document the pending ecological crisis. While her warnings were about the dangers to both human health and that of the ecosystem, it may be—in reference to the previous criterion—that her book generated action in large part because of the former threat. Nevertheless, her status as a genuinely reparative environmental leader remains clear. The success of this leadership lay in the lyricism of her writing, the passion of her defense of nature, and her combined appeal to science, sentiment, and common sense. She spoke with a prophetic voice at a time when no one else was making her point and maintained a calm conviction when initially ridiculed by the chemical industry. Most importantly, through her book she had the crucial ability to mobilize a broad range of people around the goal of environmental protection. We may think also of a myriad of local and lesser-known reparative leaders of groups such as the Sierra Club, Greenpeace, the Nature Conservancy, and regional Public Interest Research Groups (PIRGs).[43]

When imagery of nature as our wounded mother does succeed in spurring environmental action, what kind of action does it produce? In the wake of the Seattle World Trade Organization protests in November 1999, *Rolling Stone* magazine featured a story on a young hard-core revolutionary known only as "Swamp," who was at the center of the Seattle protests. Along with a group of about twenty Oregon anarchists, Swamp brawled with police and security guards and practiced direct action and vandalism (breaking store-front windows, shoplifting, setting fires, spray-painting stores with anti-corporate graffiti). The story discusses how the radical anarchist movement in America today draws inspiration from the environmental group

Earth First! whose founding motto is "No compromise in defense of Mother Earth." Indeed, Swamp explains his tactics with this powerful hypothetical scenario: "If people broke into your house and were raping your mother, would you fight back by any means necessary? What about Mother Earth?"[44]

Swamp's imagery is quite brilliant, for when the question is framed this way, who could say no? Who would not try to stop their mother from being raped? Swamp as eco-warrior is justified because his civil disobedience is actually the loving defense of a mother under vicious attack. The point that interests me is that it is precisely the Hurt Mother Earth language that serves to compel agreement with his tactics. Yet at the same time, most people would disagree with his destruction of property, advocacy of armed resistance against the state, and defense of the Unabomber as his hero. I am not trying to claim that Hurt Mother imagery breeds violence and inevitably leads to Swamp-style tactics, but when someone like Swamp chooses metaphorical imagery to explain his actions, the resonance and intense emotional evocations of the Hurt Mother may serve his cause more easily than most other imagery.

IS THE IMAGERY FREE FROM DESIRE FOR CONTROL?

As a final criterion, does the healing imagery betray contempt, triumph, or desire for control—all signs, according to the Kleinians, of reparation that is actually manic or mock? Some images, for example, seem to fall prey to the ridiculous. Environmentalists can take metaphors too far, overdramatizing and exaggerating them into the realm of hyperbole. Such language reveals, if not hidden contempt, then an inadvertent belittling of its subject that turns the serious into the absurd. Fox's blood-soaked imagery may well display this danger: "In its nuclear testing of bombs since 1945 in the Nevada desert, the United States alone has already ruptured Mother Earth's womb 845 times." He continues: "Already the human race has begun to feel the effects of the wounds that we have inflicted on Mother Earth. We have begun to put our hands in her lanced side and in her crucified hands and feet."[45] While this language may work for some, for me it verges into the realm of the ridiculous as I try to picture nature as a mother with womb, side, hands, and feet all dripping blood from hundreds on hundreds of puncture wounds. While I do appreciate

what Fox is trying to accomplish, I must confess that the gory detail
of the imagery leads me less to an impulse to heal than to a raised
eyebrow at the bathos of it all.

The notion of "cosmic redemption" in contemporary Christian ecotheology raises related issues. Some ecotheologians interpret this religious view of nature as granting the environment high value; however, it seems to me that desire for control over nature and fear of
dependency on it may be present as motives also. The idea of cosmic
redemption derives from biblical roots. It entails belief in the goodness
of the creation as made by God (Genesis 1); the creation's subsequent
curse or fall as a result of Adam and Eve's disobedience (Genesis 3:17;
also 9:2–3, after the flood); and the eschatological hope, realized
proleptically with Christ's death and resurrection, of redemption for
all the created world (Isaiah 11:6–9, 65:17–25; Romans 8:18–25). In
the Peaceable Kingdom, predation will cease and lion will lie down
with lamb. Sickness, decay, and death will be no more; all creatures will coexist in peaceful harmony, redeemed to their full vigor.
Such notions combine with a cosmological Christology that identifies
Christ not simply with the historical Jesus but with the entire cosmos. This Cosmic Christ is the immanence of God in God's creation
and the power by which the creation will be renewed. Within the
history of Christian thought, this complex of ideas forms a minority
tradition, but it is revived today by ecotheologians such as James
Nash, Matthew Fox, and (more cautiously) by Rosemary Radford
Ruether. The last two thinkers also cast cosmological Christology into
the feminine language of Mother Earth (Fox) or Gaia (Ruether).[46]

From the point of view of a relational model of self, such theological
portrayals of the meaning and end of nature hold both benefit and
risk. On the positive side, they recognize relationality by insisting that
human existence is inseparable from the whole of creation. We are
not uniquely privileged and alone worthy of God's salvific love, but
together with other animals we form the indivisible family of life.
Furthermore, cosmic redemption entails a sacramental vision of nature as revealing God and of God as indwelling the cosmos. Nash, for
example, finds here "confirmation of nature's ultimate value" and a
firm basis for ecological healing, since "if the natural world as a whole
will participate in God's redemption, then all things must be treated
with respect in accordance with divine valuations."[47] Creating or re-

creating Edenic paradise becomes not only God's work in a millennial future but also our work in the present. What better motivator for environmentalism?

On exactly this point, however, the hope for nature's glorification reveals a dark underside. Paradoxically, the task of redeeming the cosmos has been abused as a mandate for environmental exploitation. Merchant analyzes this problem in terms of a "recovery narrative" at work in modern Western Christian culture. This narrative is about how Christians can "recover Eden" and establish an improved earthly lot for all: they achieve this aim not only by reconciling their souls with God but also by regaining the dominion over nature lost by Adam and Eve after their first, or original, sin.[48] Such dominion comes about through the combined forces of Christianity, capitalism, and science. Francis Bacon, for example, writes in defense of the Scientific Revolution that "man by the fall fell at the same time from his state of innocency and from his dominion over creation. Both of these losses however can even in this life be in some part repaired; the former by religion and faith, the latter by arts and sciences."[49] Furthermore, Merchant shows how, in the recovery narratives, nature is cast as submissive female resource whose purpose is to serve and perfect the human (or, more accurately, the male). The narratives teach that human mastery over nature is justified as part of God's plan and as a means of redeeming both humanity and the earth. Dominion comes to be seen as God's will and as in the best interests of nature and humanity. Notions of the creation's past and future Edenic perfection make the environment appear tailor-made to serve humans' most exploitative desires.

America as the New Eden, the garden of the world, figures with special prominence in such narratives.[50] While this New Eden image was originally popular in seventeenth-century colonial narratives, twenty-first-century America continues to revel in a self-identity as the New Eden or world leader of capitalist democracy and cutting-edge science. We see here the truism that America is not just a country but an ideology. Present-day America recovers any glory lost in a biblical narrative of fall by exerting dominion over nature through tools of commodification, capitalism, and consumerism. The retail industry and the media make everything into a commodity, including nature, and America literally gorges itself in an orgy of capitalist consumerism. American markets make nature over into any commodity one could possibly want—and many I did not know it was possible to want. (My son has slippers with tiny red lights that blink on and off when he walks: how did I get through my own childhood without such a pair?) Science and technology seem aimed at controlling nature in every way possible (cloned sheep, designer babies grown in test tubes, SUVs that promise to tame the elements). America is a country that remakes nature to suit its own triumphalist desires and to prove its control over nature and its superiority over other cultures.

In the Christian theological notion of cosmic redemption, the remaking of the created world goes even further. The concept actually works to *negate* nature—to make it into a non-nature upon which any human dependency is erased. As such, it entails a notion of nature that seems created or controlled by human desire to be free from naturalness itself. We revisit here the fantasy of aseity. Cosmic redemption effectively erases nature by taking the impulse to heal its wounds to the ultimate conclusion. In the eschaton, the healing is so total that never again will any creature suffer predation, sickness, or death. Instead, in the words of Calvin, "their constitution will be such, and their order so complete, that no appearance either of deformity or of impermanence will be seen." The Apostle Paul writes that the creation will be set free from its slavery or bondage to what is variously translated as corruption, transience, or decay (Romans 8:21). Nash affirms this hope: God will "fulfill the creation, leading it through the process of becoming perfectly good," beyond its present "constricted conditions." God, in fact, *must* do so, for the "finality of death for any living being threatens the integrity of the Christian faith." From this perspective, redemption—for both humanity and nature—involves overcoming mortality. Transience and death are viewed as ultimately evil and as punishment for original sin.[51]

But what is nature, what is life, without change and even death? There is a glaring problem for environmental ethics in seeing transience and corruption—really only negative terms for life—as bondage, in assuming that creation is fallen and awaiting renewal from the curse of decay. We come here to an important contradiction at the heart of the relational model of self when it is expressed in biblical or Christian terms. Niebuhr expresses it as the contradiction between freedom and finiteness; Ruether, as that between consciousness and transience. Both authors refer to the Christian claim that humans are made in the image of God yet are suffering and imperfect beings who must sicken and die. Like all other creatures, we are finite and transient, yet we have freedom and consciousness to a degree claimed to be greater than that of other beings.[52] The solution offered by Christian cosmic redemption is ultimately to deny finitude and transience: the soul is immortal; the body is resurrected; Christ defeats death; in the eschaton, all is reborn as the New Creation.

This solution is in line with the transcendent thrust of much Christian thought in its hierarchical oppositions of body/soul, nature/ spirit, this world/heaven. I fear that ecotheology's project of healing and its relational model may be burdened or pulled in the direction of mock reparation by that aspect of Christian thought that values the severing of relations—dividing the soul from the body, the believer from unbelievers, the saved from the damned, the nun and priest from family life, the "lower goods" of nature (one of Augustine's phrases) from the higher spiritual realm of God, the Christian from "this world."

This analysis points again to a fundamental human ambivalence about relation, here expressed in these strands of Christian thought. When ecotheology accents the transcendent dimension, it risks undermining environmental intent. For this reason, feminist theologians and ecotheologians such as Sands and Ruether agree that we should reject notions of the immortal soul and the transfigured body, no longer prey to change or death. Ruether, for example, argues that in the "quest to escape from mortal life," this proposed solution of the immortal soul threatens life itself. Ethics and spirituality need instead to accept and even cherish the embodied transience of all selves.[53]

My reading here finds mock reparation in cosmic redemption's imagery of environmental healing. In an unfinished paper on religion, Klein offers an analysis of heaven that may apply equally well to this notion of redemption: she sees heaven as a reparation phantasy. This phantasy assuages fears about our eventual suffering and death and that of our loved ones, and controls anxiety over feelings of fragmentation.[54] From this perspective, it seems to me that the need for God or humans to save the world from transience and death in a "cosmic redemption" is misconceived. Mortality is not the problem; but our killing, degrading, and polluting of fellow creatures and natural eco-

systems is. Despite rhetoric of restoring the cosmos, the vision of redemption has an aura of contempt for nature. It seems fundamentally
world-fleeing, fueled by human desire to escape nature and the constraints of these inevitably failing bodies that are us. Cosmic redemption is part of the Christian tradition's ambivalence toward nature:
proclaimed good—but never as good as it was (before the Fall) or as
good as it will be (in the eschaton)—and perhaps never quite good
enough.

This reading also reveals limits to the relational and reparative
models of self in general. Programs of healing can become hurtful,
and understandings of personhood that frame the moral task as one
of reconnection and relationality can be oppressive. Their rhetoric
can mask intentions to control instead of heal, to evade instead of
embrace. "Making whole" sometimes glosses over the sufferings of
the wounded, the marginalized, and the oppressed. It can mean ex-
cluding the messy diversity of the human community that renders
wholeness such a challenge. At its worst, it can pose as a cover for an
elitist program of hegemony and control.

These, then, are the dangers of mock reparation and the criteria for
care, in any effort toward healing. To conclude by returning to the
case study that opened this chapter, what evaluation do these relational criteria yield of ECO's public service announcement, "Mother"?
In terms of the first criterion of avoiding idealizations and demonizations, "Mother" does seem just a little too beautiful. It presents nature
in rather ideal terms. Although the voiceover stresses the loss of species and the fact that "our mother needs our help," the imagery is
almost all of gorgeous and intact natural landscapes. If this mother is
wounded, the camera only shows her good side. Nature becomes a
Hollywood diva. A hint of demonization emerges also, as I noted, in
the threat that she will get angry and "speak her mind" in angry vol-
canic eruption.

In terms of the second criterion of whether the concern is for
the environment or human self-interest, "Mother" itself seems genuinely concerned about environmental degradation and the fate of the
planet. I by no means question the sincerity of its makers. The tone
and feeling of the public service announcement are loving, protective, and impassioned. That is why I was all the more surprised by

the information sheet that came with the copy I had ordered and that warned: "It is our health, not the earth's that is really at stake." Human self-interest comes rather abruptly to the forefront here, in an eruption of its own.

I am very interested in the third criteria of whether the imagery actually motivates action. Again, this is a place for social scientific studies on some of the 100 million people who have viewed it worldwide. Did it make them do anything in particular for the cause of conservation, or did it just provide aesthetic pleasure and fantasy entertainment with its story of endangerment and rescue?

On the final criterion of whether the imagery betrays desire for control, I do wonder a bit about the personal empowerment messages in ECO's refrain, "You have the power. Use it." The mandate to help Mother Nature is channeled through a lens of human control: we are the ones with power, and we get to decide how and when to use it. Is part of the appeal of this piece that it makes us feel big and strong, even in reference to the Great Mother of nature? My two-year-old son's favorite refrain is "I'm a big boy now; I can do it myself." Is "Mother" predicated on the same sentiment?

Environmentalists—while clearly very diverse in their range from Swamp-style Earth First! anarchists to benign backyard birders—are all loosely united around a common goal of protecting and healing nature. Using the above relational criteria, my evaluation of the environmental movement as a loose group is that it may be fed by the depressive position and show reparation at work, but it also shows failure to maintain reparation. Chances of success seem at best uncertain for the strategy of promoting habits of ecological protection through imagery of nature as the dying mother we are called to resuscitate. When the strategy backfires—or falls back into manic reparation—it does so for the same reason as does much of the other Mother Nature imagery I have discussed. The projection of gendered human relations burdens the imagery. This "image-laden language," Kolodny writes about land-as-female, "inhibits change" because it stems from the patterns of our infancy.[55] Nature is not really our mother who loves us; nature does not really get mad if we fool her; nature is not really a damsel in distress. At a surface level, these images are meant metaphorically. But looking deeper, their metaphors are phantasies that we play out on the screen of nature. They disclose deep passions, personifications, idealizations, and demonizations. Overall, the imagery reveals positions toward nature, in the Kleinian sense of patterns of response.

This interpretation finally explains how nature can be Good, Bad, and Hurt Mother all at once, within a heart of darkness environmental ethic of right relation and abuse. Paranoid-schizoid split images of nature serve to reinforce an anti-environmentalist stance. Here nature is either such an ever-giving goddess that she needs no protection at all (the Good Mother) or she is so wicked that she deserves to be mastered and her value aggressively extracted for human benefit (the Bad Mother). Depressive imagery about healing the mother's wounds begins to question this stance and feeds efforts at ecological conservation and renewal (the Hurt Mother). While such imagery can spring from manic reparation and fail to motivate environmentalism, genuinely reparative imagery can also furnish authentic support and has the best chance of changing behavior.

The next chapter looks, finally and in conclusion, at how we can nurture this chance.

SEVEN

Healing Mother Nature

We are now in a window of historic time during which it is still possible to act. We estimate the window at 50 years. If we do nothing it may soon be too late to do anything.

—*National Audubon Society, 1994*

If we detect the healing impulses of the relational self in Hurt Mother imagery—despite the imagery's failure to consistently exhibit genuine reparation—how can such impulses be encouraged? How much hope do we have for making amends and enacting reparative morality? Is it really possible to create communities of healing that embody our ethical ideals? Or, tragically, will evil always be with us? These last two issues are central to reflection in religion, philosophy, and literature and are among the oldest and most painful questions to plague us. The critical contemporary problem of environmental abuse clearly reveals such themes of evil, self-delusion, and tragedy. One of my guiding questions all along has been why people damage the environment when we have compelling evidence that such harm is not in our species' long-term best interests. My exploration of these points, winding now to a close, leads to conclusions that integrate (eco)feminism, psychoanalytic ecopsychology, and Christian (eco)theology together into a vision that is in some ways tragic but also ultimately hopeful.

ENVIRONMENTALISM AND THE TRAGIC

These conclusions focus, first of all, on the category of the tragic. Throughout the book, I have spoken of a "heart-of-darkness environmentalism" that looks deep within the human heart at darker realities of rage, hate, fear, and aggression and at the role of these realities in the nature imagery I have examined. I want to focus these reflections now on the category of the tragic.

Environmentalism needs to be deeply steeped in the lessons of tragedy. The tragic view, in fact, suggests the task of environmentalism for the twenty-first century. This view summarizes much that popular nature imagery has to teach about human-nature relations and sets the agenda for how we might proceed in order to nurture the reparative impulse. Theologian Ralph C. Wood in *The Comedy of Redemption* claims that the tragic perspective is incomplete and argues that Christianity's message is instead fundamentally comic. Christianity encompasses a tragic vision without being limited to it, he says. Wood labels Reinhold Niebuhr the foremost modern Christian theologian to emphasize the tragic, and on this point he finds Niebuhr's theology ultimately unsatisfying. For example, Niebuhr stated in his book of sermonic essays, *Beyond Tragedy,* that Christianity's view of history is tragic "insofar as it recognizes evil as an inevitable concomitant of even the highest spiritual enterprises"; however, "it is beyond tragedy inasfar as it does not regard evil as inherent in existence itself but as finally under the dominion of a good God." Niebuhr's vision here, for Wood, "lies just barely beyond tragedy" and fails to embrace sufficiently Christianity's comic truth, which is a celebration of love.[1]

Such debates are perennial.[2] While there are undoubtedly dangers to the tragic perspective—fatalism, toleration of injustice, lack of joy—the comic has dangers too: shallowness, a blinkered attitude toward the reality of evil, empty optimism. In the end, I find the lessons of the debate to be in defense of the tragic. I believe, furthermore, that these lessons have important implications for contemporary environmentalism. For example, contrary to Wood's claim, the tragic perspective strikes me as fully compatible with a celebration of love. It does not lack love but actually teaches keen lessons about love's preciousness and fragility. It directs us to care well for each other because we are frail and vulnerable, both physically and morally. Life is often hard and easily lost, and love turns all too readily to hate. Tragic love is thus poignant, even sad, because we know how often we will fail at the moral life we are called to live. Furthermore, this very poignancy ensures that the tragic is often a more compassionate view than that of the comic. Consider, for example, the New Testament story of the woman caught in adultery (John 8:1–11). Jesus says to the scribes and Pharisees who bring this woman to him for judgment, "Let the man among you who has no sin be the first to cast a stone at her." A strong view of sin leads here to a wider compassion as the crowd disperses one by one.

Augustine, too, belongs in this tradition of tragic theology. He emphasizes original sin against Pelagian notions of human perfectibility partly because he thinks the Pelagian view leads to intolerance of others' failings, to a lack of compassion for their struggles, and ultimately to a lack of *love*. If one can be perfect and without sin, as the Pelagians teach, then one logically should be so, without excuse.[3] In pragmatic terms, the tragic vision attends more closely to the cries of the wounded, whereas the comic vision tends to say, "Yes, but look on the bright side" and "Don't worry, it will all work out." In other words, comedy teaches that the human story has a happy ending. Suffering is finally worth it, and all is made right.[4] This happy ending closes the Book of Job, where God's faithful servant, made to suffer all the sorrows Satan can fling at him, receives new children and riches to replace all he has lost. However, as with cosmic redemption, such a program of healing and making whole can have an oppressive underside. Can Job's children, killed in the bet between Satan and God, really be replaced?

Religion loses compassion—as does environmentalism—when it moves too quickly or easily beyond tragedy to the comic. Within any of the world's faith traditions, the religious project becomes noxious if it insists on wholeness without attending closely to lived experiences of suffering, especially of those less privileged. While theological formulations may provide answers that point beyond tragedy toward wholeness, religious experience is often that of grappling with the tragic and with the disorienting, disjointed brokenness of life. This is indeed the project of religion, as suggested by one Latin etymology: *re-ligare*, "to re-bind or re-tie," to knit back together that which is torn apart. Such re-connection involves recognition both of the brokenness and of the possibility—indeed the longing—for repair.

From this perspective, religion is and must be a paradoxical poise of comic and tragic. It balances between quest for reconnective healing (sought in the Western traditions in the individual at one with God, the soul at peace with itself, the union of all believers, or the "brotherhood of man") and the deeply felt knowledge that the divisiveness of sin and suffering will always be with us in this world.

As noted before, this knowledge is no excuse for complacency, but instead it sets the task both for ecotheology and for environmentalism in general. If the task of environmentalism is anything, it is surely this *re-ligare:* to acknowledge the difficulties of achieving reparation, but to commit oneself to the task of reconnecting anyway, with an appreciation of frailty and an ethic of love.

The project of religion shares important characteristics with the depressive position, and these shared qualities point finally toward a "psychoanalytic ecotheology" or a "theological ecopsychology." Both theological discourse and object relations discourse, as I discussed in the last chapter, are about dynamics of separation and connection in the relational self. The complex of depressive passions and phantasies may even help fuel religion, which seems motivated by anxiety over feelings of separation or lack (concern about being fallen, lost, in need of enlightenment, in a state of suffering or sin: in other words, the mourning of the depressive position) and desire for reconnective healing (enlightenment, reconciliation, redemption: the process of reparation and integration).[5] Such an approach gets us beyond the arguments that Freud hated religion and that psychoanalysis and religion are enemies to the fact that both psychoanalysts and religious thinkers are centrally concerned with many of the same questions, namely, the complexity, suffering, and uneasiness of being human and what we can hope to do about it.

Where psychoanalysis and theology come together on these themes of tragedy and human evil, their roots attain a common ground. Both Niebuhr and fellow theologian Paul Tillich, for example, found Freud a "powerful ally" in "their opposition to the Enlightenment gospel of salvation through self-improvement" and in their common emphasis on human perversity in the problem of evil.[6] In the context of environmentalism, their shared common ground of the tragic highlights the ethical challenge for a psychoanalytic ecotheology or theological ecopsychology: how to get beyond human perversity and the problem of evil to a lived ethic of environmental care. Or to put it in more concrete terms, how, in America, to rein in rampant consumerism when all we seem to want is more, more, more, and bigger all the time, please; how to change entrenched institutional structures and societal patterns that favor consumption and make difficult a low-impact lifestyle (e.g., urban sprawl, lack of recycling facilities or vegetarian eating options, office buildings with lights that do not turn off, etc.).

Expressing this challenge in Kleinian terms, a central concern is the ethical one of developing the human capacity for love and caring. For Klein, unity, harmony, and wholeness constitute the good. Morality is grounded in the depressive position's reparative impulse to restore this good, to heal or create it anew, as in the healing of the Good but Hurt Mother Nature.[7] This morality, as Alford explains, "has to do with the victory of love over hate. Even in mature and well-integrated individuals, however, this balance is always fragile and temporary, liable to be tilted toward hatred by stress and loss. It is the fragility of this balance, its vulnerability to external events, that is tragic."[8]

Kleinian ecopsychology thus has a tragic quality to it, but one that nevertheless points out future directions for environmental sustainability. Klein's work, for example, suggests that if we idealize the divine realm as all-good, we will see the human realm wherein we live as fallen and sinful. Such a negative view presents little motivation for an environmental ethic, for why bother trying to keep healthy the physical context of such a tainted life? To the extent that the Christian tradition has promoted an other-worldly focus, it has contributed to the devaluation of nature in Western thought and practice. Developing this Kleinian angle, Goldenberg argues that the concepts of heaven, the soul, and an all-good, transcendent God encourage "a hostility to life" by taking aggression out of context through splitting and idealization. The practice of reparation and integration counsels less insistence on the absolute goodness of heaven or of God. A richer and more tolerant way of being could then result, one less hostile toward nature, the female, and the body.[9]

There is, however, no guarantee of a moral outcome. Daisaku Ikeda, founder of the Boston Research Center for the 21st Century, echoes the conviction of many environmental thinkers when he urges that "we must begin with revolution within the individual heart—the human revolution—through which we can then realize a revolution in the human relationship with the environment and thereby a revolution of 'global civilization.'"[10] The plan may well be sound, but how to carry out such a revolution is a question tragically difficult to address. Kant used some of the same language as Ikeda to point out the problem of even knowing whether this change of heart occurs: "Man cannot attain naturally to assurance concerning such a revolution, however, either by immediate consciousness or through the evidence furnished by the life which he has hitherto led; for the deeps of the heart . . . are inscrutable to him."[11]

The tragic character of life lies partly in this inscrutability, in this heart of darkness. We need a change of heart, but we can never be sure it has happened. Yet even more so, tragedy lies, in an environmental context, in the irredeemable conflicts and irreducible complexities of the human-nature relation: our seemingly deep ambivalence toward nature, the mixed and sometimes tainted motives of environmentalism, the hidden roots of how nature imagery represents the environment, the distorting lens of gendered family relations, and the sheer difficulty of working through these multiple layers to achieve major change of mind, will, and action.

Whether we move quickly enough to make reparation and restore health to the environment remains to be seen. The overall perspective developed here leans toward the tragic, for as Alford observes, "The problem of integrating our love and hate is so profound—and so constitutive of reality—that it will remain a severe problem in any imaginable society."[12] It is hard to envision a (this-worldly) future in which humanity consistently behaves in a moral fashion. The prognosis for the environment is indeed serious. But although the problem of human badness is real, so too is the human capacity for relatedness, for healing connectivity. The vision may be tragic, but it by no means yields to despair. Indeed, instead it yields insight. Prospects for hope lie in the greater clear-sightedness gained by squarely facing the complexity of human response to nature. Models of relation and reparation, rooted in our real potential for mature love and caring, offer paths to earth healing. And hope inheres in the tragic view itself, which allows us to see with eyes particularly open to love, compassion, and the moral life.

MOTHER NATURE, HUMAN NATURE: CONCLUDING APPRAISALS

Mother Nature imagery tells us much about how the human relation to nature is imagined in American popular culture, but it also says something important about how that same cultural context imagines the project of being human. The imagery seems to suggest that what is most problematic is a felt contradiction, a conflict or tension not only in relation to nature but in the human condition itself. It is, of course, an ancient idea that the human condition is divided and in tension. Attending to the rhetoric of two thinkers as diverse as the nineteenth-century Christian theologian Albrecht Ritschl and the feminist psychoanalytic theorist Dorothy Dinnerstein is instructive on this point. Their comparison helps us to arrive at final conclusions about the overall message of the nature imagery.

Both Ritschl and Dinnerstein claim that it is the nature of humans to be at the same time natural and somehow other than natural. Ritschl writes that "in every religion what is sought with the help of superhuman power reverenced by man is a solution of the contradiction in which man finds himself as both a part of nature and a spiritual personality claiming to dominate nature." Dinnerstein puts the point this way: "Myth-images of half-human beasts like the mermaid and the Minotaur express an old, fundamental, very slowly clarifying communal insight: that our species' nature is internally inconsistent; that our continuities with, and our differences from, the earth's other animals are mysterious and profound; and that in these continuities, and these differences, lie both our sense of strangeness on earth and the possible key to a way of feeling at home here."[13]

Niebuhr uses the Ritschl passage to analyze the duality that, he concurs, "underlies all religion" and that constitutes or produces this contradiction, inconsistency, sense of strangeness, or ambiguity in human experience.[14] To the extent that we stand "in nature," Niebuhr writes, we are finite creatures: limited, bound, and blind, characterized by ignorance and insecurity. In contrast, to the extent that we stand "above nature," we are free: made in the image of God, strong, far-seeing, and limitless. Such is the paradox of our "weakness" and our "greatness." Niebuhr uses "nature" here, not strictly in an ecological sense but more in a philosophical one, to signify the finiteness that comes from physicality and embodiment.[15] He is careful to insist that the human problem lies, not in the physical environment or in finiteness, nor even in the contradiction that we stand both in and above nature. He corrects Ritschl on this point: the real problem is sin, or prideful attempts to transcend the contradiction and "claim divinity" for ourselves and infallibility for our opinions. This claim of divinity was the heart of the fantasy of aseity probed in chapter 4. From this perspective, sin lies in a willful self-deception about the nature of being human.[16]

In environmentalist terms, I have spoken about this contradiction as our ambivalence toward nature: feeling ourselves part of nature but also "above" it, tempted to dominate and control it. And I have agreed that the real problem is not the ambivalence itself but our "sin" or badness in seeking to resolve the ambivalence through destructive relations toward nature. Niebuhr recognizes such sin as the pride of power: "Sometimes this lust for power expresses itself in terms of man's conquest of nature, in which the legitimate freedom and mastery of man in the world of nature is corrupted into a mere exploitation of nature. Man's sense of dependence upon nature and his reverent gratitude toward the miracle of nature's perennial abundance is destroyed by his arrogant sense of independence."[17]

From the environmental and feminist standpoint of this book, the fault lines of such analysis are readily apparent. This standpoint claims that the problem is not only our "exploitation of nature," but more fundamentally it is the negative valence imputed to our naturalness (as opposed to our freedom) and the notion of "man's" legitimate mastery over nature. Such a view of human-nature relations— quoted here because it is so standard for Christianity and modernism —is not "corrupted" by sin into exploitation, but it is itself already corrupt. One important conclusion is that this view is inconsistent with an environmental ethic and perhaps incompatible with continued life on earth. Niebuhr was of course writing in 1941 before an era of widespread ecological consciousness, and he would likely add to his analysis today, as has happened in the burgeoning literature of ecotheology (although it is important to note that the notion of mastery remains common in the general populace[18]). Dinnerstein, for example, writing some thirty-five years later, shares the conviction that human nature is divided and that analysis of such division is an important key to ethical community. But gone is the sense that we rightly dominate nature, and emphasized instead is the value of our continuities with other animals; and added elsewhere is the pernicious connection between humans' sense of mastery over nature and man's sense of mastery over woman.

The imagery I have examined gives evidence that we bear toward nature conflicted passions of loving restoration and of hateful domination. At their most intense, these latter passions go far beyond any moderate notion of "legitimate mastery" and become uncoupled from any sense of "reverent gratitude," to recall Niebuhr's phrasing. The reparative urge is genuine and has real potential to tame our destructive relations to the environment, but genuine also is the rage. Imagery reflecting both poles of the conflict thrives in the popular American imagination.

We have seen that the reasons for the conflicted response are complex. The answer lies partly in how nature functions as the ultimate source or context of life but also of constraint and death. In this sense, the temptation toward mastery is great, and the ambivalence toward nature justified. It does represent our finitude. We are physical bodies bound by limit and necessity; we are insecure and vulnerable in the face of natural events. (Just last week a tornado touched down in Tuscaloosa; Ted and I held our son in the basement, hoping that the 1932 construction date of our house meant it would survive one more night. Though we were fine, eleven other people across the county lost their lives.) Niebuhr expresses this source of our ambivalence well: to be human is to be "a child of nature, subject to its vicissitudes, compelled by its necessities, driven by its impulses, and confined within the brevity of the years which nature permits its varied organic forms, allowing them some, but not too much, latitude."[19] However, the deeper problem is our exacerbation of such ambivalence in unconscious phantasy and in too-often misogynist associations of nature with the female that subordinate both women seen as nature and nature seen as woman. We seek to ease our frightening sense of vulnerability and dependence by casting nature as bountiful protectress, devoted to our needs; or as wrathful bitch, deserving of our attacks; or as wounded damsel, herself dependent on our healing powers.

Mother Nature imagery is hardly the sole means by which we represent the environment in the cultural imagination. It is, however, popular, pervasive, widespread, and immediately understood. The fact that groups as diverse as environmental organizations and auto manufacturers use it for their ends indicates that this imagery elicits powerful and conflicting responses in a large and varied audience. The imagery reveals that we resist and refrain from a committed environmentalism because it is easy to feel that nature's provisions are ever-abundant and guaranteed. It is also easy to feel anger and hate toward nature—to want to conquer, subdue, and control it. Such activities can feel gratifying and, at some level, right. And it is easy for even a committed environmental stance to slip back into these feelings under cover of the loving Mother Nature rhetoric. We think we can choose new images, models, and symbols of nature to express our ecological sentiments and to encourage better behavior. More accurately, however, the images seem to choose—or even to possess—us. They hold sway from deep recesses of personal and cultural phantasy. We are influenced unwittingly, even unwillingly, by these ingrained and compelling patterns. Even when we try to use the patterns deliberately for an end of environmental good, the outcome can surprise. We think we have adopted inspirational notions of nature as the Good or Hurt Mother, but suddenly the Bad Mother catches us unaware with the ferocity of her presence.

Given the weight of the book's analysis, what must we conclude about Mother Nature imagery? Is it too fraught and problematic ever to be used? A comment by Henry Nash Smith is helpful in answering this question. He contemplates the relation between "mind" and "environment," or between symbolic imagery and the lived experience it reflects, in the context of nineteenth-century conceptions of the American West as "garden of the world":

> History cannot happen—that is, men cannot engage in purposive group behaviour—without images which simultaneously express collective desires and impose coherence on the infinitely numerous and infinitely varied data of experience. These images are never, of course, exact reproductions of the physical and social environment. They cannot motivate and direct action unless they are drastic simplifications, yet if the impulse toward clarity of form is not controlled by some process of verification, symbols and myths can become dangerous by inciting behavior grossly inappropriate to the given historical situation.[20]

Such is the problem with Mother Nature. We need images to express and guide our relations to nature, yet if these images do not correspond well to that which they represent—as I have suggested is often the case with the various motifs of Mother Nature—then such imagery backfires and can incite "behavior grossly inappropriate to the given historical situation." Our present situation is one of ecological imperilment, and Mother Nature imagery, in many ways, seems only to render matters worse. Images of the Good Mother make environmental destruction appear less of a problem, for the bounty of nature is then inexhaustible. When the Bad Mother is invoked, striking back against nature becomes a good. And the Hurt Mother, while offering possibilities for true reparative healing, also carries risks of ineffectual response. Given such problems, one may well wonder whether Mother Nature imagery is ever a good idea.

Notions of women having a special affinity with nature and of nature as female, although ambiguous, have been damaging. Making nature "mother" is problematic in any society still shaped by patriarchy. As a result, environmentalists need to be careful in their use of Mother Nature imagery, since it offers clear support to neither feminist nor environmental goals. Some ecofeminists conclude from this analysis that we need a total ban on such imagery. Heller, for example, calls for a "moratorium" on such metaphors "until all women are free"; and Gaard maintains that until sexism and misogyny are eradicated, "the Mother Earth metaphor will continue to be a harmful one and one that must be rejected."[21]

Despite these problems, I do not agree that associations of nature and the female need to be completely jettisoned and replaced with new images and metaphors. My point has been precisely that these associations *cannot* be banished and supplanted through conscious act of will alone. A better response, I have suggested, is to trace and expose the imagery's psychosocial roots. The more we understand how the imagery works and what it evokes, the less controlled by it we will be and the more we can instead control its content and effects. I have been asked several times while doing this study, "What bumper sticker would you make up for your car?" I have so far declined the attempt, lacking the creative genius of the Madison Avenue types (although I did briefly consider this entry by one of my colleagues: "The earth is a transvestite, and she/he is pissed").[22] But my point, really, is not to find or create perfect imagery. Instead, I think we need to pay closer attention to the complex connotations and resonances of whatever imagery we use and of the emotional wellsprings from which it draws. The insight that results helps us choose and use nature imagery responsibly, for reparative purposes, and not just as another salvo in the war against nature.

In what sense, then, can we speak of Mother Nature, of women as close to nature, of "loving our mother"? And how can we avoid or minimize the problems attendant on such imagery? While I am not completely opposed to feminine or maternal language for the nonhuman surround, I do think some expressions are best avoided; the slogans "Love Your Mother, Don't Become One" and "Control your Mother" come to mind. However, there is undoubtedly a positive role played by Mother Nature imagery and a way in which it remains compelling, important, and apt. Maternal metaphors do express the environmental truth that nature provides all life and sustenance, as does the childbearing mother. The endorsement of the twelfth-century Christian mystic Hildegard of Bingen, quoted by Matthew Fox, rings equally true for many today: "The earth is at the same time mother. She is mother of all that is natural, mother of all that is human. She is the mother of all, for contained in her are the seeds of all."[23]

Mother Nature language makes much intuitive sense to feminists and nonfeminists alike. It can also serve the important role of facilitating connection with nature. Linda Vance, for one, explains that "if I didn't think of nature as female, I wouldn't be able to feel such enormous pleasure in her presence."[24] Vance, a self-avowed lesbian and self-admitted wisecrack, is also making a joke here. Such humor is an important means to avoid taking too seriously or literally images of nature as mother. In this regard, some of the imagery I have criticized can also be read as having a humorous edge. Chevy's "Control Your Mother"—to reconsider an example I just suggested abandoning—is in part meant playfully. Its central slogan is a play on words, teasing tree-hugging environmentalists who "love their mother" that controlling her would really be much more fun—and certainly more manly. Critique of nature imagery should not cost us our sense of humor. Indeed, one of the most effective ways to undercut problems of such imagery is simply to laugh at it or, if one is feeling more charitable about its intent, to laugh with it.

Another way to address such problems follows from how the earth has functioned as a very powerful and ancient center for worship and for seeing the divine as female. Merchant tells us that, for Westerners before the Scientific Revolution, nature was "active teacher and parent" instead of "mindless, submissive [female] body."[25] Feminists and environmentalists today are reviving such meanings and ritual practices. Artist Judith Anderson, for example, combines her commitment to environmentalism and to woman-centered spirituality in a powerful etching entitled *Missa Gaia: This Is My Body* (see Figure 13). Anderson's work has become my favorite Mother Nature image and the one that strikes me as least problematic among all the contemporary imagery I have examined in this book.[26] Here the Great Mother sits in a birthing position. The world's animals flow from her and merge with her, boundaries of self and other barely discernible. The animals are her body, and she is them. Her face is old, dark, half-hidden; her gaze is empty—or perhaps all-seeing—fixed on the viewer. Her breasts sag; her belly spreads. No Hollywood diva, she. Although fertile, this mother cannot easily be called Good—her face is too menacing. It holds no warmth of welcome or promise of love. But she is not the Bad Mother either. There is no threat of active violence or harm from her, and the animals cleave loyally, twine sensuously around her body. Nor is she the Hurt Mother, although she does look very weary and worn. Anderson describes her Great Mother as embodying "both celebration and profound grief and anger."[27] This Mother, in other words, is at once Good and Bad and Hurt. Anderson manages—quite brilliantly, I think—to express all of these motifs, and none of then, at the same time. Her image is one of complex emotion, both in terms of what Gaia seems to be experiencing and in terms of the emotional response evoked in the viewer. We are at once drawn and repulsed, scared and awed.

John C. Elder, in a commentary on the etching, suggests that Anderson's figure exudes a sense of brooding. Furthermore, he argues that "troubled brooding"—in the double sense of "sorrowful contemplation and devotion to the development of fresh life"—may be an appropriate response for us as well, given our era of ecological endangerment. Elder calls for a collective process of "creative grieving" that sounds much like what I have discussed in terms of reparation. Through the reparative aspect of brooding and grieving, "sorrow and remorse can also lead us to a new maturity, fostering humility in our daily actions, as well as an enhanced sense of the preciousness of

Figure 13. *Missa Gaia: This Is My Body,* 1988. Etching by Judith Anderson
www.JudithAnderson.WomanMade.net. Photograph by Jim Colando.
Used with permission.

nature's many remaining gifts."[28] Art such as Anderson's, in other words, can lead to recognition of loss and then re-connection, to mourning and then reparation. Her Great Mother both broods and seems to inspire reparative brooding in her viewers. Anderson's feminist, environmentalist, and spiritual sensibilities, in combination with her artist's vision, have birthed a powerful Mother Nature indeed.

"Love Your Mother" can take on new life through such experimentation within contemporary ecofeminism, feminist spirituality, and ecotheology. In such contexts, women might well sometimes see themselves as "closer to nature," as when celebrating their bodies, their ability to create new life, or the interrelation of all species. Gnanadason suggests that "the fear of what is being done to the earth is giving women the urgent imperative to assert their connectedness with nature . . . more specially in the Third World where the struggle for survival is the most acute."[29] At other times women could place greater emphasis on seeing themselves as "closer to culture," or, as Susan Griffin puts it, seeing themselves as "nature seeing nature . . . nature with a concept of nature . . . nature speaking of nature to nature."[30] Understandings of mother will also change as shared parenting becomes more common. "Love Your Mother" could turn into a more effective environmental slogan if "mother" meant less exclusively the ever-giving nurturer. As we saw, however, equal parenting might also make nature seem less exclusively our mother.

This last point raises the issue of alternate images: if nature is not mother, what else might it be? Imagistic possibilities abound, ranging over the familial, personal, theistic, organic, and inorganic. Indeed, relations to the nonhuman surround are too complex to be captured by any single metaphor or set of metaphors. Yet another way to guard against problems of Mother Nature imagery, then, is to avoid its exclusive use. We benefit from drawing on many different forms of symbolic language when talking about the environment. Such imagery should be plural, flexible, and fluid; and it should consist also of partial and local images that reflect our participation in regional biospheres and place. As Yaakov Garb asks, "Isn't the fantasy that we can somehow contain the Earth within our imagination, bind it with a single metaphor, the most mistaken presumption of all?" His solution is a rousing challenge: "Bring on the Sky Goddesses, the Earth Gods, and all the wild and fecund creatures of psychic life—restore to both men and women those richly creative images of self-hood and earth-hood so long banished from our culture."[31]

Alternate familial metaphors include nature as father, parent, sister, brother, or child. One famous example is Saint Francis's references in the *Canticle of the Sun* to "brother sun," "sister moon," "brother wind," "sister water," "brother fire," and—in an intriguing precursor to the Jim Morrison reference from chapter 5—to "our sister, mother earth."[32] Imagery can be personal but not familial, as in metaphors that Merchant develops of nature as our "equal partner" and as a "free autonomous actor."[33] Ancient traditions of theistic options associate nature with the divine in, for example, Hinduism, early European pagan religion, and Native American cultures. Organic metaphors such as McFague's earth as the body of God are also possibilities.[34] And inorganic notions of nature as web of interrelations or as home or neighborhood offer other alternatives.

Illustrating this last point are two recent posters I came across that picture the planet from outer space. The caption on the first reads: "This is our neighborhood. Let's care for it." The second is even more direct: "Earth—Home Planet." Environmental bioregionalists often use these metaphors of neighborhood and home. Linda Willoughby suggests, however, that if nature is "home," responsibility for keeping it clean may well be left in the hands of those "homemakers"—women—traditionally considered best suited for such tasks.[35] Her point reminds us that we need to stay aware of the subtle meanings, emotional evocations, and deep roots of the nature imagery we use in order to determine how biodegradable and reparative it is. If images are never "exact reproductions," as Henry Nash Smith told us, and if a symbol, as Willoughby adds, is "rarely harmless, because it contains the power to transform consciousness," then the only course of action is one of maintaining a critical or evaluative distance from the nature imagery that surrounds us, even as we use or celebrate it.[36] Otherwise, we may fall into traps of perpetuating in backhanded ways the ecological unhealthiness we seek to avoid.

TOWARD THE FUTURE

When King Agamemnon returns home victorious from the Trojan War in the *Oresteia*, his wife Clytemnestra strews the ground before his feet with robes tinted regal purple from the dye of sea mollusks.

He protests the extravagance and is reluctant to spoil such treasures by walking on them, but she insists. "The sea is there," says the queen, "and who shall drain its yield?" If Agamemnon crushes the robes, more can be made, for the water "breeds precious as silver, ever of itself renewed, the purple ooze wherein our garments shall be dipped."[37] (Of course, she is flattering the conqueror only to set him up for murder, but that is another story.) She is as confident that the sea will continue to yield treasure as we are certain that the sun will rise tomorrow. Ever self-renewing, the water's bounty cannot be exhausted. To her, and throughout all of history until now, the thought of humans causing permanent and worldwide ecological damage has been simply unimaginable. We were too small, too few, too weak in comparison with nature's force and vastness. Today, however, we not only imagine such a fate but begin to fear we are living it. We number six billion and counting; there is arguably no wilderness left; our technological might matches that of nature, and we seldom hesitate to use it.

As we enter the twenty-first century, we find our millennial ideals sadly entangled in a net of interrelated and seemingly intractable social problems, of which ecological degradation forms one crucial strand. Where does this study leave us as we attempt to untangle the net? How does it help us realize, if not millennial ideals—for surely ideals, as Kathleen Sands suggests, need a "cooler place than earth to live"—then basic goals of ecological and economic sustainability and commitment to social justice?[38] I have found no simple answers on how to achieve these goals, but I have found insight and guidance and reasons to pursue the untangling of the net. By exploring psychosocial meanings of nature imagery, we learn much simply about being human. We learn about the challenges and possibilities facing us as creatures finite and fragile yet "free," part of a world both more and less finite and fragile than ourselves. To close, I offer some modest recommendations toward untangling the net.

First, there are obvious limits to the appeal to people's goodness. We cannot rely on virtuous intentions alone because of the persistent problems of human badness and ambivalence, as witnessed in the nature imagery. Environmental protection requires strong governmental legislation. We also need creative public policy—and, yes, advertising campaigns—to encourage, on the part of industry and individuals, voluntary conservation and innovations in maintaining or restoring environmental sustainability. These measures will sometimes require us to act in advance of absolute scientific proof, since such proof may only come too late (as in, for example, the case of global warming).

Second, since there are limits to the appeal to goodness, we should appeal also to people's pragmatic, long-term self-interest. To this end, we need greater ecological literacy. Students from kindergarten through college as well as the general public need more scientific education about local bioregions; the interdependence of ecosystems; criteria for sustainability; current and potential problems of pollution and ecological degradation; and the interrelation of ecological, public health, economic, and social justice issues. Such educational efforts about what we stand to lose can help to trigger and support reparation toward nature.

Third, we live in a consumer culture that bombards us with slick marketing and flashy advertising. To cope, we need media literacy and education about how the media seeks to manipulate imagery, emotion, and behavior. Bumper stickers and printed T-shirts are not innocent, nor are they insignificant. Their visions of nature shape individual and collective sensibility, alter our imagination, and affect the way we live. We should subject to continual scrutiny nature images and slogans from consumer-oriented ad campaigns as well as those from the environmental movement. We need to learn to read and critique and to responsibly use such imagery in popular culture.

Fourth, we should uncouple nature imagery from any too-exclusive female gendering. Furthermore, environmental agendas, especially in their focus on Third World development, will not succeed without, and will best proceed with, attention to "women's issues." These issues include birth control, reproductive healthcare, equal opportunity for women in education and in the workplace, equal social status, public health concerns of children and childbearing women, and shared parenting.

Finally, those academics working in environmental studies seek to influence people's understandings of nature and responses to the natural environment. I have suggested that this work would be carried further by a depth perspective or a heart-of-darkness environmentalism that reveals this understanding and response to be complex and ambivalent: shaped by unconscious factors; by phantasy, position, and defense; by gendered familial relations; by destructiveness and hate; by love and reparation. Such a perspective acts as a sounding line to probe the depths and contours of the psyche. In doing so, it charts the tangled wilderness of human response to nature and helps us to find paths toward earth healing.

Notes

1. WILDERNESS—WITHIN AND WITHOUT

1. Lester R. Brown et al., *State of the World 2000*, 80.

2. Jhally, "Advertising and the End of the World," cites studies showing that while in the 1980s Americans were "appealed to as consumers" about 1,500 times a day, by the late 1990s that figure had risen to 3,600 commercial impressions daily.

3. I thank Robert Sloan, senior sponsoring editor at Indiana University Press, for feedback on an earlier version of the manuscript that was of great help in clarifying these issues of audience and of interdisciplinary conversation. For examples of Sut Jhally's authored and co-authored works, see: Jhally, Leiss, and Kline, *Social Communication in Advertising*; Jhally, *Codes of Advertising*; Angus and Jhally, eds. *Cultural Politics in Contemporary America*; Jhally, "Advertising and the End of the World"; Jhally, "Advertising at the Edge of the Apocalypse."

4. Oelschlaeger, *Idea of Wilderness*, 1.

5. Conrad's novella is sometimes interpreted and criticized as racist and as participating in the oppressive history of African colonialism. For discussion of these issues, see essays by Chinua Achebe, Frances B. Singh, and C. P. Sarvan in the Norton Critical Edition of *Heart of Darkness*, edited by Kimbrough. I therefore use language of the heart as dark cautiously and with concern over what might feed its deeper roots but also with appreciation for the richness and complexity of this ancient metaphor.

6. Lester R. Brown et al., *State of the World 1996*, 16.

7. Within this highly interdisciplinary field of environmental studies, natural and social scientists explain ecological ills in terms of population pressures, increases in economic production (including technology and the consumption of resources), and the growing social inequities of worldwide income distribution (see, e.g., Lester R. Brown et al., *State of the World 1994*, 5–8). Humanists readily acknowledge these factors but insist also on the importance of worldview, or understandings of how or what the world is and of one's place in the world. See, for example, the influential work of Carolyn Merchant, who shows how worldview supports other sources of ecological damage by arguing that the modern mechanistic worldview "legitimates the use of nature as commodity" and so upholds the economic production system of industrial capitalism (*Radical Ecology*, 11; see also her *Death of Nature*). Note that the scientific and humanistic approaches to environmental studies are themselves expressions of worldview.

The humanist prescription, then—which I share—is to change behavior by altering imagination, by transforming sensibility and self, by reshaping the worldview of how people see nature. Without such fundamental alterations in the ideas,

175

attitudes, and values that underlie our behavior, environmental humanists insist that real and long-lasting behavioral change is impossible. Of course, despite general agreement on these points, as within any healthy ecosystem there is much diversity among environmental humanists, and disagreements run broad and deep. On the question of how worldview contributes to environmental degradation: is it mainly a problem of patriarchal hierarchy, of anthropocentric Jewish-Christian values, of modernism, or of techno-centered mechanism? How should we reform worldview: should we fight social injustice, industrial capitalism, patriarchal oppression? Should we support a land ethic, biospheric egalitarianism, conservation, or bioregionalism? What notion of the self should we adopt in our relations to the environment: are we partners, divinely-appointed stewards, resource managers, children of Mother Nature, one equal part of an interrelated whole? This book explores only some of these questions; readers seeking further exploration are invited to turn to the wide literature of environmental thought.

8. Bender, review of *Earth's Insights* by Callicott, 269.

9. To my knowledge, this book is original in its depth of focus on Mother Nature imagery in contemporary popular culture; no other such extended and critical study exists. For one examination of such imagery in a different context—that of scholars' construction of Mother Earth as a major goddess of Native American religion—see Gill, *Mother Earth*. And for a psychosocial historical examination of the metaphor of land as female in American life and literature, see Kolodny, *Lay of the Land*.

10. Jhally, "Advertising and the End of the World" and "Advertising at the Edge of the Apocalypse." For examples of environmentally inclined communications scholars who read the media images of advertising and consumer culture in order to access social construction of concepts of nature, see the work of Jhally, as well as Davis, "'Touch the Magic,'" and the anthology *Uncommon Ground*, edited by Cronon. Davis studies how the idea of nature is constructed in the Sea World theme parks. See also Rose, a feminist and ecofeminist theorist, who looks at popular science fiction representations of Gaia in "The Good Mother."

11. Jhally, "Advertising at the Edge of the Apocalypse." I thank my friend Joy Young for sharing the fish's talents with me and Nick Street for conversation about America that helped me think through some of these ideas.

12. For insight into the connotations, history, and usage of the term "nature," see Glacken, *Traces on the Rhodian Shore*, and Collingwood, *Idea of Nature*.

13. I form these definitions from a synthesis of my reading, in particular from Ortner, "Is Female to Male as Nature is to Culture?" See Warwick Fox, *Transpersonal Ecology*, 8, for an example of intention to break down these distinctions.

14. Oelschlaeger, for example, notes the difficulty of developing environmentally sound philosophy when the modern mind is almost precluded from seeing nature as anything other than "environment"; that is, "as standing apart from and inferior to us, serving only as resource to fuel the human project." "Paradox of paradoxes," he writes, "we are people who conceive of the world in terms of the learned categorical scheme of Modernism. It seems impossible to understand any

alternative, for that would entail abandoning the cultural project on which we have been so long embarked: the modern mind is inescapably enframed by language and history" (*Idea of Wilderness,* 321, 338, 318).

15. Glacken, *Traces on the Rhodian Shore,* xiv.

16. Fisher, "Radical Ecopsychology," 20. On "nature" and "human nature" as falsely monolithic terms, see Cronon, "Introduction," 34–36.

17. For such a critique of the concept of human nature, see Parekh, "Is There a Human Nature?"

18. Ortner, "So, *Is* Female to Male as Nature Is to Culture?" 179. For another defense of a type of universalism in an anthropological description of what it means to be human, see Donald E. Brown, *Human Universals.*

19. Ortner, "So, *Is* Female to Male as Nature Is to Culture?" 179.

20. Forsyth, *Freud, Jung, and Christianity,* viii.

21. While many of the works in environmental studies draw on religious studies and/or feminism, and while a few are psychological, almost none synthesize insights from the study of religion, feminism, and psychology. Elizabeth Dodson Gray is a notable exception. In terms of interdisciplinary reach, I have been inspired by and have attempted to build on her work as well as that of Dorothy Dinnerstein, Annette Kolodny, Rosemary Radford Ruether, Catherine Keller, and Naomi R. Goldenberg. See Gray, *Green Paradise Lost* and *Patriarchy as a Conceptual Trap;* Dinnerstein, *Mermaid and Minotaur;* Kolodny, *Lay of the Land* and *Land Before Her;* Ruether, *Gaia and God;* Keller, *From a Broken Web;* Goldenberg, *Returning Words to Flesh.*

22. "Cathedral of Life" poster available through www.beyondthewall.com.

23. For example, Marshall, *Nature's Web;* Gottlieb, ed., *This Sacred Earth;* Callicott, *Earth's Insights;* Tucker and Grim, eds., *Worldviews and Ecology.* Furthermore, there are "ecotheologies" from other religious traditions besides Christianity, for instance, a huge literature of Buddhist ecological consciousness (e.g., Badiner, *Dharma Gaia*).

24. One of the first in contemporary environmental thought to receive a broad hearing for the idea of a dominant Western worldview judged to be environmentally unsound and grounded in religious notions of human-nature relations was Lynn White Jr., in his highly influential and much reprinted article from 1967, "The Historical Roots of Our Ecological Crisis." White argues that the Western Christian worldview is responsible for much of the ecological crisis. He blames its anthropocentrist ideas of nature as separate from us and as intended by God for us to dominate and exploit. Consequently, White tells us that we need to "find a new religion, or rethink our old one." The pagan worldview "protected nature from man"; Christianity revised on the model of Saint Francis might do so again ("Historical Roots of Our Ecological Crisis," quotations from reprint in *Ecology and Religion in History,* 24, 25, 28–31).

25. I take the phrase "ecological promise" from ecotheologian and historian of Christianity H. Paul Santmire, in his book *Travail of Nature.* For an influential example of stewardship theology, see Hall, *The Steward.*

26. Two feminist theorists who have served as models for me of how one can work on the boundary of theology are Mary Daly and Kathleen Sands. See Daly, *Beyond God the Father,* 6–7 and Sands, *Escape From Paradise.*

27. James, *The Varieties of Religious Experience,* 507–508; emphasis his.

28. Examples of privileging theology are found in James Forsyth's "psychologically based natural theology," in which psychoanalysis supports theological truths (*Freud, Jung, and Christianity,* 19, and all of chapter 1, "Psychology of Religion as Natural Theology") and in Paul Tillich's correlational method, where theology provides answers to culture's most fundamental questions (*Systematic Theology;* see also Kelsey, "Paul Tillich," 136–37, 149).

29. Noddings, *Women and Evil,* 104–105.

30. Dinnerstein, *Mermaid and Minotaur,* 104n.

31. See, for example, Heller, "For the Love of Nature," especially 225–26, 228, 236–241. Heller blames environmental collapse on inherently flawed economic and social systems and the greed of elite males. She is critical of those who assume "the flaw [is] inherent within 'human nature.'" I agree with her analysis of the false romanticization of Mother Nature imagery; however, I find perhaps equally romantic her plan of abolishing domination, for I do not think its cause is purely social. I argue instead that systems of domination are at least partly psychological, rooted, if you will, "within human nature."

32. These remarks come from Bradford Woods, a colleague from the College of Education at the University of Alabama, in one of the working sessions of our junior faculty Interdisciplinary Writing Group, 2000–2001.

33. See James, *Will to Believe* (especially "The Will to Believe," "The Sentiment of Rationality," and "The Moral Philosopher and the Moral Life") and *Pragmatism* and *Meaning of Truth.* For an extended application of pragmatism to ecological issues, see Farber, *Eco-Pragmatism,* and its extensive review in Heinzerling's "Pragmatists and Environmentalists" (I thank my father, Joseph E. Roach, for finding me these texts). For an argument about how James's pragmatism supports an environmental ethic and shares similarities with early Buddhist traditions, see Kalupahana, "Toward a Middle Path of Survival."

34. Lester R. Brown et al., *State of the World 1996,* 11–12.

35. Lester R. Brown et al., *State of the World 1994,* 5.

2. "LOVE YOUR MOTHER"

1. As my discussion of universalism in chapter 1 notes, whether this association holds outside the West is a debated point. For an analysis of the cultural limitations of ecofeminism, see Li, "Cross-Cultural Critique of Ecofeminism." Li uses the example of China to argue that the women-nature association is not found cross-culturally, although others such as Ortner ("Is Female to Male as Nature Is to Culture?" and "So, *Is* Female to Male as Nature Is to Culture?") have disagreed with this assessment. Gaard concludes from Li's work that ecofeminism needs to avoid cultural imperialism and can better ensure its global solidarity by a praxis focused on women's crucial role in issues of health, land rights, world

hunger, development, poverty, and anti-nuclear protest than by the "culture-specific concept of an affinity between woman and nature." Within the West, however, Gaard argues that it remains crucial to analyze "ways in which feminizing nature and naturalizing or animalizing women has served as justification for the domination of women, animals, and the earth" ("Living Interconnections," 10, 5; see also 4, 9–10).

2. Kolodny, *Lay of the Land*, 4.

3. Kirtley F. Mather, *Enough and to Spare: Mother Earth Can Nourish Every Man in Freedom* (New York: Harper & Brothers, 1944); Pennsylvania State College, *Known Sources of Primary Wealth: Plants, Animals, Minerals, Fundamental Products of Mother Earth* (State College, Pa.: Depts. of Agriculture, Commerce, Internal Affairs, Mines, 1948); Rudolph J. Birsic, *The Geothermal Steam Story: Or a Hot Tip from Mother Earth* (Fullerton, Calif.: 1974); Dick Gregory, *Dick Gregory's Natural Diet for Folks Who Eat: Cookin' with Mother Nature!* (New York: Harper & Row, 1973).

4. Collard with Contrucci, *Rape of the Wild.* Yale, "Rhodell Letter," 79.

5. I thank Nick Street for very astute comments on an earlier version of my manuscript that helped me think through some of these issues. Of course, I may still have got them totally wrong; and if so, I want to assure readers that it is not Nick's fault but my own.

6. Oelschlaeger, *Idea of Wilderness*, 16; see also 16–24.

7. Sjöö and Mor, *Great Cosmic Mother*, 84; image on 83. For further discussion, see also Milne and Miller, *Visions of the Goddess*, 16–17; and Johnson, *Lady of the Beasts*, 307, 320–21.

8. The Homeric hymn to Gaia is quoted in Getty, *Goddess*, 10. For further references to the Greek Goddess Gaia, see Downing, *Goddess;* Spretnak, *Lost Goddesses;* Joseph, *Gaia*, 223–26. For the hymn to Tellus Mater, see Getty, *Goddess*, 4.

9. Philo, *On the Account of the World's Creation Given by Moses*, quoted in Glacken, *Traces on the Rhodian Shore*, 14. Glacken identifies the Plato reference as *Menexenus* 238 A.

10. Sophocles, *Antigone*, lines 338–41, 569. For commentary on this passage in the context of human control over nature, see Glacken, *Traces on the Rhodian Shore*, 120.

11. John Donne, "Elegy XIX. To His Mistress Going to Bed."

12. Bachofen, *Mother Right*, 109–10. See, in general, Bachofen's lengthy "Introduction" for a fascinating, although sexist and uncritical, example of the woman-nature association.

13. Documenting associations of nature and the female throughout history and exploring their cultural and historical particularities lies beyond the scope of this book. I refer interested readers to the researchers—on many of whom I draw—who study the woman-nature relation in a variety of contexts. Examples include Sherry Ortner (in anthropology); Carolyn Merchant (in history); Erich Neumann and Dorothy Dinnerstein (in psychology); Carol Bigwood and Patricia Jagentowicz Mills (in philosophy); Monica Sjöö, Barbara Mor, Adele Getty, and Buffie Johnson (in the overlap of women's studies, religion, and art history); Sam Gill

(in Native American religious studies); and Susan Griffin, Andrée Collard, and Elizabeth Dodson Gray (in ecofeminism). All explore perceptions of women as closer to nature than men and/or of nature as female.

14. In connection with the whole-earth image of Mother Nature, object relations theorist Jessica Benjamin's *Bonds of Love* is interesting for its analysis of the evolution of the infantile psyche. Her theorizing about the relation to the mother as object and to the "other" in general as object might help explain why this distant and objectified image of the earth is chosen to accompany the slogan instead of a more everyday and proximal image of the environment. For further analysis of the whole-earth image, see Garb, "Perspective or Escape?"

15. McFague, *Models of God,* 33–35.

16. For brief references to nature as female, see Glacken, *Traces on the Rhodian Shore,* 13 (the earth mother as primordial), 14 (as irrational), 197 (as pagan); see also 120, 136, and 244 for identifications of the female and the plowed earth. Leiss, *Domination of Nature,* 60.

17. Cronon, "Introduction," in *Uncommon Ground.*

18. Ortner, "Is Female to Male as Nature is to Culture?" 73: woman are "identified or symbolically associated with nature . . . more rooted in, or having more direct affinity with, nature." Or see Gaard: "The way in which women and nature have been conceptualized historically in the Western intellectual tradition has resulted in devaluing whatever is associated with women, emotion, animals, nature, and the body, while simultaneously elevating in value those things associated with men, reason, humans, culture, and the mind" ("Living Interconnections," 5). See also Guillaumin, "Pratique du pouvoir et idée de Nature,"; Dinnerstein, *Mermaid and Minotaur;* Merchant, *Death of Nature;* Gray, *Green Paradise Lost;* Ruether, "Motherearth and Megamachine," *New Woman/New Earth,* and *Gaia and God;* Griffin, *Woman and Nature.*

19. Dinnerstein, *Mermaid and Minotaur,* 108.

20. I thank my colleague Jenefer Husman for this comment, in one of the working sessions of our junior faculty Interdisciplinary Writing Group, 2000–2001.

21. Dinnerstein, *Mermaid and Minotaur,* 36–37. See generally her section, "The Mother as Representative of Nature: The Semi-Sentient 'She,'" 105–110.

22. Ortner, "Is Female to Male as Nature is to Culture?" 86.

23. Merchant, *Death of Nature,* 20–22, 127, 169–71. This material is also summarized in her *Radical Ecology,* chap. 2, "Science and Worldviews," and in her article "Mining the Earth's Womb."

24. Rich, *Of Woman Born,* 285.

25. Several sources discuss the schema of these three options. See, for example, King, "Ecology of Feminism and Feminism of Ecology," 22–23; Diamond and Orenstein, "Introduction," in *Reweaving the World,* ix–xii; Merchant, *Radical Ecology,* chap. 8, "Ecofeminism."

26. Some proponents include Carol P. Christ, Starhawk, Sjöö, Mor, and Eisler. Griscom ("On Healing the Nature/History Split in Feminist Thought") suggests

the term "nature feminism," whereas others, such as Merchant (*Radical Ecology,* 190–94), use "cultural ecofeminism."

27. D'Eaubonne, "Feminism or Death," quoted in Adams, *Ecofeminism and the Sacred,* xi.

28. For example, Ruether, *Gaia and God:* "The roots of this evil lie, as we have suggested, in patterns of domination, whereby male elites in power deny their interdependency with women, exploiting human labor and the biotic community around them" (200). See also Heller, "For the Love of Nature," 228.

29. Daly, "Foreword," *Rape of the Wild,* ix, xiv.

30. May, "Gaia Women," 249, emphasis hers. I thank my father, Joseph Roach, for bringing this book to my attention.

31. Personal telephone conversation with Jane Evershed, March 2002; Heller, "For the Love of Nature," 233. I thank my colleague Natalie G. Adams, in the College of Education at the University of Alabama, for a critique that helped me think through this image more fully in one of the working sessions of our junior faculty Interdisciplinary Writing Group, 2000–2001.

32. Wittig, *Guérillères,* 89; quoted, for example, in Christ, *Laughter of Aphrodite,* 121, and in Daly, *Gyn/Ecology,* 47. For examples of feminists and ecofeminists who work with versions of these new stories of the Fall, see Christ, *Laughter of Aphrodite;* Daly, *Gyn/Ecology;* Stone, *When God Was a Woman;* Sjöö and Mor, *Great Cosmic Mother;* Gimbutas, *Goddesses and Gods of Old Europe;* and Eisler, *Chalice and Blade.*

33. Ruether, *Gaia and God,* 8; see her chap. 6, "Paradise Lost and the Fall into Patriarchy," for excellent and thorough analysis of this issue and its literature. Merchant also analyzes this material in terms of a reversal of traditional Western recovery narratives in "Reinventing Eden: Western Culture as a Recovery Narrative," 154–56.

34. Culpepper, "Contemporary Goddess Thealogy," 62–65.

35. These patterns of male and female socialization are presented in, for example, the widely influential works of Chodorow, *Reproduction of Mothering,* and Gilligan, *In a Different Voice.* See Plaskow, *Sex, Sin, and Grace,* 70–73, for reflection in a theological context on whether women's experience results in positive attunement to nature.

36. King, "Ecology of Feminism and Feminism of Ecology," 23.

37. Keller, *From a Broken Web,* 13 and chap. 1, "The Separate and the Soluble." See also chapter 4, note 33 below for discussion of similar work by Saiving and Plaskow.

38. Gaard, for example, draws on Gilligan and Chodorow in the introductory essay of an ecofeminist anthology to present women's typically "interconnected sense of self" as the "theoretical base" of ecofeminist ethics and to suggest that the male disconnected sense of self is "at the root of the current ecological crisis." However, she includes no discussion such as that offered by Saiving, Plaskow, or Keller of the problems to which an interconnected sense of self may lead. See Gaard, "Living Interconnections," 1–3.

39. See Merchant, *Radical Ecology,* 188–90, for discussion of liberal ecofemi-

nism; see King, "Ecology of Feminism and Feminism of Ecology," 22, on socialist feminists. Some proponents include Simone de Beauvoir, Sherry Ortner, Colette Guillaumin, and Nicole-Claude Mathieu.

40. Ortner, "Is Female to Male as Nature Is to Culture?" 73.

41. Warren, "Feminism and Ecology," 14–15. See also Griscom, "Healing the Nature/History Split," 8–9.

42. I thank Naomi R. Goldenberg for suggesting this use of the term "biodegrade."

43. I thank Trey Roden for the phrase and the insight.

44. Willoughby, *Mother Earth*, 197. See in particular her chap. 14, "Ecofeminism Enriched by Jungian Theory."

45. Kheel, "From Heroic to Holistic Ethics," 251.

3. MOTHERS AND MOTHER NATURE

1. Callicott and Ames, "Epilogue," 287, 285, 289, emphasis theirs; Hargrove, "Foreword," xix–xx.

2. These examples are drawn from Gottlieb, ed., *This Sacred Earth*.

3. Allen, *Sacred Hoop*, especially the section "Who Is Your Mother? Red Roots of White Feminism." Smith, "For All Those Who Were Indian in a Former Life." For an analysis of the racism and classism that can result from efforts of Western environmental appropriation, see Guha, "Radical American Environmentalism and Wilderness Preservation" and Gaard, "Ecofeminism and Native American Cultures." For debate on the extent to which native Americans were "environmentalists," see Deffenbaugh, "Ecological Indian Revisited"; Kretch, *Ecological Indian*; Hughes, *North American Indian Ecology*.

4. MacCannell, "The Unconscious," 442.

5. Meissner, *Psychoanalysis and Religious Experience*, 207. Meissner adds that "the existence of unconscious mental processes forms the fundamental postulate of and the basic source of data for psychoanalytic thinking" (206).

6. Roszak, *The Voice of the Earth*, 320.

7. The lists of theologians come from Tillich's *Theology of Culture*, 114–17, except for my addition of Paul and Augustine; quotes from 115, 123. Meissner, *Psychoanalysis and Religious Experience*, 206. Meissner does add that today "the philosophical and religious orientation has come to accept as a basic and essential part of human nature man's unconscious life and its implications" (216–17).

8. Peter Brown, *Augustine*, 366, 178 (quoting Augustine's *Confessions* 10: 32), 155, 170. Augustine, *Confessions*, 10: 32, 8:7.

9. Kant, *Religion Within the Limits of Reason Alone*, 57.

10. Quoted by Pagels, "The Social History of Satan," 6.

11. James, *Varieties of Religious Experience*, 73–74.

12. Warwick Fox, *Transpersonal Ecology*, 218, 217, quoting Arne Naess, "Self-realization: An Ecological Approach to Being in the World," (Fourth Keith Roby Memorial Lecture in Community Science, Murdoch University, Western Australia, 12 March 1986). Fox draws on Naess and others to advocate a field-like, expansive self that unfolds into the ecosphere.

13. McFague suggests a model of the earth as the body of God as a way to develop an environmental ethic based on respect, love, and the interconnection of all beings. She maintains that "remythologized" doctrines of God, nature, and humans result in "embodied knowing" and "internalize a new sensibility" so that "one would, or at least might, act differently." She asks: "What if we were not only allowed but encouraged to love the earth? What if we saw the earth as part of the body of God . . . ? What if we also saw this body as overlain by the body of the cosmic Christ . . . ? Would we not then feel obliged to love the earth and all its many bodies? . . . Christians have a mandate to *love* the earth" (*Body of God*, 81, 83, 102).

14. Eliot, "The Hollow Men," 58–59.

15. Heller, "For the Love of Nature," 232.

16. Merchant, *Death of Nature*, 3; reprinted in revised context in her *Radical Ecology*, 43. Merchant argues that as a result of these changes in the Scientific Revolution of the sixteenth and seventeenth centuries, "the constraints against penetration associated with the earth-mother image were transformed into sanctions for denudation" (*Death of Nature*, 189; see also chap. 2 of *Radical Ecology*).

17. The ad, for American Express Financial Advisors, appeared in the *Wall Street Journal*, 11 April 1996, A10.

18. Noddings, *Women and Evil*, 114, see also 103–18.

19. Analyses of traditional patriarchal constructions of mother and mothering are found in Gray, *Patriarchy as Conceptual Trap*, 102–105, and in Gaard, "Ecofeminism and Native American Cultures," 301–305. See also Dally, *Inventing Motherhood*, and Thurer, *The Myths of Motherhood*, both of whom have chapters on the exaltation and idealization of the mother.

20. Auerbach, *Woman and the Demon*, 66–69.

21. Virginia Woolf, "Professions for Women," in *Collected Essays* (London: Hogarth Press, 1966) 2:285, quoted in Noddings, *Women and Evil*, 59; see Noddings' chap. 3, "The Angel in the House."

22. Woolf, in Noddings, *Women and Evil*, 59. Auerbach, however, notes that the Victorian cultural imagination grants "unprecedented spiritual power" to the angel and thus to women, albeit within the limits of a "constricted posture" and "prisonlike space" (*Woman and the Demon*, 72; see also her chap. 3, "Angels and Demons: Woman's Marriage of Heaven and Hell").

23. Rich, *Of Woman Born*, xxiv. Rich is speaking in a different context here, disagreeing with the politics of women's peace groups that "celebrate maternality as the basis for engaging in antimilitaristic work." Mothers can use children, she says, in morally questionable ways. I suggest that one contributing factor might be a too-narrow cultural focus on women's roles as mothers.

24. The British Airways advertising campaign appeared both in print and on television and used a variety of images to promote their Club World service. The image examined here comes from the *Wall Street Journal*, 5 March 1996, A5. The Northwest Airlines ad also appeared in the *Wall Street Journal*, 26 May 1994, A9.

25. Dally, *Inventing Motherhood*, 95.

26. Gaard, "Ecofeminism and Native American Cultures," 302. Gaard men-

tions the work of Chodorow and Rich as evidence here and cites Marilyn Waring's *If Women Counted: A New Feminist Economics* (San Francisco: HarperCollins, 1988) on the point that Western culture devalues maternal giving by crediting it with no economic value.

27. *Wall Street Journal,* 9 August 1996, section B. The article concludes that "valuing unpaid labor, usually by women, and deciding whether and how to include it in a nation's gross domestic product statistic is a hot topic in world economic circles."

28. Dally, *Inventing Motherhood,* 92.

29. Kahn, "Hand That Rocks the Cradle," 73.

30. Firestone, *Dialectic of Sex,* 206.

31. Ecclesiasticus 25:23. This book, also called Sirach, was written by a Jewish sage in the second century B.C. and is part of the canon of the Bible for Catholics but considered apocryphal by Protestants and Jews. John 3:1–21, also 1:12–13.

32. Shakespeare, *King Lear* 4.11.126–35; *Macbeth* 4.1.80–81 and 5.3.16–17. Simon, *Tragic Drama and the Family,* 117. Simon discusses this theme of the demonization of woman in tragic drama throughout his study; the Shakespeare examples are drawn from his book and his Harvard undergraduate course, "Tragic Drama and Human Conflict." I am indebted to him for his insights.

33. See, for example, Benjamin, *Bonds of Love;* Chodorow, *Reproduction of Mothering;* Dinnerstein, *Mermaid and Minotaur;* Keller, *From a Broken Web;* Neumann, *Fear of the Feminine;* Ruether, *Gaia and God,* chap. 6; Simon, *Tragic Drama.*

34. Aeschylus, *The Eumenides* in *Oresteia,* lines 658–60. Euripides, *Medea,* lines 573–75. Paul, 1 Corinthians 11:8; see all of chapter 11 for the tension between gender equality and hierarchy in Paul's anthropology. He writes both of the interdependence of man and woman ("in the same way that woman was made from man, so man is born of woman," v. 12) and of woman's submission and inferiority ("man is the image of God and the reflection of his glory; woman, in turn, is the reflection of man's glory," v. 7).

35. Euripides, *Medea,* lines 250–51.

36. Rich, *Of Woman Born,* 22. See also narratives on mothering in Parker, *Mother Love/Mother Hate,* 4–5, 19–21, 67–73, etc., and in Suleiman, "Writing and Motherhood."

37. Dinnerstein, *Mermaid and Minotaur,* 100. Kahn analyzes the lingering effects of this "powerful ambivalence that the mother inspires," especially for the man in patriarchal culture ("Hand That Rocks the Cradle," 88).

38. Rose, "Good Mother," 151. Rose is here summarizing part of Merchant's work in *Death of Nature* and in *Ecological Revolutions.*

39. For discussion of the modernist worldview in relation to nature, see Oelschlaeger, *Idea of Wilderness,* 285–89 and chap. 3; Merchant, *Radical Ecology,* 44–59, 63–70, 90–91; Warwick Fox, *Transpersonal Ecology,* 152–53; Stenmark, "An Ecology of Knowledge."

40. Gaard, "Ecofeminism and Native American Cultures," 305, quoting Elizabeth Dodson Gray, "Nature: Our Cultural Assumptions," *Creation* 5 (May–June 1989): 32.

41. Gupta, "Ganga."

42. Heller, "For the Love of Nature," 223.

43. Ibid., 220, 224–25.

44. Ibid., 223–24, quoting Kirkpatrick Sale, *Dwellers in the Land: The Bioregional Vision* (San Francisco: Sierra Club Books, 1985), 3.

45. Lovelock, "Gaia," 96.

46. Vance, "Ecofeminism and the Politics of Reality," 131.

47. Heller, "For the Love of Nature," 232. In chapter 7, I discuss further this issue of whether and under what circumstances Mother Nature imagery can be positive.

48. Gaard, "Ecofeminism and Native American Cultures," 303.

4. "SHE WILL TRY TO DROWN YOU"

1. Although I find such imagery problematic, the imagination and verve that went into this commercial's production are quite amazing, and I thank Nissan for their help.

2. Lovelock, *Ages of Gaia*, 212.

3. I wonder here about the possibility of a fourth motif: that of the Sexual Mother. Generally, in Mother Nature imagery, the mother's sexuality is a buried theme, represented only indirectly through her fertility. She is rarely presented as directly sexual (e.g., flirtatious, seductive, desirous, sated) but is often pictured as fertile, fecund, as powerful because of her reproductive ability to create new life. Her sexuality, in other words, is not something that serves for either her own sensual pleasure or that of any imagined partner; Mother Nature seems not to be a sexual being in this way. This holds true for the Nissan Pathfinder ad, except for the sensuality of the narrator's sultry voice and the moaning background vocals—both female. Neither are directly associated with Mother Nature, but they do set a certain sensual tone for the commercial. One of the only outright sexual representations I have come across of Mother Nature is a sculpture entitled *Nature Reveals Itself* by Louis-Ernest Barrias (French, 1840–1905; reproduced in Merchant, *Death of Nature*, 191). Here nature is a beautiful young woman, her breasts bare, in the act of lifting her veil to reveal still more of herself to her implied partner of science. The motif of the Sexual Mother may bear further study.

4. Solomon, "A Few Choice Words," 8. Most people above the age of thirty for whom I play or describe this commercial immediately remember it with amusement.

5. For example, for a helpful prefeminist account of misogynist bias, see Hays, *The Dangerous Sex.* A major feminist treatment of this subject is Noddings' excellent *Women and Evil,* which traces associations in theology, philosophy, and psychology as well as reconstructing notions of evil from the perspective of women's experience. See also Daly, *Beyond God the Father* and *Gyn/Ecology;* Auerbach, *Woman and the Demon.* In psychology, see Gilligan, *In a Different Voice,* and Sagan, *Freud, Women, and Morality.*

6. Noddings, *Women and Evil,* 52, quoting Tertullian, *De cultu feminarum,* emphasis in original. For an extended study of Eve, see Phillips, *Eve.* Ruether analyzes misogyny in the early church in "Misogynism and Virginal Feminism." See also Daly, *Beyond God the Father,* chap. 2.

7. The story of Pandora is found in Hesiod, *Works and Days* (lines 47–105) and

Theogony (lines 506–616), in Morford and Lenardon, *Classical Mythology,* 39–43. For an analysis of the Pandora story's treatment of gender, see Zeitlin, "Signifying Difference."

8. Kramer and Sprenger, *Malleus Maleficarum,* 42, 47. For one of many available studies on this material, see Klaits, *Servants of Satan.*

9. Freud, "Some Psychological Consequences of the Anatomical Distinction between the Sexes" (1925), *Standard Edition,* 19:257–58. The tongue-in-cheek commentator is James A. C. Brown, *Freud and the Post-Freudians,* 29.

10. Fisher, "Ecopsychology," 20; second set of ellipses in original.

11. Cartoon by Tom Toles, reprinted from the *Buffalo News,* in Fisher, "Ecopsychology," 23.

12. Samuel Taylor Coleridge, *Aids to Reflection,* 1848, 1:270, quoted in the *Oxford English Dictionary* (1933); definitions also consulted from *Webster's Third New International Dictionary,* the *Random House Dictionary of the English Language,* and the *Encyclopedic Dictionary of Religion.*

13. Freud, *Civilization and Its Discontents,* 38–39.

14. Niebuhr, *Nature and Destiny of Man* 1:150; see also his chap. 7, "Man as Sinner."

15. Chapter 5 takes up Klein's model. In an interesting parallel, Augustine agrees with Klein that the suckling infant exhibits all the greed and rage of full-blown badness. "If babies are innocent," he comments, "it is not for lack of will to do harm, but for lack of strength" (*Confessions* 1:7).

16. I am not the first to draw this comparison. Phyllis Grosskurth sees "close parallels" between Klein's theories on constitutional envy (an expression of the death drive) and doctrines of original sin (*Melanie Klein,* 84). Similarly, D. W. Winnicott writes in reference to Freud and Klein that "the concept of the death instinct could be described as a reassertion of the principle of original sin" (*Playing and Reality,* 70). See also comparisons of psychoanalytic and theological views of evil in Schwarz's *Evil.*

17. Niebuhr, *Nature and Destiny of Man,* 1:121.

18. Sophocles, *Oedipus the King,* line 1449.

19. Compare, for example, these formulations, the first by Freud and the second by Niebuhr, on the problem of badness for society: "In all that follows I adopt the standpoint, therefore, that the inclination to aggression is an original, self-subsisting instinctual disposition in man, and I return to my view that it constitutes the greatest impediment to civilization" (Freud, *Civilization and Its Discontents,* 69). "The selfishness of human communities must be regarded as an inevitability. Where it is inordinate it can be checked only by competing assertions of interest; and these can be effective only if coercive methods are added to moral and rational persuasion" (Niebuhr, *Moral Man and Immoral Society,* 272). Niebuhr also writes that evil is "at the very centre of human personality: in the will" (*Nature and Destiny of Man* 1:16).

20. In generally rejecting an emphasis on human badness, environmental thought seems part of a larger trend toward optimistic anthropology. Reinhold Niebuhr, for instance, argues that "modern man has an essentially easy con-

science." Modern anthropology, he says, presents us with either "rational man" or "natural man":

> If modern culture conceives man primarily in terms of the uniqueness of his rational faculties, it finds the root of his evil in his involvement in natural impulses and natural necessities from which it hopes to free him by the increase of his rational faculties. . . . On the other hand, if it conceives of man primarily in terms of his relation to nature, it hopes to rescue man from the dæmonic chaos in which his spiritual life is involved by beguiling him back to the harmony, serenity and harmless unity of nature.

In both cases, Niebuhr notes that "either the rational man or the natural man is conceived as essentially good" (*Nature and Destiny of Man* 1:23–24, 16; see also chap. 4, "The Easy Conscience of Modern Man").

21. For a survey and evaluation of Niebuhr's role in theological realism, see Lovin, "Theology, Ethics, and Culture," 75–81, 84–87, as well as Lovin's *Reinhold Niebuhr and Christian Realism*.

22. Sands, *Escape from Paradise*; Burack, *Problem of the Passions*.

23. Ecophilosopher Warwick Fox, for example, in a comprehensive overview of the environmental movement and environmental thought, finds four different notions of personhood among the various approaches adopted to nature-human relations. First, he characterizes the non-environmentalist approach as one of unrestrained exploitation and sees it as emphasizing an impulsive, primitive, id-like self that desires and functions "without particular regard for others, the future, or the constraints that are imposed by reality in general." Second, the conservation approach of mainstream environmentalism has a rational ego-like self that mediates among the competing demands of personal desire, ethical obligation, and the constraints of reality. Third, he finds the intrinsic value approach of radical ecology to favor a judgmental superego-like self that "decrees what *ought* to be and demands conformance with a certain code of conduct." Fourth, his own preferred form of radical ecology, transpersonal ecology, holds to a wide, expansive, field-like self (*Transpersonal Ecology*, 206; emphasis his; see generally all of his chap. 7). Note that only the anti-environmental position of unrestrained exploitation has a notion of destructiveness as a strong element in the human condition, and this position claims destructiveness as central in order to justify it, a move no environmentalist wants to endorse. The other notions of self that Fox surveys and the one he advocates encourage us to be good—somewhat ineffectively, I fear—without taking into account that we are also bad, and why we are so.

24. McFague, *Body of God*, 107.

25. Ruether, *Gaia and God*, 115, 139–42 and chap. 5. Ruether and other feminist thinkers (e.g., Noddings, *Women and Evil*; Sands, *Escape from Paradise*; Suchocki, *Fall to Violence*) provide important critiques of Christian notions of sin and evil in the context of contemporary feminist theology and philosophy.

26. In the psychological context, see, for example, Harry Guntrip: "There is reason to believe that [Freud's] theories of . . . instinctive aggression have done as

much harm to our general cultural orientation in this century, especially in the atmospheres engendered by two world wars, as his opening up of the field of psychotherapy in depth has done good" (*Psychoanalytic Theory, Therapy, and the Self,* 137). See also Holbrook, *Human Hope and the Death Instinct;* Zinn, *Declarations of Independence,* especially chap. 3 "Violence and Human Nature."

27. Phrasing it differently, Walter Lowe says that emphasis on the problem of evil and human perversity "scuttle[s] the Pelagian optimism inherited from the Enlightenment" (Lowe, *Evil and the Unconscious,* 74n).

28. Alford, *Melanie Klein and Critical Social Theory,* 125, 124.

29. Klein, "The Early Development of Conscience in the Child" (1933), in *Writings of Melanie Klein* 1:257 (hereafter cited as *Writings*).

30. Kant, *Religion Within the Limits of Reason Alone,* 46.

31. Eliot, "The Hollow Men." Eliot gives this poem an epigraph from Joseph Conrad's novella, *Heart of Darkness:* "Mistah Kurtz—he dead."

32. These feminist theologians maintain that the notion of sinfulness looks different when theology gives equal hearing to women's self-understandings and when it takes seriously feminist theologizing. Valerie Saiving inaugurates this discussion with her 1960 essay, "The Human Situation: A Feminine View." She argues that notions of sin are based on male experience of sinfulness and of the human condition and that they fail to describe adequately the experience of women. She and Jewish theologian Judith Plaskow, who expands on Saiving's work, suggest that women's sin is more likely to be that of "underdevelopment or negation of the self," of caring too much for others and not enough for oneself, of taking too far the traditional Christian prohibitions against "pride" and "self-assertion." This sin of pride they characterize as more typical of men. They further argue that male theories of sin are themselves sinful, in that they ignore or devalue women's experience and label women's desire for independence and self-assertion as "sin or temptation to sin." Such theology provides harmful moral guidance for women, in that the last thing a woman with a weak sense of self needs is injunction to selflessness. In most egregious form, for example, the worst advice for a battered woman would be to turn the other cheek. Saiving, "The Human Situation," 37, 39; Plaskow, *Sex, Sin, and Grace,* 68. See also Ruether, *Gaia and God,* 142; Suchocki, *Fall to Violence;* Christine M. Smith, "Sin and Evil in Feminist Thought."

Judith Plaskow develops a critique of Reinhold Niebuhr's work as one-sided and androcentric for its identification of pride or self-love as the root of sin. "Niebuhr not only fails to convey the nature of women's sin," she argues, "he actually turns it into a virtue," by not appreciating the truly "destructive element in the nature of self-sacrifice" (*Sex, Sin, and Grace,* 151–52; see also 62–73). There is probably middle ground between Niebuhr and his feminist critics. Both Plaskow and Gabriel Fackre, for example, point out how Niebuhr is not always consistent or systematic in his use of key terms such as "pride" and "sensuality." If Niebuhr intends sensuality as "escape from freedom," as he sometimes indicates, and if he did not insist on the primacy of pride and on sensuality as its derivative, then his doctrine of sin could much better account for women's experience, with pride and sensuality as complementary forms of characteristically male or female sin involving either the exaltation or abdication of freedom (Plaskow, *Sex, Sin, and Grace,* 60–63).

Similarly, Fackre proposes that Niebuhr's concept of pride be understood primarily as a fundamental "egocentricity" or "universal self-regarding tendency" underlying both the arrogance of those with power ("pride" in a secondary sense, more typical of men) and the refusal of the powerless to risk self-assertion (the flight from freedom that more often tempts women). Furthermore, to the extent that Niebuhr understands pride as this egocentricity that distorts all relationship by distorting one's relationship to God, his work is not incompatible with feminist relational theology. Fackre, "Relevance of Niebuhr," 9; see also 8–10.

33. My reference is to the previously discussed work of Nel Noddings, *Women and Evil.*

34. Psychologist Anne Campbell examines differences between how men and women understand aggression and act aggressively. She presents evidence that women get angry as often and as intensely as men and that they are violent against domestic partners as often as are men. Women, however, understand, experience, and act out such violence differently. They tend to view such aggression as a loss of self-control, whereas men tend view it as a means to exert control. Furthermore, when men and women aggress against each other in the home, women suffer graver harm due to men's usually greater size and strength (*Men, Women, and Aggression,* 70, 71, 103–104).

35. The seminal work in this field is that done by feminist psychologist Carol Gilligan, who reviewed traditional psychological theories of women's development to argue that psychology had based models of moral development on male experience, largely by ignoring the experience of girls and women. When it found women to differ from a male norm presumed universal, it concluded women to be deviant and lacking. Gilligan uncovers a "bias of developmental theory toward ordering differences in a hierarchical mode" and maintains that women's different moral voice is not a less-perfect version of the male but a distinct and equally valid conception of morality stressing care, relationship, and context instead of rights, rules, and abstract thinking (*In a Different Voice,* 33; for her review of psychological literature that faults women's moral development, see her chap. 1, "Woman's Place in Man's Life Cycle").

36. Kolodny, *The Land Before Her,* xiii; see generally her text as a whole, as well as Norwood's *Made From This Earth,* which, in a historical study of nineteenth- and twentieth-century American women's relations to nature, also addresses whether men and women's concepts of nature differ.

37. Goldenberg, *Returning Words to Flesh,* 171. Goldenberg expresses this point in the context of feminist theory as the conviction that "all humans are beings whose destructiveness is as basic as their love" (170). Note Adrienne Rich's similar comment: "Theories of female power and ascendancy must reckon fully with the ambiguities of our being, and with the continuum of our consciousness, the potentialities for both creative and destructive energy in each of us" (*Of Woman Born,* 283).

5. SPLITTING MOTHER NATURE

1. The quote is from Klein, "Love, Guilt and Reparation," (1937), *Writings* 1:336. This essay is one of Klein's most accessible; it is nontechnical and ranges widely over adult emotional life.

2. Dinnerstein, *Mermaid and Minotaur;* and Alford, *Melanie Klein.* I am deeply indebted to the excellent and original work of both writers in applying Klein's ideas to the wider cultural realm.

3. Greenberg and Mitchell, *Object Relations in Psychoanalytic Theory,* 2, 145; Burgin, "Object," 277–80; Segal, *Introduction to the Work of Melanie Klein,* 127–28.

4. Mitchell, "Introduction," in *The Selected Melanie Klein,* 23; Mitchell also calls phantasy "the key concept of her [Klein's] theory" (23). See also Greenberg and Mitchell, *Object Relations,* 124; Segal, *Introduction to Klein,* 12. The simile about phantasy draws on Mitchell (*Selected Klein,* 23) and on Alford's discussion of the group as a screen for the projection of phantasy (*Melanie Klein,* 64–74).

5. Alford, *Melanie Klein,* 62.

6. In *Beyond the Pleasure Principle* (1920) and *Civilization and its Discontents* (1930), Freud develops a theory of organic life as motivated by the balanced and opposing forces of the death drive (*Thanatos*) and the life drive (*Eros*). These two instincts are intimately yet acrimoniously intertwined (e.g., *Pleasure Principle,* 47, 55n; *Civilization and Its Discontents,* 66). They work within the individual and are also projected outward as cultural forces of either antisocial aggression or of community building. The death instinct drives the organism to reduce the tension of life (to seek, in essence, death). Since all occasions of union produce tension, it drives us away from such unions and tends toward retraction, destruction, and disintegration. The life instinct, in contrast, tends toward extension, creation, and combination. Eros makes civilization possible by driving us to build community, a task first instigated by the exigencies of reality (*Civilization and Its Discontents,* 86). However, while our physical limitations and the uncertainties of life require that we band together, our aggressive tendencies would outweigh this necessity were it not for Eros.

The task of civilization is to counteract or control the ubiquitous aggressivity that is "the derivative and the main representative of the death instinct which we have found alongside of Eros and which shares world-dominion with it." "Civilization," Freud says, "is a process in the service of Eros, whose purpose is "to combine single human individuals, and after that families, then races, peoples and nations, into one great unity, the unity of mankind" (*Civilization and Its Discontents,* 69). Eros, the power of love, makes us bind together even while Thanatos, our aggressivity and destructiveness, makes us hostile to one and all. We are in this way split and fundamentally ambivalent: we need and love our fellow humans, yet are irremediably inimical to them. The extent to which we tolerate such ambivalence is the work of Eros, the "preserver of all things" (*Beyond the Pleasure Principle,* 46). Such love is what makes life possible, bearable, and desirable.

7. Greenberg and Mitchell, *Object Relations,* 146; see also 144–46.

8. Klein, "Schizoid Mechanisms," *Writings* 3:4.

9. Although Klein originally used the term *persecutory phase* or *paranoid position* to describe what psychoanalyst W. R. D. Fairbairn was also calling the schizoid position, by 1952 she had combined the two terms and was referring to the *paranoid-schizoid position* (Klein, "Notes on Some Schizoid Mechanisms" [1946], *Writings* 3:2n). Klein labels the first of the two positions paranoid-schizoid to express her conviction that paranoid and schizoid anxieties and defenses are at work in early infantile life. Such anxieties and defenses are normal at this point of development, but they are characteristic of paranoia or schizophrenia if they persist as the primary means of dealing with reality.

10. Klein picks up on Freud's notion of the conflict between the life drive and death drive as fundamental to the human condition. She believes, however, that Freud "never fully worked out his discovery of the two instincts" and was "reluctant to extend it to the whole of mental functioning." Klein interprets the drives in terms of love and hate and places them in a developmental schema of infancy and childhood. The depressive position—based on struggles between the life and death drives—becomes for Klein the "nodal" point in the child's development, a place Freud reserved for the Oedipal complex. Klein, "On the Development of Mental Functioning" (1958), *Writings* 3:245; "A Contribution to the Psychogenesis of Manic-Depressive States" (1935), *Writings* 1:289, recapitulated in "Notes on Some Schizoid Mechanisms" (1946), *Writings* 3:3. Important essays for Klein's understanding of the depressive position and reparation are "A Contribution to the Psychogenesis of Manic-Depressive States" (1935); "Love, Guilt and Reparation" (1937); and "Mourning and Its Relation to Manic-Depressive States" (1940), all in *Writings*, vol. 1.

11. Klein, "Schizoid Mechanisms," *Writings* 3:5.

12. Klein, "Some Theoretical Conclusions Regarding the Emotional Life of the Infant," (1952), *Writings* 3:62; see also "Schizoid Mechanisms," *Writings* 3:2. Note Dinnerstein's comment: "The mental processes that Klein seems to attribute to three- or six-month-old infants, for example, should not be taken literally; her formulations are based on the play, dreams, and transference behaviors of older children and adults, who have recast memories of very early feelings into words and images that the infant did not possess. For this same reason, the term 'breast' as she uses it must be understood not solely in its literal sense but also as a metaphor for 'source of good'" (*Mermaid and Minotaur,* 96n).

13. Klein, "Schizoid Mechanisms," *Writings* 3:5; see also 3:6–7.

14. Ibid., 3:2, 5.

15. Ibid., 3:6, 2, 5. Many analysts consider Klein's explanation of the dynamics of projective identification to be "her greatest contribution to psychoanalysis" (Grosskurth, *Melanie Klein,* 373).

16. Merchant, *Death of Nature,* 3; reprinted in revised context in her *Radical Ecology,* 43. My previous discussion of this point was in chapter 3.

17. Klein, "The Early Development of Conscience in the Child," (1933), *Writings* 1:253. See also Segal, *Introduction to Klein,* 13.

18. Gill, *Mother Earth,* 54, quoting J. W. MacMurray, "The 'Dreamers' of the Columbia River Valley, in Washington Territory," *Transactions of the Albany Institute*

(Albany, 1887), 247–48; see also all of Gill's chap. 3, especially 40–41, 52–55. For Merchant's references to Smohalla, see, for example, *Death of Nature*, 28; *Radical Ecology*, 43–44.

19. "When the Music's Over," from the album *Strange Days*. Published by Doors Music Co., released Oct. 1967.

20. Kolodny, *Lay of the Land*, 3–4, 146, quoting a poem credited to Book Jones appearing in the People's Park Committee leaflet, distributed May 1969.

21. Gaard, describing a cartoon from the *Duluth News Tribune*, 24 October 1989, in "Ecofeminism and Native American Cultures," 304.

22. Billboard advertisement, Boston subway platform, January 1998. Print ad for Tourney golf outerwear, *Wall Street Journal*, 10 April 1998, W5; emphasis theirs.

23. Dinnerstein, *Mermaid and Minotaur*, 105, 93, 100; see generally all of chap. 6.

24. Ibid., 108; again, see generally all of chap. 6. Kolodny, *Lay of the Land*, 156.

25. Kahane, "The Gothic Mirror," 336–37.

26. Dinnerstein, *Mermaid and Minotaur*, 100.

27. Merchant, *Death of Nature*, 127.

28. For the extensive Web site of this "online resource for stay-at home dads," see www.slowlane.com. The 1993 statistic comes from a Census Bureau survey reported in "At-home Dads Find They Are Not Alone," *Tuscaloosa News*, 2 January 2000.

29. Dinnerstein, *Mermaid and Minotaur*, 102; see also 113–14, 149–56. Keller, *From a Broken Web*, chaps. 3–5; however, see 120–21 for Keller's differentiation of her project from that of Dinnerstein. Note also that some feminist scholars are wary of the argument that shared parenting is the solution to maternal ambivalence; see, for example, Jean Bethke Elshtain's critique of Dinnerstein as somewhat apolitical and utopian in *Public Man, Private Woman*, 286–90.

30. Alford, *Melanie Klein*, 46.

31. Ibid.

32. I used the line "If Mother Nature has proved one thing, it is that she can be a real bitch" as the epigraph of chapter 4. It is quoted by Cronon, "Introduction," *Uncommon Ground*, 48, from a letter to the editor by Jeff Outcalt in *Time* magazine (21 February 1994, 7) after the Northridge, California, earthquake.

33. Alford, *Melanie Klein*, 57, 21, 83; see also 38–42. Niebuhr explores this same problem of the difference between individual and group morality in *Moral Man and Immoral Society* and in "Collective Egoism," in *Nature and Destiny of Man* 1:208–19. See Alford's comparison of his own project with that of Niebuhr in *Melanie Klein*, 20. See also Kolodny, *Lay of the Land*, for an analysis of American gendered language about nature as part of the "psychic content of the group's shared fantasies—however unacknowledged or unconscious these may have been" (148).

34. Alford, *Melanie Klein*, chap. 3, "A Psychoanalytic Theory of the Large Group," 62–64, 74–76, 79. Alford uses role theory here to distinguish between how we act as members of groups and how we act as individuals.

35. McPhee, *Control of Nature*, 7, ellipses in original.

36. Alford, *Melanie Klein*, 82–87.

37. Ibid., 75–76.

38. Linda Daigle, quoted in "Fran's Victims Begin Cleanup," Cambridge, Mass. *Crimson,* 9 September 1996, A4, in reference to Hurricane Fran's damage of North Carolina. The storm killed at least twenty-two people and left Daigle and other residents of Raleigh, N.C., without electricity or drinking water.

39. Klein, "Love, Guilt and Reparation," *Writings* 1:336.

40. Jerome Kagan, "A Conversation with Jerome Kagan," *Harvard Gazette,* 22 September 1989, 6, quoting Richard Feynman.

41. Freud, *Future of an Illusion,* 19.

42. Alford, *Melanie Klein,* 188.

43. Dinnerstein, "Survival on Earth," 193.

6. "OUR MOTHER NEEDS OUR HELP"

1. Earth Communications Office (ECO), promotional material on "The Public Service Announcement Campaign (PSA)," received in a personal communication from ECO, 22 July 1996. ECO can be reached at 12021 Wilshire Blvd., Box 557, Los Angeles CA, 90025; at (310) 571-3141; or at their Web site www.oneearth.org.

2. Ibid. Readers with access to the Web can view the piece for themselves; see "Mother," Earth Communications Office Public Service Announcement, written and produced by ECO Chairman Larry Kopald, 1995, at www.oneearth.org.

3. Ibid.; emphasis mine. Lovelock, *Ages of Gaia,* 212.

4. Merchant, *Death of Nature,* 30, quoting Pliny, *Natural History;* see also 29–41.

5. Conversation with Smohalla reported by E. L. Huggins, quoted by Gill, *Mother Earth,* 52–53. Alexandre Hogue's studies and oil painting of *Mother Earth Laid Bare* (1936) are reproduced in DeLong, *Nature's Forms / Nature's Forces,* 39, 120–23 (note that the date is in error in DeLong's text); the quote is by Hogue from his own description of the painting, 120. I learned of Hogue's work in a lecture by Merchant, "Reinventing Eden: Landscape as Narrative."

6. The series mythology, profiles on Gaia, and information about the Captain Planet Foundation—an educational and granting agency aimed at K-12—can all be found at www.turner.com/planet/.

7. Matthew Fox, *Coming of the Cosmic Christ,* 33, 145, 147, 245. See, generally, his sections "A Dream—'Your Mother Is Dying'—A Crucifixion Story for Our Times" and "Jesus Christ as Mother Earth Crucified and Resurrected."

8. Gnanadason, "Feminist Eco-Theology for India," 77–78.

9. Klein, "Love, Guilt, and Reparation," *Writings* 1:337; emphasis and parenthesis hers.

10. Winnicott, *The Maturational Process and the Facilitating Environment.* I thank Bennett Simon for finding the reference for me.

11. For some influential contemporary relational models, see: in philosophy and women's studies, Noddings, *Caring;* in psychology and religion, Jones, *Contemporary Psychoanalysis and Religion;* in theology, Suchocki, *Fall to Violence.* See also Merchant, *Earthcare;* here Merchant develops a partnership ethic of "earthcare" specifically grounded in the concept of relation.

12. Gablik, *Reenchantment of Art,* 1, quoting D. H. Lawrence; emphasis his.

13. In ecofeminism and feminist theology, for example, Ruether concludes that sin "lies in distortion of relationship, the absolutizing of the rights to life and power of one side of a relation against the other parts with which it is, in fact, interdependent" (*Gaia and God*, 142). Suchocki, in *Fall to Violence*, develops a notion of original sin within a relational theology that stresses relationship as central and primary to all existence. And Christine M. Smith, in "Sin and Evil in Feminist Thought," a review essay of current feminist understandings, finds emphasis on "right relation" in the theologies of Rita Nakashima Brock, Mary Potter Engel, Carter Heyward, and Beverly Harrison.

14. Oelschlaeger, *Idea of Wilderness*, 295, quoting Holmes Ralston.

15. Freud, *Beyond the Pleasure Principle*, 35.

16. James, *Varieties of Religious Experience*, 507–508; emphasis his. See Keller for an argument that James "lifts the notion of relation into conceptual prominence" and "credits relations with full ontological and epistemological status" (*From a Broken Web*, 177; see generally 177–79).

17. Ruether, *Gaia and God*, 141.

18. Ibid., 213, 214; see generally 211–15 and 256.

19. Juliet Mitchell calls the depressive position the "hallmark of Kleinian theory" (*Selected Klein*, 115). It is in the depressive position that the baby first realizes that "the loved object is at the same time the hated one" and that real objects and phantasized ones "are bound up with each other" (Klein, "Manic-Depressive States," *Writings* 1:286). These feelings are intensified by the process of weaning, in which the infant mourns "the mother's breast and all that the breast and the milk have come to stand for in the infant's mind: namely love, goodness, and security" (Klein, "Mourning," *Writings* 1:345).

20. See Segal's helpful chapter, "Reparation," in *Introduction to Klein*. The concept of reparation, notes Harriet Lutzky, "is original, and thought by some to be [Klein's] most important contribution to psychoanalytic theory" ("Reparation and Tikkun," 449).

21. Klein, "Some Theoretical Conclusions Regarding the Emotional Life of the Infant" (1952) *Writings* 3:74. Klein, "Love, Guilt and Reparation," *Writings* 1:308; "Mourning," *Writings* 1:347; Segal, *Introduction to Klein*, 37.

22. Klein, "Love, Guilt and Reparation," *Writings* 1; Alford, *Melanie Klein*. Hanna Segal notes that "the depressive position is never fully worked through. The anxieties pertaining to ambivalence and guilt, as well as situations of loss, which reawaken depressive experiences, are always with us" (*Introduction to Klein*, 80).

23. Klein, "On the Theory of Anxiety and Guilt" (1948), *Writings* 3:34, 41; "Envy and Gratitude" (1957) *Writings* 3:232.

24. Klein, "Envy and Gratitude," *Writings* 3:232–33; "Schizoid Mechanisms," *Writings* 3:8; "On the Sense of Loneliness" (1963), *Writings* 3:301. As Naomi Goldenberg remarks: "Klein thinks that the most fundamental psychological achievement of childhood is the sustained capacity to feel both love and hate toward the same people and things. This ability is essential for both intellectual and moral development," and allows for more "balanced" and "caring" lives (*Returning Words to Flesh*, 159, 163).

25. Segal, *Introduction to Klein*, 95–96, 128. Alford, *Melanie Klein*, 34.

26. I thank Diane Jonte-Pace for feedback that pointed out this danger. For a critique of Mother Nature language as emerging from a romantic tradition condescending toward the female and exploitative toward the environment, see Heller, "For the Love of Nature." For the metaphor of the damsel in distress, see Kheel, "From Heroic to Holistic Ethics."

27. Sophia Center pamphlet, unsolicited mailing received 25 June 1997. The school can be reached at Holy Names College, 3500 Mountain Boulevard, Oakland CA, 94619-1699 or at (510) 436-1046.

28. Segal, *Introduction to Klein*, 95.

29. Fackre, *The Promise of Reinhold Niebuhr*, 41; Niebuhr, *Nature and Destiny of Man* 1:104, 106.

30. Matthew Fox, *Original Blessing* and *Cosmic Christ*, 148–49. For a discussion of Matthew Fox in the context of ecofeminist thought, see Ruether, *Gaia and God*, 146, 241–42.

31. Fackre, *Promise of Niebuhr*, 57, 38–41.

32. Sands, *Escape from Paradise*, 168. See also Alford, *Melanie Klein*, 88–91.

33. See, for example, Western and Wright, eds., *Natural Connections*.

34. Dillard, *Pilgrim at Tinker Creek*, 227.

35. Alford, *Melanie Klein*, 34.

36. Matthew Fox, *Cosmic Christ*, 13.

37. The front of the bookmark indicates that it is from the "Jane Evershed Card Collection." I thank Harriet Lutzky for it. Evershed is the artist whose *Women Wiping Up the World* was discussed in chapter 2.

38. On a related point, commentators sometimes criticize Klein as being too focused on the child's psychic life and insufficiently attentive to the child's actual relationships. While the maternal object figures prominently in her theory, it is quite true that she focuses much less on the individual role of the real-life mother. See, for example, Greenberg and Mitchell, *Object Relations*, 146–47.

39. Sachs, *Global Ecology*, xvi–xvii.

40. Posted to WiRESlist, the listserv for Women in Religion, Ethics and the Sciences, a program of the Center for Theology and the Natural Sciences, Berkeley, Calif. (ctnswest @ ctns.org); 4 May 2001.

41. Klein, "Love, Guilt and Reparation," *Writings* 1:337.

42. Ruether, *Gaia and God*, 255.

43. Alford, *Melanie Klein*, 90. For discussion of Carson in the context of other women naturalists and environmental activists, see Breton, *Women Pioneers for the Environment*, and Norwood, *Made From This Earth*.

44. Wright, "Swamp's Last Day on Earth," 50.

45. Matthew Fox, *Cosmic Christ*, 15, 16.

46. See Ruether, *Gaia and God*, chap. 9; Matthew Fox, *Cosmic Christ*; James A. Nash, *Loving Nature*, 124–33. All discuss Christian thinkers who have written in this tradition: Paul, Irenaeus, and Teilhard de Chardin (Ruether); Meister Eckhart, Hildegard of Bingen, and Julian of Norwich (Fox); Paul, Calvin, and John Wesley (Nash).

47. James A. Nash, *Loving Nature*, 132, 133.

48. Merchant, "Reinventing Eden: Western Culture as a Recovery Narrative"; see also her *Death of Nature*.

49. Leiss, *Domination of Nature*, 49, quoting Bacon, *The New Organon;* see generally Leiss's section on Bacon entitled "The Recovery of the Divine Bequest," 48–57.

50. For the theme of America as garden of the world, see Henry Nash Smith, *Virgin Land.*

51. James A. Nash, *Loving Nature*, Calvin commentary on 126, 132, 133, 130; Ruether, *Gaia and God*, 235–36, 234.

52. For example, Niebuhr, *Nature and Destiny of Man* 1:178–86; Ruether, *Gaia and God*, 251.

53. Ruether, *Gaia and God*, 141; see also 251–53. The concept of the immortal self, Ruether urges, "must be recognized, not only as untenable, but as the source of much destructive behavior towards the earth and other humans" (*Gaia and God*, 251). Sands, *Escape from Paradise*, 166.

54. According to Grosskurth, Klein makes this point in notes for a projected paper on religion, wherein she analyzes heaven as a place where there is "no hate, only love" and where "wholesale reparation" is possible (*Melanie Klein*, 455).

55. Kolodny, *Lay of the Land*, 147.

7. HEALING MOTHER NATURE

1. Wood, *The Comedy of Redemption*, 8; Niebuhr, *Beyond Tragedy*, x–xi, 155. See also Fackre, *Promise of Niebuhr*, 43.

2. Apart from Wood's defense of the comic in theology, for a defense of the comic and critique of the tragic in psychoanalysis, see Holbrook, *Human Hope*. For a defense of the tragic within theology and feminism see Sands, *Escape from Paradise;* within theology, see Suchocki, *Fall to Violence;* within feminism and psychoanalysis, see Burack, *Problem of the Passions*. For an application to psychoanalysis of Northrop Frye's typology of the tragic, comic, romantic, and ironic, see Schafer, "Psychoanalytic Vision of Reality."

3. See Peter Brown, *Augustine*, chaps. 30–31.

4. John Hick, for example, concludes his *Evil and the God of Love* with a defense of his anti-Augustinian theodicy: "We believe or disbelieve, ultimately, out of our own experience and must be faithful to the witness of that experience; and together with very many others, I find that the realities of human goodness and human happiness make it a credible possibility that this life, with its baffling mixture of good and evil, and including both its dark miseries and its shining joys, including both man's malevolence and his self-forgetting love, is indeed part of a long and slow pilgrim's progress towards the Celestial City" (*Evil and the God of Love*, 386).

5. Psychologist of religion Harriet Lutzky affirms "the power of the concept of reparation to interpret religious myth" ("Reparation and Tikkun," 457). As Winnicott remarks, Klein has shown "why there exists a relationship between the

deepest conflicts that reveal themselves in religion . . . and the depressed mood" (quoted in Lutzky, "Reparation and Tikkun," 457).

6. This quote and the metaphor of common ground come from Lowe, *Evil and the Unconscious*, 74–75, 91. See Niebuhr, "Human Creativity and Self-Concern in Freud's Thought," and Tillich, "The Theological Significance of Existentialism and Psychoanalysis," in *Theology of Culture*. Tillich speaks in that essay of the common roots and "mutual interpenetration" of theology and psychoanalysis (114), and of the "inseparability of depth psychology . . . from theology" (117).

Despite this appreciation, Tillich and Niebuhr (who produced the first two major theological responses to Freud) both ultimately dismiss psychoanalysis as unsatisfactory from the perspective of Christian theology. Tillich charges that Freud sees only "existential man"—the human predicament of estrangement (theologically, the Fall)—and recognizes neither original goodness nor "teleological man" (the possibility of salvation). Niebuhr, for his part, dismisses the "romantic pessimism" of Freud's system and labels it an untenable one of despair. What Freud misses, they both say, is redemptive hope, an understanding of the human capacity for freedom, the dimension of transcendence (Tillich, *Theology of Culture*, 120; Niebuhr, *Nature and Destiny of Man* 1:121, 52–53; Homans, *Theology after Freud*, 21). See Homans' study for detailed analysis of the theological response and critique offered by Tillich and Niebuhr to Freud.

Freud's vision *is* tragic, in the sense developed in my text, although I disagree that it is one of despair. As Homans says, "Freud, too, had his doctrine of grace as well as of sin" (*Theology after Freud*, 27). In my reading, however, what constitutes such "grace" in Freud's thought differs from Homans' interpretation, which stresses sublimation and the work of psychoanalytic therapy. Neither Tillich nor Niebuhr credits Freud for his notion of the life drive or Eros. Yet precisely in this concept lies hope. Freud sees in Eros the ability to bind people together in communities where love tempers hate and fellow-feeling balances tendencies to destructiveness.

7. Klein, "Envy and Gratitude," *Writings* 3:232; Wollheim, *Mind and Its Depths*, 52, 57–59; Alford, *Melanie Klein*, 34–35, 38–42.

8. Alford, *Melanie Klein*, 11.

9. Goldenberg, *Returning Words to Flesh*, 163. Sands advocates the same perspective in her work of postmodern feminist theology; see, for example, *Escape from Paradise*, 15, 90, 167. Ruether, too, argues against the concept of an immortal soul (*Gaia and God*, 251–53).

10. Daisaku Ikeda, "1997 Peace Proposal," quoted in the newsletter of the Boston Research Center for the 21st Century, 8 (Spring 1997) 14.

11. Kant, *Religion Within the Limits of Reason Alone*, 46.

12. Alford, *Melanie Klein*, 135.

13. Albrecht Ritschl, *The Christian Doctrine of Justification and Reconciliation*, quoted in Niebuhr, *Nature and Destiny of Man* 1:178; Dinnerstein, *Mermaid and Minotaur*, 2.

14. The term "ambiguity" comes from Niebuhr, *Nature and Destiny of Man*

1:178, in his commentary on Ritschl's passage; "contradiction" is Ritschl's term; "inconsistency" and "sense of strangeness" derive from the Dinnerstein quote.

15. Niebuhr, *Nature and Destiny of Man* 1:178, 181, 13, 182. See Homans, *Theology after Freud*, 28–29 for Niebuhr's definition of nature.

16. Niebuhr, *Nature and Destiny of Man* 1:178, 98; see also his chaps. 7 and 8, "Man as Sinner." In a subordinate analysis, Niebuhr defines sin as our "sensual" attempts to hide our freedom and lose ourselves in this world (see, e.g., 179, 228–40). See also my chapter 4, note 33.

17. Niebuhr, *Nature and Destiny of Man* 1:190.

18. As evidence of how commonplace this view remains, note this introduction to the final term paper of one of my students recently: "It is, and has always been obvious that man was placed on this planet to conquer and rule it; however, we have taken this concept or idea entirely too far. God blessed us with a brain that was capable of thinking, learning, and retaining vast amounts of useful knowledge. With this unique benefit and feature, mankind has evolved from its original primal state into a magnificent mini-God, if you will."

19. Niebuhr, *Nature and Destiny of Man* 1:3.

20. Henry Nash Smith, "Preface to the Twentieth Anniversary Printing," *Virgin Land*, ix–x.

21. Heller, "For the Love of Nature," 232; Gaard, "Ecofeminism and Native American Cultures," 313.

22. I thank Jerry Rosiek for this entry, as well as for his ever-amusing and inspired leadership of our junior faculty Interdisciplinary Writing Group and CRAPS (the Committee to Retain Assistant Professors in the System) at the University of Alabama.

23. Matthew Fox, *Cosmic Christ*, 11, 13, quoting Hildegard of Bingen.

24. Vance, "Ecofeminism," 136.

25. Merchant, *Death of Nature*, 190.

26. I thank Steven C. Rockefeller for bringing this image to my attention.

27. From an artist statement by Judith Anderson, about her 1988 etching *Missa Gaia: This Is My Body*. The statement and etching appeared as part of an art exhibit accompanying a symposium held at Middlebury College in fall 1990 called "Spirit and Nature: Religion, Ethics, and Environmental Crisis." From it emerged the volume *Spirit and Nature*, edited by Rockefeller and Elder, in which the etching is reproduced (194).

28. Elder, "Epilogue," 195–96, 198.

29. Gnanadason, "Feminist Eco-Theology for India," 77–78. For an example of feminist spirituality that draws on Mother Nature imagery, see Sjöö and Mor, *Great Cosmic Mother*.

30. Griffin, *Woman and Nature*, 226.

31. Garb, "Perspective or Escape?" 278, 277.

32. Saint Francis, "Canticle of the Sun," in Ross and McLaughlin, eds., *Portable Medieval Reader*, 517–18. For Francis's "embrace of nature," see Santmire, *Travail of Nature*, 106–19. Griffin uses imagery of nature as sister (*Woman and Nature*, 219); Vance advocates "Sister Nature" ("Ecofeminism," 133); Morrison and Gnanada-

son, as we saw, refer to the earth respectively as "our fair sister" (in "When the Music's Over") and "sister earth" ("Feminist Eco-Theology for India," 78). For nature as brother, see Santmire's *Brother Earth*. Peggy Cleveland in an unpublished paper (in the author's possession) explores imagery of nature as our child in "Mothering the Earth or Nurturing Nature" (1985).

33. Merchant, *Earthcare*, 218, 221; see also 216–24.

34. McFague says this model is "indispensable" today "because it unites us to everything else on our planet in relationships of interdependence" (*Body of God*, viii, x).

35. Willoughby, *Mother Earth*, 197–98. See, for example, feminist bioregionalist Judith Plant, who emphasizes the specificities of place and community ("Toward a New World" and "The Circle Is Gathering").

36. Willoughby, *Mother Earth*, 199. For examples of such vigilance, see Willoughby's analysis of water symbolism and rituals ("Ecofeminist Consciousness and the Power of Symbols") and Culpepper's "sympathetic critique" of Mother Earth ritual and thealogy ("Contemporary Goddess Thealogy").

37. Aeschylus, *Agamemnon* in *Oresteia*, lines 958–60.

38. Sands, *Escape from Paradise*, 167.

Bibliography

This bibliography lists all the works to which I refer in the text and footnotes, as well as some additional titles that helped shape my thinking but to which I make no specific reference.

Adams, Carol, ed. *Ecofeminism and the Sacred.* New York: Continuum, 1993.

Aeschylus. *Oresteia.* Translated by Richmond Lattimore. Chicago: University of Chicago Press, 1953.

Alford, C. Fred. *Melanie Klein and Critical Social Theory: An Account of Politics, Art, and Reason Based on Her Psychoanalytic Theory.* New Haven, Conn.: Yale University Press, 1989.

Allen, Paula Gunn. *The Sacred Hoop: Recovering the Feminine in American Indian Traditions.* Boston: Beacon Press, 1986.

Angus, Ian, and Sut Jhally, eds. *Cultural Politics in Contemporary America.* New York: Routledge, 1989.

Auerbach, Nina. *Woman and the Demon: The Life of a Victorian Myth.* Cambridge, Mass.: Harvard University Press, 1982.

Augustine. *Confessions.* Translated by R. S. Pine-Coffin. Penguin Classics, 1961.

———. *City of God.* Translated by Henry Bettenson. Penguin Classics, 1984.

Bachofen, J. J. *Mother Right: An Investigation of the Religious and Juridical Character of Matriarchy in the Ancient World.* 1861. In *Myth, Religion, and Mother Right: Selected Writings of J. J. Bachofen.* Translated by Ralph Manheim. Princeton, N.J.: Princeton University Press, 1973.

Badiner, Allan. *Dharma Gaia: A Harvest of Essays on Buddhism and Ecology.* Berkeley, Calif.: Parallax Press, 1990.

Bender, Frederic L. Review of *Earth's Insights: A Survey of Ecological Ethics from the Mediterranean Basin to the Australian Outback,* by J. Baird Callicott. *Philosophy East and West* 46 (April 1996): 269–72.

Benjamin, Jessica. *Bonds of Love: Psychoanalysis, Feminism, and the Problem of Domination.* New York: Pantheon, 1988.

Bigwood, Carol. *Earth Muse: Feminism, Nature, and Art.* Philadelphia: Temple University Press, 1983.

Breton, Mary Joy. *Women Pioneers for the Environment.* Boston: Northeastern University Press, 1998.

Brown, Donald E. *Human Universals.* Philadelphia: Temple University Press, 1991.

Brown, James A. C. *Freud and the Post-Freudians*. Harmondsworth, U.K.: Penguin, 1961, 1964.

Brown, Lester R., et al. *State of the World: A Worldwatch Institute Report on Progress Toward a Sustainable Society*. New York: Norton. Published annually.

Brown, Peter. *Augustine of Hippo*. Berkeley: University of California Press, 1967.

Burack, Cynthia. *The Problem of the Passions: Feminism, Psychoanalysis, and Social Theory*. New York: New York University Press, 1994.

Burgin, Victor. "Object." In *Feminism and Psychoanalysis: A Critical Dictionary*, edited by Elizabeth Wright. Oxford: Blackwell, 1992.

Callicott, J. Baird. *Earth's Insights: A Survey of Ecological Ethics from the Mediterranean Basin to the Australian Outback*. Berkeley: University of California Press, 1994.

Callicott, J. Baird, and Roger T. Ames, eds. *Nature in Asian Traditions of Thought: Essays in Environmental Philosophy*. Albany: State University of New York Press, 1989.

Campbell, Anne. *Men, Women, and Aggression*. New York: Basic Books, 1993.

Cantrill, James G., and Christine L. Oravec, eds. *The Symbolic Earth: Discourse and Our Creation of the Environment*. Lexington: University Press of Kentucky, 1997.

Carson, Rachel. *Silent Spring*. 1962. Twenty-fifth anniversary edition: Boston: Houghton Mifflin, 1987.

Chodorow, Nancy. *The Reproduction of Mothering: Psychoanalysis and the Sociology of Gender*. Berkeley: University of California Press, 1978.

Christ, Carol P. *Laughter of Aphrodite: Reflections on a Journey to the Goddess*. San Francisco: Harper & Row, 1987.

Christ, Carol P., and Judith Plaskow, eds. *Womanspirit Rising: A Feminist Reader in Religion*. San Francisco: Harper & Row, 1979.

Collard, Andrée, with Joyce Contrucci. *Rape of the Wild: Man's Violence against Animals and the Earth*. Bloomington: Indiana University Press, 1988.

Collingwood, R. G. *The Idea of Nature*. 1945. Reprint: Oxford: Oxford University Press, 1960.

Conrad, Joseph. *Heart of Darkness*. 1902. Edited by Robert Kimbrough. Norton Critical Edition, 3rd ed. New York: W. W. Norton, 1988.

Cronon, William, ed. *Uncommon Ground: Rethinking the Human Place in Nature*. New York: Norton, 1995.

———. "Introduction: In Search of Nature." In *Uncommon Ground: Rethinking the Human Place in Nature*, edited by William Cronon. Reprint: New York: Norton, 1996.

Culpepper, Emily Erwin. "Contemporary Goddess Thealogy: A Sympathetic Critique." In *Shaping New Vision: Gender and Values in American Culture*, edited by Clarissa Atkinson, Constance Buchanan, and Margaret Miles. Ann Arbor, Mich.: UMI Research Press, 1987.

Dally, Ann. *Inventing Motherhood: The Consequences of an Ideal*. London: Burnett Books, 1982.

Daly, Mary. *Beyond God the Father: Toward a Philosophy of Women's Liberation*. 1973. New edition. Boston: Beacon Press, 1985.

———. *Gyn/Ecology: The Metaethics of Radical Feminism*. Boston: Beacon Press, 1978.

———. "Foreword." In *Rape of the Wild: Man's Violence against Animals and the Earth*, by Andrée Collard with Joyce Contrucci. Bloomington: Indiana University Press, 1988.

Davis, Susan G. "'Touch the Magic.'" In *Uncommon Ground: Rethinking the Human Place in Nature*, edited by William Cronon. New York: Norton, 1996, 1995.

D'Eaubonne, Françoise. *Le féminisme ou la mort*. Paris: Pierre Horay, 1974. Translated as "Feminism or Death" in *New French Feminists: An Anthology*, edited by Elaine Marks and Isabelle de Courtivron. Amherst: University of Massachusetts Press, 1980.

Deffenbaugh, Daniel G. "The Ecological Indian Revisited." *Soundings: An Interdisciplinary Journal* 83 (Summer 2000): 477–85.

DeLong, Lea Rosson. *Nature's Forms / Nature's Forces: The Art of Alexandre Hogue*. Tulsa: University of Oklahoma Press and Philbrook Art Center, 1984.

Diamond, Irene, and Gloria Orenstein, eds. *Reweaving the World: The Emergence of Ecofeminism*. San Francisco: Sierra Club Books, 1990.

Dillard, Annie. *Pilgrim at Tinker Creek*. New York: Harper & Row, 1974.

Dinnerstein, Dorothy. *The Mermaid and the Minotaur: Sexual Arrangements and Human Malaise*. New York: Harper & Row, 1976.

———. "Survival on Earth: The Meaning of Feminism." In *Healing the Wounds: The Promise of Ecofeminism*, edited by Judith Plant. Toronto: Between the Lines, 1989.

Donne, John. "Elegy XIX. To His Mistress Going to Bed." In *The Norton Anthology of Poetry*. New York: Norton, 1970.

Downing, Christine. *The Goddess: Mythological Images of the Feminine*. New York: Crossroad, 1987.

Eisler, Riane. *The Chalice and the Blade*. San Francisco: Harper & Row, 1988.

Elder, John C. "Epilogue: Brooding Over the Abyss." In *Spirit and Nature: Why the Environment Is a Religious Issue*, edited by Steven C. Rockefeller and John C. Elder. Boston: Beacon Press, 1992.

Eliot, T. S. "The Hollow Men." In *The Complete Poems and Plays, 1909–1950*. New York: Harcourt, Brace & World, 1971.

Elshtain, Jean Bethke. *Public Man, Private Woman: Women in Social and Political Thought*. 2d ed. Princeton, N.J.: Princeton University Press, 1993.

Euripides. *Medea*. In *The Complete Greek Tragedies*. Vol. 3. *Euripides*. Edited by David Grene and Richmond Lattimore. Translated by Rex Warner. 1959. Chicago: University of Chicago Press, 1974.

Evans, G. R. *Augustine on Evil.* Cambridge: Cambridge University Press, 1982.

Fackre, Gabriel. "The Continuing Relevance of Reinhold Niebuhr." *Theology and Public Policy* 5 (Fall 1993): 4–14.

———. *The Promise of Reinhold Niebuhr.* Revised ed. Lanham, Md.: University Press of America, 1994.

Farber, Daniel A. *Eco-Pragmatism: Making Sensible Environmental Decisions in an Uncertain World.* Chicago: University of Chicago Press, 1999.

Firestone, Shulamith. *The Dialectic of Sex: The Case for Feminine Revolution.* New York: William Morrow, 1970.

Fisher, Andy. "Toward a More Radical Ecopsychology: Therapy for a Dysfunctional Society." *Alternatives Journal: Environmental Thought, Policy, and Action* 22 (July/August 1996): 20–26.

Ford, David F., ed. *The Modern Theologians: An Introduction to Christian Theology in the Twentieth Century.* 2 vols. Oxford: Basil Blackwell, 1989.

Forsyth, James. *Freud, Jung, and Christianity.* Ottawa: University of Ottawa Press, 1989.

Fox, Matthew. *Original Blessing: A Primer in Creation Spirituality Presented in Four Paths, Twenty-six Themes, and Two Questions.* Santa Fe, N.Mex.: Bear, 1983.

———. *The Coming of the Cosmic Christ: The Healing of Mother Earth and the Birth of a Global Renaissance.* San Francisco: Harper & Row, 1988.

Fox, Warwick. *Toward a Transpersonal Ecology: Developing New Foundations for Environmentalism.* Boston: Shambhala, 1990.

Freud, Sigmund. *The Standard Edition of the Complete Psychological Works of Sigmund Freud.* London: Hogarth Press, 1953–1974.

———. *Beyond the Pleasure Principle.* Translated and edited by James Strachey. 1920. New York: Norton, 1961.

———. *Future of an Illusion.* Translated and edited by James Strachey. 1927. New York: Norton, 1961.

———. *Civilization and Its Discontents.* Translated and edited by James Strachey. 1930. New York: Norton, 1961.

Gaard, Greta. "Ecofeminism and Native American Cultures: Pushing the Limits of Cultural Imperialism?" In *Ecofeminism: Women, Animals, Nature,* edited by Greta Gaard. Philadelphia: Temple University Press, 1993.

———. "Living Interconnections with Animals and Nature." In *Ecofeminism: Women, Animals, Nature,* edited by Greta Gaard. Philadelphia: Temple University Press, 1993.

———, ed. *Ecofeminism: Women, Animals, Nature.* Philadelphia: Temple University Press, 1993.

Gablik, Suzi. *The Reenchantment of Art.* London: Thames and Hudson, 1991.

Garb, Yaakov Jerome. "Perspective or Escape? Ecofeminist Musings on Contemporary Earth Imagery." In *Reweaving the World: The Emergence of Ecofeminism,* edited by Irene Diamond and Gloria Feman Orenstein. San Francisco: Sierra Club Books, 1990.

Garner, Shirley Nelson, Claire Kahane, and Madelon Sprengnether, eds. *The (M)other Tongue: Essays in Feminist Psychoanalytic Interpretation.* Ithaca, N.Y.: Cornell University Press, 1985.

Getty, Adele. *Goddess: Mother of Living Nature.* London: Thames & Hudson, 1990.

Gill, Sam D. *Mother Earth: An American Story.* Chicago: University of Chicago Press, 1987.

Gilligan, Carol. *In a Different Voice: Psychological Theory and Women's Development.* Cambridge, Mass.: Harvard University Press, 1982.

Gimbutas, Marija. *The Goddesses and Gods of Old Europe, 6500–3500 B.C.* Berkeley: University of California Press, 1982.

Glacken, Clarence. *Traces on the Rhodian Shore: Nature and Culture in Western Thought from Ancient Times to the End of the Eighteenth Century.* Berkeley: University of California Press, 1967.

Gnanadason, Aruna. "Toward a Feminist Eco-Theology for India." In *Women Healing Earth: Third World Women on Ecology, Feminism, and Religion,* edited by Rosemary Radford Ruether. Maryknoll, N.Y.: Orbis Books, 1996.

Goldenberg, Naomi R. *Returning Words to Flesh: Feminism, Psychoanalysis, and the Resurrection of the Body.* Boston: Beacon Press, 1990. Reprinted as *Resurrecting the Body: Feminism, Psychoanalysis, and Religion.* New York: Crossroads, 1993.

Gottlieb, Roger S., ed. *This Sacred Earth: Religion, Nature, Environment.* New York: Routledge, 1996.

Gray, Elizabeth Dodson. *Green Paradise Lost.* Wellesley, Mass.: Roundtable Press, 1979, 1981.

———. *Patriarchy as a Conceptual Trap.* Wellesley, Mass.: Roundtable Press, 1982.

———. "An Ecofeminist Critique of Christianity." Lecture delivered at Harvard Divinity School, Cambridge, Mass., 29 November 1989.

Greenberg, Jay R., and Stephen A. Mitchell. *Object Relations in Psychoanalytic Theory.* Cambridge, Mass.: Harvard University Press, 1983.

Griffin, Susan. *Woman and Nature: The Roaring Inside Her.* New York: Harper & Row, 1978.

Griscom, Joan L. "On Healing the Nature/History Split in Feminist Thought." *Heresies: Feminism and Ecology* 4 (1981): 4–9.

Grosskurth, Phyllis. *Melanie Klein: Her World and Her Work.* Cambridge, Mass.: Harvard University Press, 1987.

Guha, Ramachandra. "Radical American Environmentalism and Wilderness Preservation: A Third World Critique." *Environmental Ethics* 11 (1989): 71–83.

Guillaumin, Colette. "Pratique du pouvoir et idée de Nature: (2) Le discours de la Nature." *Questions féministes* 3 (May 1978): 5–28.

Guntrip, Harry. *Psychoanalytic Theory, Therapy, and the Self.* New York: Basic Books, 1971, 1973.

Gupta, Lina. "Ganga: Purity, Pollution, and Hinduism." In *Ecofeminism and the Sacred*, edited by Carol Adams. New York: Continuum, 1993.

Hall, Douglas John. *The Steward: A Biblical Symbol Come of Age*. Grand Rapids, Mich.: Eerdmans, 1990.

Hargrove, Eugene C., ed. *Religion and Environmental Crisis*. Athens: University of Georgia Press, 1986.

———. "Foreword." In *Nature in Asian Traditions of Thought: Essays in Environmental Philosophy*, edited by J. Baird Callicott and Roger T. Ames. Albany: State University of New York Press, 1989.

Hays, H. R. *The Dangerous Sex: The Myth of Feminine Evil*. New York: G. P. Putnam's Sons, 1964.

Heinzerling, Lisa. "Pragmatists and Environmentalists." Review of *Eco-Pragmatism: Making Sensible Environmental Decisions in an Uncertain World*, by Daniel A. Farber. *Harvard Law Review* 113:1421–47.

Heller, Chaia. "For the Love of Nature: Ecology and the Cult of the Romantic." In *Ecofeminism: Women, Animals, Nature*, edited by Greta Gaard. Philadelphia: Temple University Press, 1993.

Hick, John. *Evil and the God of Love*. 1966. Revised edition. HarperSanFrancisco, 1977.

Holbrook, David. *Human Hope and the Death Instinct*. Oxford: Pergamon Press, 1971.

Homans, Peter. *Theology after Freud: An Interpretive Inquiry*. Indianapolis, Ind.: Bobbs-Merrill, 1970.

Hughes, J. Donald. *North American Indian Ecology*. 2d ed. El Paso: Texas Western Press, 1996.

Irigaray, Luce. *Sexes et parentés*. Paris: Minuit, 1987.

James, William. *The Will To Believe*. 1897. New York: Dover, 1956.

———. *The Varieties of Religious Experience*. 1902. New York: Penguin Classics, 1982.

———. *Pragmatism*, 1907, and *The Meaning of Truth*, 1909. Cambridge, Mass.: Harvard University Press, 1975, bound as one.

Jhally, Sut. *The Codes of Advertising: Fetishism and the Political Economy of Meaning in the Consumer Society*. New York: St. Martin's Press, 1987.

———. "Advertising and the End of the World," video cassette. Northampton, Mass.: Media Education Foundation, 1998.

———. "Advertising at the Edge of the Apocalypse." Article online. No date. www.sutjhally.com. Accessed September 2002.

Jhally, Sut, William Leiss, and Stephen Kline. *Social Communication in Advertising: Persons, Products, and Images of Well-being*. Toronto and New York: Methuen, 1986.

Johnson, Buffie. *Lady of the Beasts: Ancient Images of the Goddess and Her Sacred Animals*. San Francisco: Harper & Row, 1988.

Jones, James. *Contemporary Psychoanalysis and Religion: Transference and Transcendence*. New Haven, Conn.: Yale University Press, 1991.

Joseph, Lawrence E. *Gaia: The Growth of an Idea.* New York: St. Martin's Press, 1990.

Kahane, Claire. "The Gothic Mirror." In *The (M)other Tongue: Essays in Feminist Psychoanalytic Interpretation,* edited by Shirley Nelson Garner, Claire Kahane, and Madelon Sprengnether. Ithaca, N.Y.: Cornell University Press, 1985.

Kahn, Coppélia. "The Hand That Rocks the Cradle: Recent Gender Theories and Their Implications." In *The (M)other Tongue: Essays in Feminist Psychoanalytic Interpretation,* edited by Shirley Nelson Garner, Claire Kahane, and Madelon Sprengnether. Ithaca, N.Y.: Cornell University Press, 1985.

Kalupahana, David J. "Toward a Middle Path of Survival." In *Nature in Asian Traditions of Thought: Essays in Environmental Philosophy,* edited by J. Baird Callicott and Roger T. Ames. Albany: State University of New York Press, 1989.

Kant, Immanuel. *Religion Within the Limits of Reason Alone.* 1794. New York: Harper Torchbooks, 1960.

Kaufman, Gordon. *Theology for a Nuclear Age.* Manchester: Manchester University Press, 1985.

Keller, Catherine. *From a Broken Web: Separation, Sexism, and Self.* Boston: Beacon Press, 1986.

Kelsey, David H. "Paul Tillich." In *The Modern Theologians: An Introduction to Christian Theology in the Twentieth Century,* vol. 1. Edited by David F. Ford. Oxford: Basil Blackwell, 1989.

Kheel, Marti. "From Heroic to Holistic Ethics: The Ecofeminist Challenge." In *Ecofeminism: Women, Animals, Nature,* edited by Greta Gaard. Philadelphia: Temple University Press, 1993.

King, Ynestra. "The Ecology of Feminism and the Feminism of Ecology." In *Healing the Wounds: The Promise of Ecofeminism,* edited by Judith Plant. Toronto: Between the Lines, 1989.

Klaits, Joseph. *Servants of Satan: The Age of the Witch Hunts.* Bloomington: Indiana University Press, 1985.

Klein, Melanie. *The Writings of Melanie Klein.* 4 vols. Roger E. Money-Kyrle, gen. ed. London: Hogarth Press, 1975. Reprint: New York: Free Press, 1984.

Kolodny, Annette. *The Lay of the Land: Metaphor as Experience and History in American Life and Letters.* Chapel Hill: University of North Carolina Press, 1975.

———. *The Land Before Her: Fantasy and Experience of the American Frontiers, 1630–1860.* Chapel Hill: University of North Carolina Press, 1984.

Kramer, Heinrich, and James Sprenger. *Malleus Maleficarum.* Translated by Montague Summers. New York: Dover, 1971.

Kretch, Shepard, III. *The Ecological Indian: Myth and History.* New York: Norton, 1999.

Leiss, William. *The Domination of Nature.* New York: George Braziller, 1972.

Li, Huey-li. "A Cross-Cultural Critique of Ecofeminism." In *Ecofeminism:*

Women, Animals, Nature, edited by Greta Gaard. Philadelphia: Temple University Press, 1993.

Lopez, Barry. *Arctic Dreams: Imagination and Desire in a Northern Landscape.* New York: Bantam, 1986.

Lovelock, James. "Gaia: A Model for Planetary and Cellular Dynamics." In *Gaia: A Way of Knowing,* edited by William Irwin Thompson. Great Barrington, Mass.: Lindisfarne, 1987.

———. *The Ages of Gaia: A Biography of Our Living Earth.* New York: Bantam Books, 1990.

———. *Gaia: The Practical Science of Planetary Medicine.* London: Gaia Books, 1991.

Lovin, Robin W. "Theology, Ethics, and Culture." In *The Modern Theologians: An Introduction to Christian Theology in the Twentieth Century,* vol. 2. Edited by David F. Ford. Oxford, U.K.: Basil Blackwell, 1989.

———. *Reinhold Niebuhr and Christian Realism.* Cambridge, U.K.: Cambridge University Press, 1995.

Lowe, Walter. *Evil and the Unconscious.* Chico, Calif.: Scholars Press, 1983.

Lutzky, Harriet. "Reparation and Tikkun: A Comparison of the Kleinian and Kabbalistic Concepts." *International Revue of Psycho-Analysis* 16 (1989): 449–58.

———. "The Sacred and the Maternal Object: An Application of Fairbairn's Theory to Religion." In *Psychoanalytic Reflections on Current Issues,* edited by Howard B. Siegel et al. New York: New York University Press, 1991.

MacCannell, Juliet Flower. "The Unconscious." In *Feminism and Psychoanalysis: A Critical Dictionary,* edited by Elizabeth Wright. Oxford, U.K.: Blackwell, 1992.

MacIsaac, Sharon. *Freud and Original Sin.* New York: Paulist Press, 1974.

Marshall, Peter. *Nature's Web: An Exploration of Ecological Thinking.* London: Simon & Schuster, 1992.

Mathieu, Nicole-Claude. "Homme-culture et femme-nature?" *Homme* 13 (July–September 1973): 101–13.

May, Elizabeth. "Gaia Women." In *Rescue the Earth! Conversations with the Green Crusaders,* by Farley Mowat. Toronto: McClelland & Stewart, 1990.

McFague, Sallie. *Models of God: Theology for an Ecological, Nuclear Age.* Philadelphia: Fortress, 1987.

———. *The Body of God: An Ecological Theology.* Minneapolis: Fortress Press, 1993.

McPhee, John. *The Control of Nature.* New York: Farrar, Straus & Giroux, 1989.

Meissner, William W. *Psychoanalysis and Religious Experience.* New Haven, Conn.: Yale University Press, 1984.

Merchant, Carolyn. *The Death of Nature: Women, Ecology, and the Scientific Revolution.* San Francisco: Harper & Row, 1980.

———. "Mining the Earth's Womb." In *Machina Ex Dea: Feminist Perspectives on Technology,* edited by Joan Rothschild. Pergamon Press, 1983.

——. *Ecological Revolutions: Nature, Gender, and Science in New England.* Chapel Hill: University of North Carolina Press, 1989.

——. *Radical Ecology: The Search for a Livable World.* New York: Routledge, 1992.

——. "Reinventing Eden: Western Culture as a Recovery Narrative." In *Uncommon Ground: Rethinking the Human Place in Nature,* edited by William Cronon. New York: Norton, 1996, 1995.

——. *Earthcare: Women and the Environment.* New York: Routledge, 1996.

——. "Reinventing Eden: Landscape as Narrative." Part of the 1997 American Landscape Lecture Series. Harvard University Graduate School of Design. 3 April 1997.

Miles, Margaret. *Augustine on the Body.* AAR Dissertation Series. Scholars Press, 1979.

Mills, Patricia Jagentowicz. *Woman, Nature, and Psyche.* New Haven, Conn.: Yale, 1987.

Milne, Courtney, photographs by, and text by Sherrill Miller. *Visions of the Goddess.* Toronto: Penguin Studio, 1998.

Mitchell, Juliet, ed. *The Selected Melanie Klein.* New York: Free Press, 1986.

Morford, Mark P. O., and Robert J. Lenardon. *Classical Mythology.* New York: David McKay Co., 1975.

Naess, Arne. "The Shallow and the Deep, Long-Range Ecology Movement. A Summary." *Inquiry* 16 (Summer 1973): 95–100.

Nash, James A. *Loving Nature: Ecological Integrity and Christian Responsibility.* Nashville: Abingdon Press, 1991.

Nash, Roderick. *The Rights of Nature: A History of Environmental Ethics.* Madison: University of Wisconsin Press, 1989.

Neumann, Erich. *The Fear of the Feminine and Other Essays on Feminine Psychology.* 1953. Translated by Boris Matthews et al. Princeton, N.J.: Princeton University Press, 1994.

——. *The Great Mother: An Analysis of the Archetype.* 1955. Translated by Ralph Manheim. Princeton, N.J.: Princeton University Press, 1972.

Niebuhr, Reinhold. *Moral Man and Immoral Society: A Study in Ethics and Politics.* 1932. New York: Scribner, 1960.

——. *Beyond Tragedy: Essays on the Christian Interpretation of History.* New York: Charles Scribner's Sons, 1937.

——. *The Nature and Destiny of Man: A Christian Interpretation.* 2 vols. 1941. New York: Scribner, 1964.

——. "Human Creativity and Self-Concern in Freud's Thought." In *Freud and the Twentieth Century,* edited by Benjamin Nelson. New York: Meridian Books, 1957.

Noddings, Nel. *Caring: A Feminine Approach to Ethics and Moral Education.* Berkeley: University of California Press, 1984.

——. *Women and Evil.* Berkeley: University of California Press, 1989.

Norwood, Vera. *Made From This Earth: American Women and Nature.* Chapel Hill: University of North Carolina Press, 1993.

Oelschlaeger, Max. *The Idea of Wilderness: From Prehistory to the Age of Ecology.* New Haven, Conn.: Yale University Press, 1991.

———. *Caring for Creation: An Ecumenical Approach to the Environmental Crisis.* New Haven, Conn.: Yale University Press, 1994.

Ortner, Sherry B. "Is Female to Male as Nature Is to Culture?" In *Woman, Culture, and Society,* edited by Michelle Zimbalist Rosaldo and Louise Lamphere. Stanford, Calif.: Stanford University Press, 1974.

———. "So, *Is* Female to Male as Nature Is to Culture?" In *Making Gender: The Politics and Erotics of Culture,* by Sherry B. Ortner. Boston: Beacon Press, 1996.

Pagels, Elaine. "The Social History of Satan." *Harvard Divinity Bulletin* 24 (1995): 3.

Parekh, Bhikhu. "Is There a Human Nature?" In *Is There a Human Nature?* edited by Leroy S. Rouner. Notre Dame, Ind.: University of Notre Dame Press, 1997.

Parker, Rozsika. *Mother Love/Mother Hate: The Power of Maternal Ambivalence.* New York: Basic Books, 1995.

Phillips, John Anthony. *Eve: The History of an Idea.* San Francisco: Harper & Row, 1984.

Pitcher, W. Alvin. *Listen to the Crying of the Earth: Cultivating Creation Communities.* Cleveland: Pilgrim, 1993.

Plant, Judith. "Toward a New World: An Introduction" and "The Circle Is Gathering." In *Healing the Wounds: The Promise of Ecofeminism,* edited by Judith Plant. Toronto: Between the Lines, 1989.

———, ed. *Healing the Wounds: The Promise of Ecofeminism.* Toronto: Between the Lines, 1989.

Plaskow, Judith. *Sex, Sin, and Grace: Women's Experience and the Theologies of Reinhold Niebuhr and Paul Tillich.* Lanham, Md.: University Press of America, 1980.

Ponting, Clive. *A Green History of the World: The Environment and the Collapse of Great Civilizations.* New York: St. Martin's Press, 1991.

Pratney, Winkie. *Healing the Land: A Supernatural View of Ecology.* Grand Rapids, Mich.: Chosen Books, 1993.

Primavesi, Anne. *From Apocalypse to Genesis: Ecology, Feminism and Christianity.* Minneapolis: Fortress, 1991.

Rich, Adrienne. *Of Woman Born: Motherhood as Experience and Institution.* Tenth anniversary edition. New York: Norton, 1986.

Rigby, Paul. *Original Sin in Augustine's Confessions.* Ottawa: University of Ottawa Press, 1987.

Rockefeller, Steven C., and John C. Elder, eds. *Spirit and Nature: Why the Environment Is a Religious Issue.* Boston: Beacon Press, 1992.

Rose, Ellen Cronan. "The Good Mother: From Gaia to Gilead." In *Ecofeminism and the Sacred,* edited by Carol J. Adams. New York: Continuum, 1993.

Ross, James Bruce, and Mary Martin McLaughlin, eds. *The Portable Medieval Reader.* New York: Penguin Books, 1977.

Roszak, Theodore. *The Voice of the Earth: An Exploration of Ecopsychology.* New York: Simon & Schuster, 1992.

Roszak, Theodore, Mary E. Gomes, and Allen D. Kanner, eds. *Ecopsychology: Restoring the Earth, Healing the Mind.* San Francisco: Sierra Club, 1995.

Rowthorn, Anne W. *Caring for Creation: Toward an Ethic of Responsibility.* Wilton, Conn.: Morehouse, 1989.

Ruether, Rosemary Radford. "Misogynism and Virginal Feminism in the Fathers of the Church." In *Religion and Sexism,* edited by Rosemary Radford Ruether. New York: Simon & Schuster, 1974.

———. *New Woman/New Earth: Sexist Ideologies and Human Liberation.* New York: Seabury Press, 1975.

———. "Motherearth and the Megamachine: A Theology of Liberation in a Feminine, Somatic, and Ecological Perspective." In *Womanspirit Rising,* edited by Carol P. Christ and Judith Plaskow. San Francisco: Harper & Row, 1979.

———. *Gaia and God: An Ecofeminist Theology of Earth Healing.* HarperSanFrancisco, 1992.

———, ed. *Women Healing Earth: Third World Women on Ecology, Feminism, and Religion.* Maryknoll, N.Y.: Orbis Books, 1996.

Sachs, Wolfgang, ed. *Global Ecology: A New Arena of Political Conflict.* London: Zed Books, 1993.

Sagan, Eli. *Freud, Women, and Morality: The Psychology of Good and Evil.* New York: Basic Books, 1988.

Saiving, Valerie. "The Human Situation: A Feminine View." *Journal of Religion* 40 (April 1960): 100–112. Reprinted in *Womanspirit Rising,* edited by Carol P. Christ and Judith Plaskow. San Francisco: Harper & Row, 1979.

Sands, Kathleen M. *Escape From Paradise: Evil and Tragedy in Feminist Theology.* Minneapolis: Fortress, 1994.

Santmire, H. Paul. *Brother Earth: Nature, God, and Ecology in Time of Crisis.* New York: Thomas Nelson, 1970.

———. *The Travail of Nature: The Ambiguous Ecological Promise of Christian Theology.* Philadelphia: Fortress, 1985.

Schafer, Roy. "The Psychoanalytic Vision of Reality." In *A New Language for Psychoanalysis.* New Haven, Conn.: Yale University Press, 1976.

Schwarz, Hans. *Evil: A Historical and Theological Perspective.* Translated by Mark W. Worthing. Minneapolis: Fortress, 1995.

Segal, Hanna. *Introduction to the Work of Melanie Klein.* 2d ed. New York: Basic Books, 1974.

Sessions, George, ed. *Deep Ecology for the Twenty-first Century.* Boston: Shambhala, 1995.

Simon, Bennett. *Tragic Drama and the Family: Psychoanalytic Studies from Aeschylus to Beckett.* New Haven, Conn.: Yale University Press, 1988.

Sjöö, Monica, and Barbara Mor. *The Great Cosmic Mother: Rediscovering the Religion of the Earth.* San Francisco: Harper & Row, 1987.

Smith, Andy. "For All Those Who Were Indian in a Former Life." In *Ecofeminism and the Sacred,* edited by Carol Adams. New York: Continuum, 1993.

Smith, Christine M. "Sin and Evil in Feminist Theology." *Theology Today* 50 (July 1993): 208–19.

Smith, Henry Nash. *Virgin Land: The American West as Symbol and Myth.* Cambridge, Mass.: Harvard University Press, 1978, orig. 1950.

Solomon, Marc. "A Few Choice Words: Ad Slogans in the Popular Media, 1980–1990." Winter 1996, on the Web site of LKM Research, Inc. http://hamp.hampshire.edu/~eprF94/LKMsample.html

Sophocles. *Antigone.* In *The Complete Greek Tragedies.* Vol. 2. *Sophocles.* Edited by David Grene and Richmond Lattimore. Translated by Elizabeth Wyckoff. Chicago: University of Chicago Press, 1974, orig. 1959.

———. *Oedipus the King.* In *The Three Theban Plays.* Translated by Robert Fagles. New York: Penguin Classics, 1984.

Spillius, Elizabeth Bott, ed. *Melanie Klein Today.* London: Routledge, 1988.

Spretnak, Charlene. *Lost Goddesses of Early Greece: A Collection of Pre-Hellenic Myths.* Boston: Beacon, 1978.

Stenmark, Lisa. "An Ecology of Knowledge: Feminism, Ecology, and the Science and Religion Discourse." *Metaviews* 6 (2001.02.05). Accessed at www.metanexus.org, Sept. 2002.

Stone, Merlin. *When God Was a Woman.* New York: Harcourt Brace Jovanovich, 1976.

Suchocki, Marjorie Hewitt. *The Fall to Violence: Original Sin in Relational Theology.* New York: Continuum, 1994.

Suleiman, Susan Rubin. "Writing and Motherhood." In *The (M)other Tongue: Essays in Feminist Psychoanalytic Interpretation,* edited by Shirley Nelson Garner, Claire Kahane, and Madelon Sprengnether. Ithaca, N.Y.: Cornell University Press, 1985.

Thoreau, Henry David. *Walden.* 1854. New York: Signet, n.d.

Thurer, Shari L. *The Myths of Motherhood: How Culture Reinvents the Good Mother.* Boston: Houghton Mifflin, 1994.

Tillich, Paul. *Systematic Theology,* vol. 1. Chicago: University of Chicago Press, 1951.

———. *Theology of Culture.* London: Oxford University Press, 1959.

Tucker, Mary Evelyn, and John A. Grim, eds. *Worldviews and Ecology. Bucknell Review.* Lewisburg, Pa.: Bucknell University Press; and Cranbury, N.J.: Associated University Presses, 1993.

Van Herik, Judith. *Freud on Femininity and Faith.* Berkeley: University of California Press, 1982.

Vance, Linda. "Ecofeminism and the Politics of Reality." In *Ecofeminism: Women, Animals, Nature,* edited by Greta Gaard. Philadelphia: Temple University Press, 1993.

Warren, Karen J. "Feminism and Ecology: Making Connections." *Environmental Ethics* 9 (Spring 1987): 3–20.

———, ed. *Ecological Feminism.* London: Routledge, 1994.

———, ed. *Ecological Feminist Philosophies.* Bloomington: Indiana University Press, 1996.

Western, David, and R. Michael Wright, eds. and Shirley C. Strum, assoc. ed. *Natural Connections: Perspectives in Community-based Conservation.* Washington, D.C.: Island Press, 1994.

White, Lynn, Jr. "The Historical Roots of Our Ecologic Crisis." *Science* 155 (10 March 1967): 1203–207. Reprinted in *Ecology and Religion in History,* edited by David Spring and Eileen Spring. New York: Harper and Row, 1976.

Willoughby, Linda Teal. "Mother Earth: Ecofeminism from a Jungian perspective." Ph.D. diss., Iliff School of Theology and the University of Denver, 1990.

———. "Ecofeminist Consciousness and the Transforming Power of Symbols." In *Ecofeminism and the Sacred,* edited by Carol J. Adams. New York: Continuum, 1993.

Winnicott, D. W. *The Maturational Process and the Facilitating Environment.* New York: International Universities Press, 1965.

———. *Playing and Reality.* London: Routledge, 1971.

Wittig, Monique. *Les Guérillères.* Translated by David LeVay. New York: Avon, 1971.

Wollheim, Richard. *The Mind and Its Depths.* Cambridge, Mass.: Harvard University Press, 1993.

Wood, Ralph C. *The Comedy of Redemption: Christian Faith and Comic Vision in Four American Novelists.* Notre Dame, Ind.: University of Notre Dame Press, 1988.

World Commission on Environment and Development. *Our Common Future.* Oxford: Oxford University Press, 1987.

Worster, Donald. *Nature's Economy: The Roots of Ecology.* Garden City, N.Y.: Anchor, 1979.

Wright, Evan. "Swamp's Last Day on Earth . . . And Other True Tales of the Anarchist Underground." *Rolling Stone* 837 (30 March 2000): 44–50.

Yale, Andy. "Rhodell Letter. The Closing of the American Mine: Oblivion Comes to a West Virginia Coal Town." *Harper's* (December 1994).

Young, Richard A. *Healing the Earth: A Theocentric Perspective on Environmental Problems and their Solutions.* Nashville: Broadman & Holman, 1994.

Zeitlin, Froma I. "Signifying Difference: The Case of Hesiod's Pandora." In *Playing the Other: Gender and Society in Classical Greek Literature.* Chicago: University of Chicago Press, 1996.

Zinn, Howard. *Declarations of Independence: Cross-Examining American Ideology.* New York: HarperCollins, 1990.

Index